DISCARD

D0778406

The Prairie Logbooks

1844-1845

THE PRAIRIE LOGBOOKS

Dragoon Campaigns to the Pawnee Villages in 1844,
and to the Rocky Mountains in 1845

By Lieutenant J. Henry Carleton

Edited, with an Introduction, by
Louis Pelzer

University of Nebraska Press
Lincoln and London

Ⅲ

Manufactured in the United States of America

First Bison Book printing: May 1983

Most recent printing indicated by the first digit below:
1   2   3   4   5   6   7   8   9   10

Library of Congress Cataloging in Publication Data

Carleton, James Henry, 1814–1873.
    The prairies logbooks.

    Reprint. Originally published: Chicago : Caxton club,
1943.
    "Bison book"—Verso t.p.
    1. Carleton, James Henry, 1814–1873. 2. Indians of
North America—Wars—1815–1875—Personal narratives.
3. Dakota Indians—Wars—Personal narratives.
4. Pawnee Indians—Wars—Personal narratives.
5. United States. Army. Cavalry, 1st—History.
6. United States. Army—Military life. I. Pelzer, Louis,
1879–1946. II. Title.
E81.C37 1983   973.5'8   82-24755
ISBN 0-8032-1422-7
ISBN 0-8032-6314-7 (pbk.)

Published by arrangement with the Caxton Club, Chicago.

CONTENTS

INTRODUCTION

THE American army of this year of 1943 is greater by almost a thousand fold than that of a century ago. Today the army is half as large as the national population of 1840 or about twice as large as the entire American population when Washington became president. In 1844 the last war was thirty years in the past and the Civil War was seventeen years in the future. Four decades had passed since the Louisiana Purchase and Chicago was a youthful hamlet of ten years. Webster and Tyler were contending with the British for the Oregon Country. Travel in the region west of the Mississippi was by foot, horseback, steamboat, and wagon.

A procession of explorers, scientists, fur traders, and military men had invaded the Great Plains since the Louisiana Purchase. Lewis and Clark, Stephen H. Long, George Catlin, Henry Dodge, Frémont, Josiah Gregg, Howard Stansbury, and R. B. Marcy are only a few of the milestones on the trails of the westward penetration—an advance that was followed by Oregon emigrants, Mormons, gold seekers, cattlemen, farmers, railroad builders, and miners. About two hundred and fifty years were required for settlement to spread from Jamestown to the Mississippi but a series of advancing frontiers caused the Trans-Mississippi West to become "settled" in about five decades.

No draft or selective service helped to form the army of a century ago. Some men had fought in Indian wars and had been in the army for years. Large numbers were enlisted in Boston, Philadelphia, New York, and other cities of the East. Hundreds of young men weary of cities and society joined regiments which were to "scour the prairies of the region beyond the Mississippi." German, Irish, and English immigrants joined the army. Americans—picked, athletic young men of good character—entered the ranks. But people then had little knowledge or pride concerning the army and some enlisted men were looked upon as "the rag-tag-and-bob-tail herd" and the "scum of population of the older States."

* * *

These frontier soldiers had never dreamed of airplanes, of machine guns, smokeless powder, or the long range cannon of today. Their Springfield muskets and the Colt's, Hall's, and Jenks' carbines would not compare with the modern Garand rifle. The ordnance department listed about one hundred Belgian, Swedish, and American howitzers and field guns. The percussion caps, flints, sabres, and cannon wads would now be more appropriate in museums.[1] But it must be recalled that the soldiers then were closer to the Revolutionary War than this generation is to the War Between the States.

Perhaps more picturesque but less serviceable was the soldiers' clothing in 1830 than of the present time. A chance visitor at Fort Leavenworth, Jefferson Barracks, or Fort Crawford could have seen a varied assortment of army clothing. The quartermaster of today could find much of interest in the soldiers' dress in that year. Privates' drilling overalls cost $.62; the price of a pair of shoes was $1.24; the army blanket sold for $2.50; the sum of $1.53 would buy a knapsack; flannel drawers were priced at $.87; and a pair of bootees at $1.48. Great coats for service in the cold winter climate were purchased for $6.56. More ornamental articles such as the pompon, band and tassell, and the cockade and eagle were on sale respectively at twenty, twelve, and six cents.[2]

A long chain of about a dozen outposts stood on the Mississippi during the forties like sentinels to guard the western frontier. Nearly all have disappeared and vanished in the river towns of today. At these posts were Indians, hunters, soldiers, and travellers, and steamboats labored from one post to another. To these outposts soldiers

---

[1] *Senate Documents*, 3rd sess., 27th Cong., I, Document 1, pp. 197–224 and *Senate Documents*, 2nd sess., 28th Cong., I, Document 1, pp. 113–304.

[2] Louis Pelzer, *Marches of the Dragoons in the Mississippi Valley* (Iowa City, Iowa, 1917), 6.

were sent, from them sent to other posts, and here they were drilled and mustered out. From Jefferson Barracks mounted troops were sent to other forts of the great West. On the plains marches and expeditions many soldiers kept diaries, notebooks, and journals, which bring stories of hunting, traders, Indians, and buffalo—almost endless numbers of shaggy buffalo. At the sites of various posts only old burying grounds link these old military stations with the present.

Life at garrisons and camps in the forties was a round of inspections, reviews, playing the "Star Spangled Banner," guard duty, and, at the smaller posts, the tasks of shoeing horses, cutting wood, cleaning the camp grounds, and repairing the chimneys.[3] A soldier's routine appears in an order of 1850 for the dragoons at Fort Leavenworth. Sleep was broken by the reveille at daybreak and fifteen minutes later was followed by the stable call. Then came the sick call at 7:10 and the call to breakfast twenty minutes later. Fatigue call, guard mounting, and orderly call followed. The dinner call at 12 M was succeeded by the fatigue call an hour thereafter and by the stable call at 1:30. Retreat was sounded at sunset. Tattoo at 9:00 P.M. meant rest for the troops—except for the sentinels who kept the long winter night watches.[4]

Horses and mules furnished the backbone of the transportation for army men and supplies a century ago. Pack mules followed scouts where wagons could not travel. The mule was sure-footed, but uncertain as to intentions and sometimes called a "stubborn fact." The Rifle Regiment marched the journey of 2,000 miles from Fort Leavenworth to Fort Vancouver in 1849. Their travels in storm, danger, hardships, and with terrible toils had required about four months—a trip now made by train in about half that number of days. Ox-teams, covered wagons, horses and mules in 1849—Pullman cars and airplanes in 1943.

The army doctor was friend, mother, nurse, and adviser to these frontier troops. No family physician had a more varied practice. Whether at a tropical fort in Florida or at a cold, northern post in

[3] William A. Ganoe, *The History of the United States Army* (Revised Edition, 1942, New York), 193, 194.
[4] *Post Records of Fort Leavenworth*, January 26, 1850.

Minnesota the doctor was present to minister to the men. On marches across the plains he carried his calomel, opium, morphine, and doses of quinine. Fevers ranked high among the one hundred and twenty-five diseases listed by army physicians in about 1852. The number of bone fractures went up to a high figure and diseases of the digestive organs gave plenty of work for these medical men. Cholera sometimes struck an army post to claim its victims. Pneumonia and paralysis were not unknown and even "Nostalgia" is listed among the ills of the army. Calomel was given for rheumatism, mumps, fevers, and even for broken bones.

William Hammond, an army surgeon, reported that at Fort Laramie in 1850 emigrants between Fort Leavenworth and that post suffered acutely from what they called "cholera" or a malady resembling it. But he regarded it as only an acute form of diarrhoea due to hardships and imprudence in diet. "The universal use of quack nostrums, called cholera mixtures, composed principally of brandy and Cayenne pepper has tended to aggravate the disease. A great many cases when fairly treated with calomel, opium, and astringents readily yielded." Two years later, another army doctor reported that at Fort Laramie the army hospital was crowded with sick emigrants. Lying in tents and in the hospital they were waited upon by hospital attendants, visited by the soldiers, and treated by the medical officer.[5]

Each year army doctors examined thousands of enlisted men to see if they were fit for service. About ninety years ago 13,000 were rejected out of 16,000 examined. Men with varicose veins made up the largest number of unfit. Others were too slender or not robust. Broken-down constitutions, habitual drunkenness, old injuries and fractures were causes for rejection. Loss of teeth, goitre, unequal length of limbs, deafness, and even stammering barred other men from service. The best men, reported the examiners, were Americans from the agricultural districts. The average weight of American and foreign-born troops—out of a group of 1800 examined in 1852— was a little less than a hundred and fifty pounds.

---

[5] *Statistical Report of the Sickness and Mortality in the Army of the United States, January 1839–January 1855* in *Senate Executive Documents*, 1st sess., 34th Cong., Document 96, *passim*. The quoted matter is from pp. 78, 80.

Before the Civil War hospitals were crude and ambulances few. The first public and successful use of ether in surgical operations is usually credited to the year 1846. The Red Cross and similar organizations were then unknown. "The American soldier," reported Secretary of War, Lewis Cass, in 1831, "is well paid, fed, and clothed; and in the event of sickness or disability, ample provision is made for his support." But he deplored that little provision existed for the mental and moral culture of the troops at the remote posts. No chaplains were stationed at some forts to minister to the moral and religious life of the soldier, to give reproof and admonition during his life, nor in death the consolations of religion.[6] After 1838 the War Department was empowered to employ chaplains at certain designated posts at $40 a month with quarters, rations, and fuel. Such chaplains "shall also perform the duties of schoolmaster."[7]

Year after year soldiers in the West drilled, marched, executed Federal laws, and shifted from post to post. These services influenced the westward drift of population, complementing the work of the explorers, the boatmen, the missionaries, and the surveyors and engineers. The annals of our western posts and prairie marches have not yet passed into such picturesque accounts as hover about Fort Pitt, Quebec, and Ticonderoga. The names of great soldiers in the frontier army are few. But homage and recognition are due to the thousands of plain, frontier soldiers for their quiet and often unheralded services—whether at lonely Mississippi River posts, in the protection of trade caravans, in travels over the cacti-covered plains, or in marches from post to post. "These little bands of trained and disciplined Americans," wrote an army historian, "wove the capillaries of civilization as thickly as they could through the wilderness."[8]

* * *

Lieutenant James Henry Carleton's first *Logbook* was published anonymously and appeared first in *The Spirit of the Times*, New York,

[6] *American State Papers, Military Affairs*, IV, 709, 718.

[7] *U. S. Stat. at Large*, V, 256–260. By this law privates were paid $8 monthly of which sum one fourth was to be withheld until the term of enlistment should expire. In place of the spirit or whiskey component part of the army ration the privates were given six pounds of coffee and twelve pounds of sugar.

[8] William Addleman Ganoe, *The History of the United States Army*, 194.

from November 9, 1844 to April 12, 1845. "It is the intention of the gifted writer," explained the editor, William T. Porter, "to give in this 'Log-Book' every information which the most curious might wish for—spiced and seasoned here and there with the record of many a thrilling incident and laughable event." The editor hoped the readers would travel with the expedition "in spirit, and partici- pate in all the delights and duties, the fun, frolic, and romance with which it was characterized." The sketches were reprinted in contem- porary newspapers, notably in the Bangor (Maine) *Daily Courier* and the *Western Democrat* of Weston, Missouri, under the title of "Occidental Reminiscences."[9]

The *Logbook* describing the second expedition (commanded by Colonel S. W. Kearny) was first printed in *The Spirit of the Times* from December 27, 1845 to May 30, 1846. Lieutenant Carleton's chapters were to be written, he announced on December 27, 1845, "mainly with a view of attempting a rude description of the recent campaign of the First U. S. Dragoons to the headwaters of the Rio Colorado of the West; and from thence to the Southward along the base of the Rocky Mountains, nearly to the sources of the Rio del Norte and the Arkansas; and then from there home by way of the Santa Fe Trace to Fort Leavenworth."

The panorama of the unsettled West appeared and receded as Lieutenant Carleton's dragoon mounts shogged westward over prai- rie and plains. Indians in their native state, "Modern Pilgrims" to Oregon, fur traders, tedious Indian councils, and frontier posts are

[9] Lieutenant James Henry Carleton (1814–1873) held the commission of second lieutenant in the First Regiment of United States Dragoons from October 18, 1839 to March 17, 1845, when he was promoted to first lieutenant. He served with dis- tinction in the Mexican War, in the Civil War, and in the New Mexican campaigns. Besides the *Logbooks*, in which the last entry is for July 13, 1845, he is the author of four other works: *The Battle of Buena Vista with the Operations of the "Army of Occu- pation" for one Month* (New York, 1848); "Diary of an Excursion to the Ruins of Abó, Quarra, and Gran Quivira, in New Mexico under the Command of Major James Henry Carleton, U. S. A." from December 14–24, 1853, in *Ninth Annual Re- port of the Smithsonian Institution* (1854), and in *House Miscellaneous Documents*, 2nd sess., 23rd Cong., Document 37, pp. 296–316; "Mountain Meadow Massacre . . . Special Report of the Mountain Meadow Massacre" (Washington, 1902), dated May 25, 1859, in *House Documents*, 1st sess., 57th Cong., 605; and "To the People of New Mexico" (1864), giving reasons for the location of the Navajo Indians at the Bosque Redondo.

recurring scenes of his *Logbooks*. The columns paused to repair broken wagons, to cross streams, to bury comrades, to rest weary men and horses, and to give succor to discouraged emigrants to Oregon.

Regimental histories of units of the First United States Dragoons and their many circuits in the West yield cross sectional views of the work of the frontier army of a century ago. Such history has been preserved in officers' reports, the accounts of travellers, diaries, journals, order books, and correspondence. This material, containing facts, descriptions, narratives, and impressions, enriches our knowledge of the staples of western history.[10]

*   *   *

In eastern-born Lieutenant Carleton the Great Plains created impressions of youthful enthusiasm and wonder. Educated in the East he became intensely alert to the contrasts between that region and the expanding West. Writing unofficially Carleton, in his jottings, does not show the official restraints of other dragoon journalists like Kingsbury, Wheelock, and Kearny. But there is direct evidence that Carleton's observations were carefully supplemented by studies of the writings of the plains travels of Frémont, Parker, Murray, and Gregg. Possessed of observing eyes, Carleton writes chapters that are marked by sustained interest, good taste, and a solvent sense of humor.

Carleton's *Logbooks* admirably supplement the journals of Major Clifton Wharton and those of Captain Philip St. George Cooke. Wharton's parallel account of the expedition of 1844 is factual, official in tone, but shows little of Carleton's idyllic love for the plains, or of his penetrating interest in the Indians, or of the daily routine of the dragoons in camp or on the march. Cooke's *Scenes and Adventures in the Army* is also a record of the expedition of 1845 but the sub-title *Romance of Military Life* affords Captain Cooke the opportunity for more extended scenic descriptions and philosophical reflections. Carleton is an observing participant of scenes which he reports

---

[10] See the Appendix for a list of the "Principal Writings of Members of the First Regiment of United States Dragoons from 1833 to 1847."

sympathetically but objectively. Wharton and Cooke are faithful ob-
servers and reporters and, like Carleton, paint vivid pictures of Fort
Laramie and its conglomerate population.

Snapshots of the Oregon emigrants by Carleton are in general accord with the Jesse Applegate record of a year or two earlier and are
among the earliest accounts of the Oregon emigration. Francis Parkman's *Oregon Trail*, written about the same time as the first *Logbook*,
was published about two years later (1847). But the young Boston
patrician looked upon the Oregon pioneers as little more than bar-
barians and was inclined to compare them with their ancestors
"scarcely more lawless than themselves" or with the Huns who had
once devastated Europe.

Carleton's observations on these Oregon pioneers is more objective and more sympathetic and is more understanding of the great
population movement of the forties. To him they were "practical
agriculturists." And to them he credited the strongest and most enduring sentiments of patriotism. "They will remain knitted to us, by
all the pride they must feel in remembering the glories of the American Past, and all the hope that must inspire them as they look forward to the power and magnificence of the American Future."

Intimate, vivid, and early pictures are given in the first Carleton
Logbook of the Pawnee Indians. A student of Indian life in Maine and
an avid reader of early writers on Indian life, Carleton's descriptions
bear the qualities of objective approach, appreciative understanding,
and freedom from romantic sentimentalism. The accounts of Pawnee
government, food, wars, family life, hunting, superstition, and religion are charged with apt data and illustrative detail and are an important contribution to the record of Indian culture on the Great
Plains.

Revealing, although less intimate, is Carleton's account of the
Dakota and their lodges, bows, arrows, and lances. The Dakota were
"quite wealthy in horses, mules and asses" and were inveterate horse
jockeys. The chase was the labor of these children of the plains and
war their pastime. Excepting the Pottawatomi, Carleton's western
tribes are described as idle, cowardly, treacherous, poor, drunken,
and dishonest and had made a profession of stealing. "The farther

you get from the influence of the whites, the better they become," Carleton shrewdly observed.

Great herds of buffalo stared at Carleton's marching columns. The *Logbooks* recall prairie dogs, hares, antelopes, and bears. Larks, curlews, blackbirds, and mocking birds rose in alarm before this dragoon invasion. At other times the troops, while smoking their evening pipes or lounging about the mess-fires, could listen to the howling of wolves, the monotones of tree-frogs, or the quavering notes of owls. The varieties and habits of animal life on the plains have been entertainingly portrayed by Lieutenant Carleton.

*   *   *

Certain deletions in the *Logbooks* of speculative and fanciful reflections have been made without impairing the narratives and descriptions. Lieutenant Carleton's spelling of "Kearney" has been changed to the correct form of "Kearny" and the reduction of some italicized forms may be more pleasing to the eye without affecting the author's meaning. Likely rough notes were jotted down at the close of the day's journey and as he sat near his tent. There is evidence of friendly cooperation and conversation among the dragoon journalists of these marches—Lieutenant Carleton, Captain Cooke, Major Wharton, and Lieutenants Franklin and Turner. On the evening of June 3 of the second march Carleton noted that the gentlemen were engaged in "what the General Regulations of the Army denominate as 'Sedentary Duties.' They are nearly all sitting upon the ground in front of their respective tents, and each one has a little bottle of ink propped up beside him to keep it from upsetting, a steel-pen in his hand, and upon his knees a roll of wrinkled and dog-eared paper."

*   *   *

Duty and pleasure merge in acknowledging the help and cooperation of the Publications Committee of The Caxton Club. Mr. Vilas Johnson furnished advice and decisions; Mr. John Merryweather, the chairman, gave friendly and patient aid; and Mr. Franklin J. Meine, discoverer of these journals, provided the verified copies of the *Logbooks* as typed from his rare set of *The Spirit of the Times*. I bow also to my colleague and former student, Dr. William J. Petersen, who can be charitable of my worst and critical of my best.

Students, readers, and writers of western history will, I hope, join in commending the policy of printing such accounts as the Carleton *Logbooks*, Jesse Applegate's *A Day with the Cow Column*, and other narratives. In the second *Logbook* Lieutenant Carleton invites the reader to join the second expedition: "And whether he visits the Emigrants during his journey, and allows himself to speculate upon their prospects—or to sympathise with them in their difficulties; or when he gets tired of that, to come back and join the Dragoons again, and so *vice versa*, it is hoped he will jog along with us in the quiet, old-fashioned manner, and at the close feel that the time has not been wholly thrown away which he has spent in glancing at the scenes of 'Farther West'."

LOUIS PELZER

The State University of Iowa
Iowa City

A Dragoon Campaign
to the Pawnee Villages in 1844

CHAPTER I

"EXORDIUM" – *The object of the campaign – Detained by rains from starting – Then by Mormon difficulties – Writer's reason for being particular in description – Fort Leavenworth – Dragoon parade – Final inspection – Officers of the Expedition – Mr. Deas the Artist – Commencement of the march.*

URING the summer of 1844, orders were received at Fort Leavenworth from the Head Quarters of the Third Military Department, for five companies of the *1st U.S. Dragoons*[1] to proceed to the Pawnee villages on Nebraska. The object of this expedition was to confirm the relations of peace and amity already existing between the Pawnees and the United States, and also, to adjust certain difficulties which had arisen between them and some of the neighboring tribes. The Sioux had for a long time been waging a most bloody war against them, to stop which, if possible, was likewise made a part of the duty of the Dragoons. On account of the heavy rains which had almost deluged the prairies from the latter part of March until the first of July, the movements of the troops in obedience to these orders was necessarily delayed. About that time, or rather just before, Gov. Ford of Illinois, made a requisition on the Commanding Office of the Department just named,[2] for a certain number of regulars to be stationed in that State—their presence being deemed necessary by him, from the great excitement which had arisen in consequence of the death of the Mormon Prophet and his brother. The order, therefore, for the campaign to the Pawnee towns was suspended until the action of the President on Gov. Ford's requisition could be known—it having been forwarded direct to Washington. Early in August this suspension was removed, the preparations were immediately made for the march to the Nebraska.

For the reason that but little can be known by those residing in the Eastern States, of the manner in which these expeditions are conducted by the regular cavalry—and for the reason that the route to be taken by the troops upon this occasion, in striking across the country from Fort Leavenworth to the Forks of the Nebraska, is entirely unknown—never having been travelled save perhaps, by the wild savages of the prairie—the writer of these rough notes wishes to be as particular as possible in his description of everything which comes under his notice, whether it relates to the movements of the troops—the country over which they are to pass—or the Indians whom they are to visit. It will therefore be his object in writing of these things to speak of them exactly as he may see them. Now and then, it is true, some little incident may occur, which in painting, he may touch here and there, just to give it a proper effect; but all these things will be seen by the reader as he goes along. It is his wish to take those who are disposed to accompany him, from the beginning to the end of the campaign; and to sketch for them all the scenes through which he is to pass, in such a manner, if possible, as to afford them sufficient interest and enjoyment to recompense them for their trouble. Having got through with all these preliminary remarks—the bell rings—hats off in front—up goes the curtain—and here is a view of Fort Leavenworth—the acknowledged Eden of the beautiful West. On the north the great Missouri washes the base of the hill upon which the fort seems almost to repose, embowered as it is amongst the huge elm and oak, and walnut trees, that fill its parade, and surround it on every hand. High above them can be seen towering aloft, the tapering flagstaff, supporting a gorgeous drapery, which, as it slowly unfolds in the breeze of the morning, reveals itself to be the magnificent banner of our country—pictured with all its brilliant emblazonry, in strong relief against the pure blue of heaven. Then away to the west, and the south, and the east, can be seen, as far as the eye can reach, hill and dale—woodland and prairie—luxuriously sleeping in the soft haze, that ever more or less pervades, during the summer season, the atmosphere of the West. 'Tis indeed a lovely scene—one which would almost make Apollo, or Pan, enamoured of earth again, could they but catch one glimpse of it. Besides, there is no Midas here to oppress either of them. It is nature—all nature! Man has not yet marred its beauty. And save those elegant buildings that seem clustered together beneath that flag—reflecting back with their pure white the morning's sunlight as it struggles down through the deep green foliage above—or the little wreaths of blue smoke, which here and there curl gently upwards from the distant groves, marking the spot where the red man has built his rude wigwam—nothing that man has done sullies the picture. In all else it is as it came from the hand of the Creator. This description, if it may be called one, is not overdrawn, but falls far short of the reality. All who have once visited this spot, will say that no pen could ever do justice to its loveliness. Well, reader, this is the first scene.

Time, 10 o'clock, A.M., August 12th. You are on the parade under those grand old trees. On three sides of the great square that surrounds you, are the quarters of the officers and men—with colonnades and piazzas about them. Don't you see on the various galleries that surround those buildings, men in military garb moving hither and thither—some packing effects—some arming themselves—some shaking hands with, and apparently bidding good bye to comrades who are to remain behind! On the fourth side of this square, and towards which you are now facing, are twelve long white buildings in a row, with immense double doors in each end. Those are the dragoon stables—calculated for holding the horses of six complete companies. So much for scenery. I have gone considerably into detail so far, because this is an important spot in my Log-book. It is the *point d'appui* of the campaign; the post, reader, from which we are about to commence our voyage.—(Allow me, if you please, to say *I*, for it is difficult always to remember to say *we*, when speaking of ourselves). Now for the actors.

Did you hear that bugle!—it blew what is called the signal, "boots and saddles." Now look at the different quarters—see the men pouring from them like bees from so many hives. Don't you hear the clang—clang—clang, of the heavy sabres as they descend the steps—

they are all completely armed and equipped. See, in addition to those beautiful and effective Prussian sabres just named, that are trailing by their sides as they walk along. Hall's patent carbine, hanging by its broad white sling, gracefully over the shoulder, and also, that each man has in his hand one of those superb Harper's Ferry pistols—they are all on their way to the stables. Ten minutes more—another bugle; that was the signal—"to horse." Now they come out—what a crowd! Each man has his hand near the bit, leading his charger. They form in two ranks on foot, each company on its own parade in front of its stables—at the same time, the officers mounted, come dashing along from their quarters to their several companies. The commands are given: the men are in the saddle at once, and the ranks are closed and dressed. Another bugle, still—that was the "assembly"—the fine brass band of the regiment, also mounted, commences a lively march. The companies break into column, move off, and take position according to rank, in line. There are five of them—first, that is Capt. Cooke's troop of blacks, just wheeling into line on the left of the Band—second, this is Capt. Burgwin's troop of greys—third, that is Capt. Moore's troop of bays—fourth, that is Lieut. Kearney's troop of chestnuts—fifth, that is Capt. Terrett's troop of blacks; hardy, dashing looking fellows, those men, tanned up in their march from Fort Scott, from whence they have just joined us. So the line is completed—the carbines are placed in the buckets by the men's sides—the pistols in the ho'sters, and the five companies are arranged as three squadrons. The adjutant now forms the parade, after which the commanding officer proceeds to make a final inspection of the men, arms, horses and equipage—all found to be in excellent order. The men are nearly all quite young, and as a body are as handsome, athletic, vigorous, and soldierly looking fellows as can be found in any service in the world, I will venture to say. They are mounted on the best American horses, all of them being upwards of fifteen hands in height—and as the serried ranks are extended before you, armed in the manner I have described, does it not occur to you, gentle reader, that such troops would be exceedingly ugly customers, of a keen frosty morning in autumn, when the air would be slightly sarcastic about the point of a man's nose, and the tips of his ears? I assure you they would.

The train of fifteen wagons left about an hour ago; it has gone on ahead—each wagon is drawn by six mules; besides, an additional number of these animals are led to provide for accidents. You must now take notice of those two brass howitzers on the left of the line— we take them with us. They are twelve pounders, and are said to be very effective against Indians. They (the Indians) say they can stand before the bow and arrow, or even the rifle pretty well, but they "object to being shot at by a wagon." Everything being now ready for a start. I'll just name over the officers who belong to the expedition, and we'll be off:—

Major Clifton Wharton, *Commanding*[3]

STAFF

Dr. S. G. I. De Camp, *Surgeon, U.S.A.*
Capt. W. M. D. M. Kissack, *Quarter-master*
Lieut. J. Henry Carleton, *Commissary*
Lieut. T. C. Hammond, *Adjutant*

LINE

Capt. Philip St. George Cooke	Lieut. Philip Kearney
Capt. B. D. Moore	Lieut. Andrew Jackson Smith
Capt. J. H. K. Burgwin	Lieut. John Love
Capt. B. A. Terrett	Lieut. George T. Mason

Rev. Leander Ker, *Chaplain, U.S.A.*

Mr. Charles Deas, the distinguished artist of the West,[4] also accompanies the dragoons on this campaign. He will, no doubt, make many fine additions to his already extensive and truly beautiful gallery of paintings.

The inspection over, the command is given, and in a moment the long line is broken into column and on its way for the still *Farther West.* A more propitious day for commencing a campaign could not have been chosen. The air is just lively enough to rustle the leaves and flowers, and raise the locks from one's cheeks. Every man is in fine spirits, and even the horses seem to be delighted at their prospect of having many a fine roll and unconstrained gambol upon the green prairies. It is indeed a noble body of troops—and I hear it remarked by many old campaigners, that they seldom, if ever, saw such a well appointed command in every particular. The Band accompanies the column for some distance, cheering their comrades with many an old and familiar air. At length they turn back, and we are fairly separated from our post, and on our way. . . .

CHAPTER II

FIRST DAY'S MARCH—*Scenery*—*Appearance of the Column*—*Arrive at a stream*—*Manner of encamping*—*Great excitement—very!*—*Young horses and old ones*—*Stillness of a military camp after "tattoo"*—*Query as to the stream*—*Second day's march*—*Manner of starting in the morning*—*"Jim Rogers"*—*Counter-marching*—*Old Council Bluff Trail*—*Polar Plant*—*Encamp again*—*Excessive heat*—*Sick report increasing.*

LET the reader picture to himself a gently undulating prairie, here and there interspersed with patches of woodland—the trees of which being so completely divested of undergrowth that they appear to have been carefully trimmed by art; then let him imagine each grove a finely kept park—each green and flower enamelled slope a favorite lawn for the dance of the wood nymphs—each vista through the arching foliage a sylvan pathway, connecting one beautiful spot with another almost to infinity, and he will have a faint idea of the country for the first three day's march from Fort Leavenworth, in almost every direction. Now, let him bring into such a picture, the immensely long column of Dragoons, marching "by twos," followed by the burnished pieces of artillery and the train of fifteen wagons, with the mounted guard some half mile in the rear of the whole, and he can imagine very readily, the grand effect of the scene. No person could view it without being almost enchanted by its peculiar beauty. The horsemen can here and there be seen emerging from some delightful grove, or winding down some gentle acclivity; some are in the strong light, some are in the deep shadows; and as they pass along, their arms and equipments sparkling in the sun, their sabres clanging against their heavy spurs and stirrups, their horses neighing and prancing, they lend a life—a charm, a picturesqueness to the already perfect view, which one must see in reality in order to appreciate it properly, for no pen or pencil could ever do it justice;—there are so many indescribable little things which give a keeping to such a picture. . . .

As new directions are taken by the column, or different parts of it, you can hear the animated commands of the officers, or the distant bugle near the commander, as the signal to *"Halt!"* or *"Forward!"* is sounded. This, with the lusty voices of the mule-drivers as they exhilarate their long eared teams, with a flourish and crack of their huge whips, together with that incessant hum and rumble, that swells upon the ear like a deep undertone—a low and heavy bass to all these other trebles—occasioned by the tramp, tramp, tramp of hundreds of feet each instant upon the reverberating ground, make up a series of exciting sounds, which, taken in connection with the picture I have vainly attempted to describe, render the march exceedingly and singularly attractive.

About four o'clock P.M., we encamp upon the head waters of a beautiful stream, which after running considerably west of north for some sixteen or eighteen miles—(following its course) gradually winds around and runs eastward into the Missouri.[5] When the Dragoons are operating upon the prairie, the following is their mode of encamping, as nearly as I can describe it. The ground is usually selected by the Quarter-master, who generally marches with the Pioneers under his command, some mile or two in advance of the troops. In choosing it he has an eye not only to beauty and strength of position, but also to its convenience to wood and water. Above all, he must be careful to have fine grass at hand in abundance, amongst which to picket the horses and mules. This selection being made, when the column comes up the Commanding officer, through the Adjutant, directs each Squadron as it arrives where to take position. If the encampment is upon a stream—and it generally is so— our Squadron is formed along its bank, and facing it. The next takes position upon its right, facing outward—the next upon its left, also facing outward. The wagons and howitzers are parked upon the fourth side, under charge of the guard. This square is usually about one hundred and twenty yards on each side—sometimes more and sometimes less, according to the nature of the ground. As soon as each Squadron has got its place the men are all dismounted, when they immediately strip their horses upon the very ground they occupy, and lead them off out of the square. After finding a good spot of grass in the neighborhood, each man there pickets his horse. This is done by having a lariette made of six eighths manilla rope, some thirty feet in length, one end of which is fastened in the halter, the other into a ring attached to an iron picket pin some fourteen inches long, which the dragoon forces into the ground with his foot. As soon as this is done all the men return to where their horses were stripped, as there the tents are to be pitched. By this time the company wagons have come up, and each one is halted a few yards in rear of where the line of tents of the troop to which it belongs will rest. It is quickly unloaded. Then about one third of each mess— (and every company is divided into several, of seven or eight men each)—take the tents away and pitch them. This they do with an extremely important air, as if everything depended upon it. There is a great deal of pacing off of ground, and *sighting* along the line to see if all is straight, and the intervals properly preserved. The next third seize the utensils for cooking with most grave and serious faces; and in taking them away do it with a sort of professional flourish, seemingly ambitious to make as much noise as possible, as if they had an extensive larder, and were fully acquainted with its value, and in fact, wished everybody else to be acquainted with it also. The remaining third take the axes, go after wood and build fires; and, as if determined not to have *their* duty considered insignificant compared with that of the others, they chop and lug their burthens along, lay their wood ready for kindling in a peculiarly solemn and scientific manner, and after having done so, (having reference all the time to the line, for they even "*dress*" the fires), they light a match, and with the help of dry leaves and grass soon get the flame going—as they kneel down and with distended cheeks blow it into a roaring condition, like so many animated bellows—they cast serious and significant glances at those at work with the tents and mess pans, as much as to say—"Well, if it wasn't for us what *would* you fellows do for a supper, anyhow!" All these duties are done at once; and when each of the parties gets into active operations, and the three various but important branches of labor are all being operated upon at the same time, there is no little noise and excitement in the camp. The click! click! click! of a hundred hatchets driving tent pins, and a hundred axes cutting wood is heard; and mingled with it, is the rattle of divers pots, kettles and pans; each mess apparently striving to outdo all others in its culinary din, as if more noise not only betokened better supper, but more of it. Then to be added to all this, is the braying of mules and the neighing of horses. They, too, are in great commotion from their delight at getting rid of their burthens, and scores of them at a time may be seen rolling, and kicking up their heels in their joy at their liberty. Here and there an old campaigner of a horse, or donkey, who has had much experience, and gained therefrom a great quantity of real hard horse sense, goes quietly to feeding as soon as he is picketed. Ever and anon such old stagers look up, and as they leisurely chew the mouthful of grass which they have just cropped, they cast a sort of sage, patronizing and slightly contemptuous glance at the young and frisky fellows about them, as much as to say—"Gad, my fine chaps, you'd better be eating your supper and leave off your rustics! Time you've seen the service *I* have, you'll learn how to cut vastly different capers from those."

Supper being over, the "stable call" is sounded, when all the animals are led into the square and again picketed, though with much less scope to their lariettes, as the ground is more limited. A chain of sentinels is thrown around the whole, and now the encampment is completed for the night. So this beautiful spot of ground, which but one hour ago was so still, so retired; almost shrinking away from view among those old trees, with its modest loveliness, is now covered with a little city, with its streets, its smokes, its noise and bustle. And, although small, it is a city it would be extremely hazardous to beleaguer—it is a perfect little fortress of itself. Those white tents cover a living wall which few would care about battering, much less to mount.

At nine o'clock in the evening "tattoo" is blown, when each company parades under arms in front of its own tents, and is inspected by an officer. This inspection is one of form entirely—the object being to see that every man has his arms, and his equipments on; for immediately thereafter he retires, and if an alarm is given in the night, or an attack made, he can leap from his blankets and place his hand upon his weapons at once. Fifteen minutes more and the bugle sounds "put out the lights"—when in an instant everything is not only as dark, but as quiet as the grave. No doubt, reader, you have been in many a place so still as almost to hear yourself think—but all that is nothing to the stillness of a military camp in the night. I can hardly think of anything more awful and sublime—for it is sublime—than that profound silence that reigns there then. A moment since, as it was, and men were passing to and fro, and knots of them were sitting around the camp fires, the light striking here and there upon their faces and forms, while all the rest of their figures would be in deep shadow. In other of the groups, a dozen young soldiers would be gathered around some old dragoon, listening to his long yarns of hair-breadth escapes—buffalo chases—campaigns to the mountains, and other wonderful events of his service. In others, some fine voice would be singing the burden of a light ballad, or patriotic song, and scores of men would join in the chorus, waking the echoes again, with their rich bursts of melody. Besides, beneath all this, was that continued and confused hum of voices, incident to all great bodies of men whose conversation had been for a long time restrained, and is just set at liberty. With these sounds, too, were mingled the noises of the various employments of men preparing the morrow's breakfast, with divers coffee mills in full and prolonged operation. *Now*, not a man can be seen, save it may be the distant sentinel, nearly obscured by the murky shadows of night; and not a sound can be heard save perhaps, the whoop of some far-off owl, as it comes borne upon the faint breeze of night—or the almost human scream of the wolf as he ventures occasionally near the encampment. It is the repose of this multitude around you that makes the profound solitude, and the contrast from the recent bustle which causes the awful stillness. You are expecting some audible manifestation of life from the hundreds of human beings whom you know are within so few yards of you, and because you are dis-

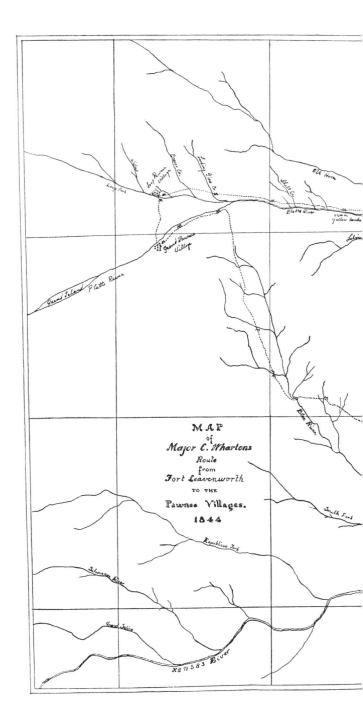

MAP
of
Major C. Whartons
Route
from
Fort Leavenworth
TO THE
Pawnee Villages.
1844

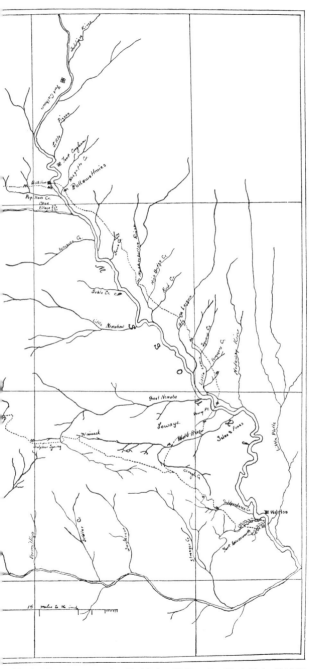

After the Wharton map as reproduced in *Collections of the Kansas State Historical Society*, Vol. XVI.

appointed is one reason why the silence seems greater than perhaps, it really is.

Such is the process of encamping every night; the only variation being in the Squadrons as they alternate in position, as do the different troops composing the same Squadron. This is done that all may fare exactly alike as to convenience to wood and water. The stream upon which this encampment is located is very clear—flowing over a limerock bed, and beautifully fringed along its banks with groves of oak, walnut, hickory, hackberry and elm. The Commanding officer is of the impression that it is a branch of the Kanzas—but probably such is hardly the fact—it being, in the opinion of many, a tributary of the Missouri, as I before described. Our course to-day has been nearly west, and we have marched not over ten miles in a straight line from Fort Leavenworth.

Tuesday, August 13, 1844

The bugles are sounding the "Reveille" at the first appearance of light in the heavens, and the men turn out and after arming themselves completely, fall into line by companies for roll call and inspection. The object in having the troops parade under arms at daybreak is to accustom them to springing up and forming ready for action at a moment's notice. Each soldier, therefore, is always very particular where he places everything the night before. This duty over, "stable call" again sounds, when the animals are led out of the square to fresh spots of grass. At the signal for "breakfast" which is blown half an hour afterwards, that meal is eaten, and the men who are for guards saddle up their horses. The "adjutant's call" is then sounded and the detail of each company is paraded by the orderly sergeants and inspected by an officer of the troop to which it belongs. The rest of the men hurry and pack up everything, but the tents, and load the company wagons. Then the "general" is sounded when in a moment the pretty little city with its white buildings and regular streets, and rows, vanishes away like the mists of morning which but now settled in the distant vallies and hung in wreaths about the tops of the trees. The ceremony of guard mounting is then gone through with, when the new guard is marched on and the old one relieved. While all this is being done the men bring in their horses, and having paraded them in line, an officer inspects each of them carefully, in order to see if they have been taken proper care of, and likewise to see if they are in every respect uninjured. Because of the moment the dragoon's horse gets out of condition or lame, that moment the man must walk and let him recover; for the horse as well as man must always be kept efficient and in fighting order. The Pioneer party now moves off, following the guide and quartermaster, and soon too the wagons are in motion. With their white covers they seem almost like a moving encampment. . . .

Our guide is a Delaware Indian named Jim Rogers. He says he is seventy-two years of age, and yet he is straight as an arrow and is as hardy and as healthy as a man of forty. Jim is a great character; he knows the general geography of the country—but never before has been in this part of it. He was out with Lieut. Frémont in his first Expedition to the mountains, and knows thoroughly all the Southern routes from the Missouri to the Nebraska, but on this one which we design taking, he is entirely at fault. Jim cuts a great figure on an old condemned white horse which had served many a long year in the dragoons before being turned over to the quarter-master's department. He is dressed from head to foot in a fringed suit of buckskin, with an old figured calico shawl upon his head which had probably seen more service than the horse even. Then upon his shoulder he carried a rifle which for length and general clumsiness of appearance would make that owned by Leatherstocking seem to be a highly finished pistol. Jim is somewhat of a wag too; that is in a quiet way. He never speaks except to answer some question, but occasionally those answers are given in a tone and manner that plainly show they are intended as much to quiz as anything else. Yesterday he led us decidedly out of our course; to-day he is making up for it by taking us in every direction but the right one in hopes to find a "big divide"; owing to these mistakes of Jim the column has made a large detour of several miles, sometimes facing directly toward Fort Leavenworth again. This is very annoying: besides we have had two wagons broken, from the badness of the ground we have been forced to travel over in order to extricate ourselves from the numerous water-courses that spread out like a net upon every hand. About ten o'clock we strike the Old Council Bluff trail and follow it up. Notwithstanding it takes us something out of our course, it is the best we can do. We are now getting along very well, except that we make too much northing. This, however, we shall be enabled to remedy as we get farther over our journey. The stream upon which we encamped last night keeps upon our left hand; distant, generally, about two miles. It circles around, crossing our trace at a point say fifteen miles from where we started this morning. The squadrons march alternate days with the left and then with the right in front—and where the ground will admit of it—one squadron marches in front of the train of wagons to beat down the high grass forward of the teams, meanwhile the other two march one upon each side of this train, distant, say forty or fifty yards. In that way we form three parallel columns and break three complete roads.

The soil we have travelled over so far has been exceedingly rich and capable of producing anything that grows in this latitude. We saw immense quantities of the *polar plant* to-day, but as a good description of it was recently published in the "Spirit of the Times," from the practised pen of Lieut. Alvord, 4th U.S. Infantry, a gentleman of high attainments, I will merely say that it grows in clusters of four or five leaves each, every leaf being usually fourteen or sixteen inches in length by six inches in width at the broadest part. This plant is of a pale green and has a rough, harsh texture. Its immense leaves face toward the east and west, with their edges north and south. A stout fibrous stalk shoots up three or four feet in height from the centre of each clump of leaves, having several yellow blossoms at and near its top very closely resembling small sun flowers. This plant is highly resinous and no doubt possesses some valuable medicinal properties. I regret that I have not a sufficient acquaintance with its botanical structure and qualities to give it a proper description. It is the Indian's compass as he traverses the great oceans of the west, and one which is as true as the magnet to the pole. Why it invariably points to the north is beyond my power to determine, unless it be that it is peculiarly sensitive so far as regards heat, and therefore presents to the sun at broad noon-day only the edges of its large leaves. Until more is known of its truly singular qualities, it will ever be a subject of much curious speculation to the voyageur of the prairies. We arrived at the stream I have spoken of at the point where it crossed our trail—flowing to the right toward the Missouri—by three o'clock P.M. We here, also, found it very finely timbered with oak, walnut, ash, sycamore and linden. . . . In descending to the stream from the high prairie the road wound around a hill which was so steep it was with much difficulty the wagons were kept from turning over. At this place one of our howitzer carriages was accidentally broken. To repair it will cause much delay. As the leading squadron approached the stream which was exceedingly clear and beautiful, with alternate pools and ripples, the order was given for the horses of it to be watered. One gentleman dashed forward into the water, and immediately found his horse struggling in quick sands. It was a very dangerous position for him to be in, as the horse began to rear and plunge in a frightful manner, and withal tried to turn and come out on the same side from which he entered the water. His rider, fearing that the horse might possibly fall with him and strike him with his feet, sprang from his back into the stream. . . .

We encamped at three o'clock this afternoon on the northern bank of this creek, the spot selected is a very desirable one, having wood and water upon three sides of it, and one of those fortress hills upon the fourth. It is a little prairie of itself, and is just large enough for a magnificent encampment. Mr. Deas made two very fine sketches of this spot after the tents were pitched and the fires lighted. At 4 P.M. the mercury stood at 84° Fah. in the shade, and twelve men are on the sick report. Many of those who in garrison had been attacked with fever and ague or intermittent fever, and had as they supposed entirely recovered, have again been visited by these diseases, relapses being brought on by the excessive heat. Besides, there are many new cases, the seeds of which were probably sown in the system during the summer, and are now making their appearance; induced to do so no doubt by the sudden change in the men's manner of living and exercise, and continual exposure to the rays of a burning sun. Reader, good night!

CHAPTER III

WEDNESDAY, AUGUST 14

WE BEGAN our march this morning at 7 o'clock, still keeping the Council Bluff trail. We had not proceeded over a mile, before the "Hospital Wagon"—a *lame* apology for an ambulance—got broken, when a halt of an hour was ordered until it could be repaired. This was the second time that wagon had broken since we started. In fact, it seemed to be a doomed vehicle from the commencement. Whether the fault was in the material of which it was constructed, or from its venerable antiquity, or both, could never be ascertained; but it broke, nevertheless. It certainly was not in the citizen teamster, Mr. Jackson—"the gentleman as drew it"— for he always protested "he drew carefuller, capting (addressing the quarter-master), than any of the boys along;" but, from the fact of his having one eye slightly shadowed by a faint knuckular abrasion remotely resembling a *bung*, he might have been mistaken. His vision was undoubtedly affected by the bandage invariably tied over his left organ of sight, (a sort of dark curtain to that window of his soul), and therefore he could not place stumps and holes in their proper location—running afoul of them every now and then with an independent kind of a looseness which was generally very much to the detriment of his carriage. This, the men (much to his annoyance) designated by the euphonious name of "Physic Cart."

Our course was about West 20° North, to-day, and for the first few miles, was over a broken and abruptly undulating prairie. One gentleman attached to the Expedition, commenced his *"Fall's Hunt"* this morning. He would have done so before we crossed Salt Creek, within a mile or so of Fort Leavenworth, but from the great scarcity of game in that region, he restrained his ardor till to-day. It perhaps would not do to say, that in volunteering to come on this campaign, he had the remotest idea of indulging his singular passion for hunting; but yet, when it is considered to what great expense he subjected himself in the way of a fit out, (the articles purchased being entirely powder and shot, and numerous boxes of percussion caps), one would be apt to believe that he had *some* notion of shooting game, even before he came, provided always that he could do so as a matter of course, without even turning out of his way to hunt it. His boy John, therefore, was placed in charge of the immense saddle-bags of ammunition at the first start from the post, and being mounted with them upon an antique horse, was directed always to keep near his master from morning till night, to deal out the rounds as they should be needed, he (John) acting in the capacity of what the sailors call a "powder monkey," only not in full commission, being but a brevet, from his inexperience in such service. This gentleman even went so far as to tell the caterer of his mess not to purchase meats for the march, as he had made such complete preparations for hunting that he would be enabled, with ease, to furnish several tables with all the animal food they could need.

On this morning the shooting was to commence, and large bets of wine was made as to the result. It was really exciting to look away across the prairie, and see him riding through the grass, with his dog, "Sport," dashing hither and thither in front, and John bringing up the rear with the ammunition, literally an animated caisson; or rather, a locomotive magazine, done, (as the painters say) in condemned horse and nigger. Every now and then "Sport" would *point;* then the hunter would dismount, give his bridle rein to John, and stealing gently forward, would sing out *"hie on!"* In a moment the bird would be in the air: bang! bang! (both barrels) and away whirrs the grouse, "Sport" keeping underneath it, and barking until he is distanced, and the bird is fairly out of sight. As the hunter comes back to his horse, chewing tobacco like fury in his keen excitement at the sport, he loads his piece, mounts up again, and pushes on as before. All this he does with the utmost relish; the only drawback being, perhaps, a reflection as to the means that any of the mess has for a supper, which unfortunately may have calculated upon his success in *killing*, and not in hunting, birds—for of his ability to perform all manner of things pertaining to the latter act, the most sceptical could never doubt, more especially could they have but witnessed his continued industry from morning till night.

Jim Rogers generally followed in this gentleman's wake, and once in a while he would bring *his* rifle to bear upon something, but as it never made a practice of going off until it has been snapped and primed, and the flint rubbed and pecked with the back of a knife, some six or eight times, he generally had about the same luck as his illustrious predecessor. They were both great hunters—indeed, perfect Nimrods in *their* way—but the fact was, they were out of luck.

We left the Council Bluff trail about 9 o'clock, A.M., for the purpose of heading the little branches of Independent River, a small tributary of the Missouri. This forenoon we have been ascending a high rolling prairie, with but few groves of timber in sight, except that which covers the great Missouri Bottom away upon our right.

In the afternoon there was a spirited wolf chase, in which several of the officers joined. The animal was perfect game, and afforded a deal of sport, but he was at length killed by a sabre stroke, given by one of the officers as he dashed past him with the speed of the wind.

We encamped at 4 o'clock P.M. upon the head waters of Independence Creek, not having marched to-day more than fifteen miles, on account of excessive heat, which was very oppressive to the animals, particularly to the mules.

Just before we arrived at the camping ground, Private Clough of "K" troop, went into a fit, and although our experienced surgeon was immediately attending him, he died in fifteen minutes! A moment ago, as it were, he was riding along with his comrades, apparently as well as they; now, there he lies upon the green turf, a stark and ghastly corpse, with his spirit in another being! It is a fearful thing thus to see one's fellow man, when in seemingly robust health —living-feeling—hoping on like one's self, thus stricken down by an unseen hand, and *so soon* removed from all known things of this world, to the unknown ones of another. The singular and sudden death of this man was a shock to our feelings which it would be difficult to forget.

We have seen but very little game, so far. We are still too near the Kickapoos and Sacs to meet with much to shoot at except prairie fowl. The sick report is becoming larger, and many of the men are so weak, we are obliged to convey them in the wagons. The dew is so very heavy that it wets the tents completely through during the nights. The soldiers on guard are exposed to it; besides, they get their feet and limbs as drenched as they can well be, in walking through the high grass, both on post and in relieving sentinels. This, with the loss of sleep, and the exposure and fatigue in the hot sun, all day, is very apt to induce sickness, more especially if their systems are partially prepared for it from previously existing causes.

THURSDAY, AUGUST 15

After the "assembly" sounded this morning, the squadrons were paraded with the men on foot "standing to horse." An escort of a corporal and eight men, mounted, led the way, when the whole command marched to the spot where poor Clough was to be buried. It was on the summit of a beautiful hill, on the east side of the stream upon which we had encamped, and where a grave had already been dug by a detail from his own company. On account of the impossibility of having a coffin made, the remains had been wrapped in a blanket and deposited in the grave—which was left open—previous to the columns having arrived at it. The squadrons formed three sides of a square about the spot, and after the chaplain had made some very appropriate remarks, and a feeling prayer, the order was given to mount, when the escort fired the last salute over the remains of their comrade, and we wheeled off on our march over the great ocean.

> "Leaving the dead
> To its own solitary rest,
> Of all lone things the loneliest"!

Our course to-day was but little north of west, and lay over the dividing ridge that separated the waters running into Stranger River —a branch of the Kanzas—from those flowing toward the Missouri. The timber upon the streams about four or five miles to our left, seemed to be very heavy and thrifty, while that on the water courses upon our right, appeared sparse, and of a small and meagre growth.

At 10 o'clock A.M., as they say at sea, we hove in sight of the homeward-bound Kickapoos, hailed them, and made them heave too. They were not carrying much sail at the time, being under a close reefed breechcloth, with only a half point blanket aloft. They were evidently privateersmen, each carrying a long rifle athwart his saddle, midships, something like a pivot Long Tom on a Letter of Marque. They had been hunting, and promised to bring some fresh deer and turkies to our camp at night. They then bore off, and the last we saw of them, they were standing close hauled upon the wind, evidently trying to weather a small island of timber away to the southward. They were the first craft of any kind, that had crossed our wake since we had been at sea.

At twelve miles from our last encampment, we came to a fine spring branch on the left of our trail. This would be a good place to halt for the night. We march on eight miles further, over a gently undulating plain, and encamped at 5 o'clock, P.M. on a small stream which also ran to the south, and at this point formed a large bend by curving in near our trail. Seventeen men on the sick report, the weather still continuing excessively dry and hot. The soil passed over to day has been evidently growing somewhat poorer. How-ever, we have kept a high dividing ridge, and but little opportunity has been offered to examine that on the lower lands, and near the water courses. We have no trouble from the green prairie-fly, seeing but now and then one. No doubt the heavy rains destroyed the most of them. Sometimes they are so thick as to almost kill the horses, causing the blood to run in large drops from whatever spot they alight upon. In fact, I have heard of instances of horses being killed by them, their deaths being occasioned, no doubt, by the prolonged and excessive nervous irritation from the innumerable swarms of these winged and ravenous blood suckers continually biting them. They are the scourge of the prairies, but so far, we have been most fortunate in escaping them.

This evening, four Mountain men, representing themselves as belonging to the "Union Fur Company,"[6] came into camp from Fort Leavenworth. They brought us some letters. They said they were on their way to Council Bluff, and begged us to let them have some provisions, as they had started from the Fort a day after we did, and had travelled so far without anything to eat except a few loaves of bread they had put in their saddle-bags. No doubt they told the truth, for from their appearance, we judged they had left there while inebriated;[7] besides, the leader of the party was violently threatened with the *tremens* when he came into camp; so much so, in fact, that his conversation was extremely wandering and incoherent. We supplied them with provisions enough to last six days, and they are encamping near us to-night. These mountain men live in a singularly wild and precarious manner: here, to-day, with plenty—there, to-morrow, with nothing—subjected to every hardship of labor and exposure, and running every risk of life—still they are happy, and so wedded to their wandering kind of existence, that all the allurements of wealth and comfort, and the charms of society, cannot wholly win them from their wild sort of freedom on the great plains, the vast rivers, the sublime mountains. However hard they may fare, they are never happy unless communing with nature herself—with nothing but the pure blue heaven overhead, the broad and beautiful prairie around. They are then at home.

CHAPTER IV

STRIKE THE OREGON TRAIL FROM ST. JOSEPH–*Noon rest–Thirteen Indians discovered–Something of a shower–Suffering of the Emigrants–The lone grave upon the prairie–Encamp on Wolf River–Quarter-master–Rocky Mountains, and Jim Rogers lost–Jim's rifle improving–Great luck of "Sport's" owner, and great exertions of "Sport" himself.*

FRIDAY, AUGUST 16

WE TOOK up our line of march at 7 o'clock, A.M., and shaped our course as nearly west as the nature of the ground would admit. After having travelled about six miles we struck the Oregon Trail, running west from St. Joseph. This trail was made by a large company which emigrated to the Columbia river early last Spring.[8] At this point some of the head waters of the Big Nemaha bore south—distant about three miles. We halted at one o'clock on a little creek emptying into Wolf river, where the horses were stripped and allowed to graze for an hour and a half. Such rests in the heat of the day are exceedingly refreshing to the poor animals, as they suffer much more than the men, from the excessive heat and want of water.

This forenoon, the officers in sweeping the horizon with their glasses, discovered thirteen Indians upon an ascent away upon our left—too far off, in fact, ever to have noticed them by the naked eye. They were evidently watching our column—which from its compactness and length, and the long train of white topped wagons, can be seen at an immense distance. We believe them to be Kanzas. In commencing our march this afternoon our course inclined considerably more towards the north.

About 4 o'clock P.M., a dense, black cloud arose in the north west, and after covering nearly half of the sky with its terrific volume, passed around to the eastward, evidently but a few miles from us. We could hear the continual roar of the thunder, and see the vivid flashes of lightning as they seemed to play from one cloud to another, and down to the prairie. Sometimes they appeared to hang in tremulous festoons, from one huge mass to another, for more than a second; and then again, would be darting like winged serpents, hither and thither, downwards and upwards, zig zag, and every other way; forming, at times, a perfect net-work of dazzling flame upon the awful darkness from whence they seemed to spring. This, together with the unceasing roar of the thunder, and that fearfully rushing sound caused by the conflict of antagonist winds, tossing the clouds this way and that in their dreadful strife, formed a scene so sublime, and created music so grand and terrible, that I am sure, all who gazed upon the one, or heard the other, can never forget either so long as they live. All this time the prairie-hawks and swallows, and various other birds, kept flying through the air as if half crazed, and screaming from very fright. As our column moved along hardly a word was spoken; all seemed intently watching the agony, as it were, of the elements. The Genius of the storms must have conducted this magnificent tempest himself—no journeyman, or even director of ordinary, every-day-sort of showers, could have had any hand in it at all.

From the unprecedented rains which commenced about the time the Oregon Emigrants began their long and dangerous journey, it was evident to us that they must have suffered extremely. Every foot of their trace seemed to have been ploughed in furrows from their wagons, having cut through the thin turf deeply into the wet and soft earth—besides, sickness and death were no strangers to them on their toilsome and hazardous march. This afternoon we passed a grave where they had buried one of their number. It had a mound of earth raised over it, which was covered with grass and flowers, but there was nothing further to tell us who it was that slept beneath.

And why did they rear even this? Who would ever again pass this way? Who, if they saw this humble hillock, would know or care for the ashes beneath? Perhaps no one! Even they who built it could never expect to see it again—and yet it was gratifying to them in their heavy bereavement, even *thus* faintly to distinguish from the surrounding level—this last resting place of their dead. Even thus to fix some little mark upon the desolate waste, which, although never more to be visited by them, still would be sacred and hallowed! Still would be *something* to arrest the flight of memory in her sad journey back to the past, to call again into being the dear departed!*

We encamped about six o'clock P.M., on Wolf river, near its source; turning off a mile and a half to the right to do so. To-day we have reached twenty-five miles. This stream has a few stinted oaks upon it, a limestone bed, and abounds with fish, many of which were caught by both the officers and men. We also found upon it some very fine specimens of marine fossils. The Quarter-master has selected a spot for an encampment some four miles and a half in advance of where we halted, and upon the left of the trail, on waters which ran to the south-west, and which were supposed to be the head branches of the Big Nemaha. There he found a fine spring, and caught some delicious fish—Jim Rogers and Rocky Mountains† were with him. They saw a great many elk "sign," but they were not sufficiently fresh to create any excitement. For a long while they waited there, expecting the column to come up; and finally, the sun went down, but no dragoons could be seen anywhere in sight. They then began to retrace their steps—this was no easy matter to do, for the shadows of night had fairly obliterated their faint trail, and they had to steer their course by the wind. We had marched so far, and the animals were suffering so much for want of water that the Commanding officer concluded to turn off to the first spot where we

---

*Although at the time we knew not who had been buried here, we afterwards learned that it was Mrs. . . . . , the wife of General . . . . , the leader of the party. She was said to have been very young, amiable and beautiful.

†The soldiers called Mr. DEAS by this name. Probably from his riding a horse which "*had* done the State some service—had a broad white hat—a loose dress, and sundry traps and truck" hanging about his saddle, like a fur-hunter. Besides, he had a Rocky Mountain way of getting along; for, being under no military restraint, he could go where he pleased, and come back when he had a mind to.

could possibly get along for the night—hence the reason we had not pushed on to the place selected by the Quarter-master. In a dry, or even in an ordinary wet season, cattle would be greatly distressed from thirst in travelling over the ground we have passed to-day. On account of the prolonged absence of the Quarter-master and his partners in difficulty, we all concluded they were lost—(which by the way was a very proper conclusion), and various trumpeters were sent off to the summits of the neighboring eminences to blow the "recall"; besides, the Adjutant had got some rockets ready to send up, when an answering *"hallo-o-o-o!"* came faintly upon our ears from the distance. The lost ones soon came in, having had the most unexpected and unprecedented good luck in sporting. Rocky Mountains had entered extensively into the fishing business, and had been quite successful. Jim had had good luck also; for his gun had gone off at the second or third trial every time; and although he had shot nothing as yet, still, it was gratifying to him to feel that there was a decided improvement in his rifle, and he got up quite an excitement upon the subject, though on a small scale, and in a private way. The owner of "Sport" had outdone even himself on this occasion. Sport had made some of his most *distingue* efforts in the way of pointing, and his master some of his most brilliant shots; from such combined exertions can it be wondered why the luck in bringing in game was so great? We all recollect with what triumph this keen sportsman held up by the neck his half a brace of grouse as he rode into camp; and with what an air he pointed at it, in reply to the numerous queries of "what luck?" He had astonished not only his friends, but himself at such unusual good fortune.

So ended this day's march. From the loss of his party, and the success of the hunter, the Commanding officer named this stream. Save that the sick report still increases nothing else had occurred during this day worthy of notice. Many bets are daily made as to the time we shall probably strike the Nebraska. There we expect to meet with incident sufficient to keep us continually interested.

CHAPTER V

COLUMN CAUGHT IN A TRAP—*Believing with Macbeth, that "it was as bad to go back, as to go o'er"—Commanding Officer pushes ahead—Suffering of Emigrants—The Nemaha—Passage of this river—Reach another stream—Build bridge—Jim's decisions as to the best of any two "divides"—His patience in adversity—Sulphur Springs discovered—Mr. Jackson begins to "see the Elephant"—Study of astronomy on the Prairies—Few birds seen—Jim's expert practice at an antelope—He sees the "Elephant," and turns back—Circular march—Misfortune of having a race track in one's road, on the night of the 8th of January.*

SATURDAY, AUGUST 17

THE "Hospital Wagon" driven by Mr. Jackson, being again broken, the squadrons did not leave the encampment on Wolf River until half-past eight o'clock this morning. The baggage train, however, started some hour or more previously, following in the trail of the Quarter-master and his pioneers, and Jim Rogers. We still kept upon the Oregon trace. This forenoon, our course was nearly west, with the head waters of Wolf River upon our right, and the Great Nemaha upon our left. This latter river forms a large bend by running nearly west for upwards of twenty miles from its source, and then sweeping entirely around the head of Wolf River, and passing off to the east towards the Missouri. We had all along supposed that much of the heavy timber seen upon our left, skirted Blue River—a tributary of the Kanzas—but by noon this day, we were undeceived on this point, by finding ourselves caught in this big bend of the Nemaha:[9] it was a perfect cul de sac, and we were handsomely pocketed in it. On every hand were immense watercourses and deep ravines. We, therefore, were obliged either to retrace our steps, and head this river entirely, or to find some ford and endeavor to cross it. The commanding officer decided upon the latter course, and search was made for a ford. Happily one was found near where we first struck the river; but as it would take some hours to prepare the high banks so that the wagons could be let down, the squadrons were ordered to encamp, and fifty men were detailed, and placed under the direction of the Quarter-master, for this purpose. It was after sundown before the banks were digged down enough to afford safe passage to the heavily laden wagons. The Oregon Emigrants had got caught in the same trap; but at the season of the year when they were here, the water was so high as to render a passage of the river impossible. They turned back and "headed" it, bearing off to the south, and circling around between it and the Blue. They must have had a dreadful march of it; wherever they went, it seemed to us that their wagons must have cut through the turf and soil, nearly up to the hubs of their wheels. They encamped upon the very spot where we now are, and here is the grave of a little child they buried!

The Nemaha is a finely timbered stream, having upon its banks, ash, elm, slippery elm, hickory, black walnut, oak, and linden. We also found in its neighborhood, limestone, sandstone, marine fossils, gneiss and iron. No doubt there is also coal in abundance in the vicinity, as we saw many indications of it.

Sunday, August 18

This morning, at about half-past six o'clock, we commenced getting our wagons over the river. Seventy-five men were detailed for each bank: each party had ropes—the first to check the vehicles in their descent to the water, the second to assist in drawing them up the opposite shore. By this means, the whole train was crossed in about an hour and a half. The banks of the river are very high and very miry; and this and another ford, half a mile below, are the only ones to be found for a great distance. The Nemaha is susceptible of the highest rises. We noticed by the drift wood and other indications, that it must have been all of thirty-five feet deep, the past summer. The view, as the columns passed this stream, was exceedingly picturesque. Just below our ford was a fine fall of water, suitable for a mill seat, with limestone bed and banks. But no mill could be built that would hardly stand the freshet of the rainy season; yet a race could be digged at this point at a very trifling expense.

Our course to-day has been but a little north of west. We travelled over a high, rolling, and partially broken prairie, with numerous streams upon each hand, all running toward the Nemaha, and all beautifully fringed with timber. The soil, however, has been very poor, being thin, gravelly, and sterile. Our march has been considerably impeded by the numerous small water-courses that spread over the country like a web, some of which we were obliged to bridge. At one o'clock, P.M., we came to a fine, large stream, running diagonally to our right, with high bluffs upon its southern banks. It took our men two hours to bridge it. While the column was halted at this place, the animals were stripped, and allowed to feed upon the wild pea-vine, which grew here in great abundance. Horses and mules prefer the leaves of this plant to the best of grass, and thrive upon them quite as well, if not better, than upon grain, even.

The bridge completed, we were up and on our way again, following a small Indian trail, which seemed to be running in nearly the direction we desired to travel. Jim Rogers seemed more at home after being told to keep this trail: he was not so erratic in his directions, as when having nothing to guide him. Jim had a very happy way of deciding doubtful questions as to the best route to be pursued when two "divides" offered themselves to our columns; each one with nearly equal pretensions to being correct, so far as we could judge, having never travelled either. In such cases, for fear of leading us astray, or into some quagmire, or stream, that we could not cross with the wagons, he would opportunely have a chill, roll himself in his blanket, and fastening his picket-rope to his foot, would lie in the grass, with his old white horse feeding around him, until nearly night, when he would mount up and joint the column: if he found it in difficulty from having taken the wrong divide, he would seem to *look*—"Well, it wasn't *my* fault, thank God!" though not a word would escape his lips. So far as we could judge from what Jim *said*, he regarded everything as a matter of course, whether for or against us.

The trail we followed took us out to the high prairie, from the broken ground near the Nemaha, giving us more sea-room and plainer sailing. We encamped at half-past six o'clock, on a fine spring branch, with timber upon three sides of our square. It is of a poor quality, however, being mostly scrub oak, hickory, and cotton-wood. We have noticed in several places, a species of dwarf oak, that grows only from one to three feet in height, and yet seems to be loaded down with acorns.

Once fairly out of the Nemaha trap, we feel much lighter in spirits. No body has seen the "Elephant"* yet, although sometimes several were on the point of doing so—Mr. Jackson in particular; for as he has unintentionally made it a rule to break down every day since we left Fort Leavenworth; he begins to get quite tired of the campaign. We think at the rate *he* has gone on, he will probably see that animal to-morrow. Two of the officers discovered a fine *sulphur spring* about a mile back of this encampment, and about two hundred yards to the left of our trace.

To night the stars appear singularly numerous and large, owing to an unusually transparency of the atmosphere; and several of the officers have been improving such a fine opportunity to add to the knowledge of astronomy, by laying upon the soft grass in front of their tents, and discussing the peculiarities of several new and beautiful constellations, and fixing some of the old ones in different parts of the heavens from those they have heretofore been accustomed to occupy. One gentleman thought he saw the Southern Cross (we were in 41° N.L.) and probably went so far as to speak somewhat at length on that beautiful cluster of stars, illustrating his conversation on this subject by numerous legends and anecdotes

*When one gets tired of the journey, and wishes to turn back, he has "seen the Elephant"—a cant phrase used by all voyageurs of Western Prairies.

which were extremely racy and to the point, being excelled in brilliancy only by the stars themselves. Another discovered in the *Southern* heavens, a very respectable Ursa Minor, which lacked only three legs and a tail of being quite perfect. This was not the case however with a Scorpion another of the gentlemen pointed out to us. *Its* tail was at least 45° long with a body in proportion. And as for legs, it had *any* number. To-day we have marched seventeen miles notwithstanding the bridges we had to build.

MONDAY, AUGUST 19

Took up our line of march at seven o'clock, our course being W.N.W. and still on the Indian trail. All the morning we were ascending a high ridge with small fringes of timber on each hand, skirting the forks of the Nemaha and which are beginning to be very much attenuated. The soil is exceedingly thin and poor. At five miles from our last encampment we came to a very beautiful stream, curving in on the left, near our trace. Here would be fine camping for a large command, there being plenty of wood, water, and grass. A few miles further on we also found water in sink holes, where we halted a while to let the animals quench their thirst and breathe, for they suffered excessively from the great heat. At half past eleven we passed a "big divide" and struck a large stream running to our left. Here we "nooned" it; and while the animals were grazing, many of the officers and men caught quite a quantity of fish. This stream is ten miles from our last encampment, and is no doubt a fork of the Blue. It is well timbered, and has a wide intervale which is exceedingly rich, from getting all the wash from the uplands. It is singular that *so far* we have seen but a very few birds. The groves of the prairies being, generally, vocal with their sweet songs—we have been struck with the silence which seems to pervade all the woods upon this route. The only birds we have seen being paroquets, grouse (*one* grouse; it being the half a brace killed in a chapter or two back, by the Nimrod of the command), partridges, black-birds, prairie-hawks, whip-'o'wills, larks, plovers and swallows—and a very few of them. This day has been the hottest of any we have had since we started. About the middle of the afternoon, however, a very sudden change took place in the weather; the mercury falling at least 25° Fah.; and we were soon shivering with cold. Six antelopes were discovered at 4 P.M. by the Pioneers, and Jim dismounted, and with his unerring rifle got within fifty yards of them. It was exciting to see how he managed to keep to the leeward of them—going through the tall grass upon his belly like a snake. By and bye, he got behind a tall tuft of weeds—raised on one knee—cocked his piece—rubbed the flint with his thumb nail, and then drew a nice, fine bead on the animals. This time we felt sure Jim would do honor to himself and tribe. He pulled the trigger! (*off went the antelope like the wind*)—puh! —Sizzle-zle-zle-le-e! Bang!—but 'twas too late—they were three hundred yards off, at least, before the bullet from *that* gun overtook them. This was something like luck thought Jim; for his piece had gone off at the *first* pull, and that was some comfort—that was.

At one time during the afternoon, the ridge we were on curved around until our course was nearly east of north. The quarter-master, at that place, asked Jim which way the Pawnee Villages lay?

Jim pointed in a wrong direction.

"No!" said the quarter-master, looking at his compass at the same time, "that is the way!" (pointing north of west.)

Jim immediately said—"Then I go back!"

"Where?"

"Home!" said Jim; and he began to unsaddle the horse which he had ridden, and to pack the effects upon his own back: the horse belonged to the quarter-master's department.

"But, Jim, how are you going?"

"On foot," said Jim.

"What will you eat?"

"Don't know."

"Well, see the Major when you meet the column, and tell him."

This, Jim promised to do, and off he started. When the Major met him, he asked him what he was going back for? He said—"Road heap crooked—maybe men laugh at me."

And this was his only reason for starting back without provisions, and carrying fifty or sixty pounds weight upon his back, and he seventy-two years old, at that. Such was poor Jim's shrinking from ridicule. He had rather run the risk of being starved to death than to be laughed at! However, he gave up the journey, and came on to camp. We encamped at sundown on a small branch of the Blue, having marched nearly all the afternoon, in a circle. Speaking of circles, our march since one o'clock, P.M., reminds me of one that was performed by a gentleman, some years since, at Fort Gibson.[10] The Dragoon Barracks at that post are some quarter of a mile from those occupied by the Infantry. On the 8th of January, that year, the officers of Dragoons had a wine party, to which several of the Infantry officers were invited. They all became quite merry on the occasion, and about twelve o'clock at night one of the latter officers started for home, but did not arrive there till nearly reveille. Upon being asked why he was so long upon the journey, he frankly confessed that "he had kept what he believed was the road, but that it had seemed awfully long, somehow." He had travelled for six hours upon the *race track* which lies between the two Barracks, and upon which he had accidentally got in the dark! We are now about three miles from where we halted at noon.

CHAPTER VI

A MILITARY CAMP ON A WET MORNING—*Employment of officers and of soldiers—doleful appearance of niggers—Witchcraft—Commanding officers' horses non est inventus—Encamp—No Wood—Building of bridges—Labor of the troops—Their cheerfulness upon every occasion—"Fairy Rings"—Speculation upon them—Dance of the Brownies—Thunder shower and curious halloing of the horses.*

TUESDAY, AUGUST 20

THIS morning everything was soaking wet from the heavy rain, which began falling about one o'clock A.M., and continued until daylight. The pioneers had been sent forward to construct a bridge over a small stream some mile or two in advance of our encampmanent. This they did not complete until nearly noon; so we remained where we were and tried to make ourselves as comfortable as possible under the circumstances.

A military encampment on a wet morning is not the most cheerful looking place in the world, that is certain. The bleak wind blowing the smoke every way but the right one; the dull, leaden sky overhead; the cold rain and fog, all tend to make it anything but pleasant. Everybody and everything seems to have the blues. Some of the officers with their military cloaks wrapped about them, may be seen in little knots here and there, either discussing the merits of the campaign, or speaking upon the best probable route to be taken—or, giving reminiscences of other expeditions; while others again, are reading in their tents, or smoking off the blues—or are, mayhap, down beside the little creek, in the wet grass, with a rod and line and flies, ambitious of sunfish and chubs, the largest of which has not over a three inch longitude. The men are rather meditative in all they do—there is no "whistling for want of thought" amongst them on such a morning as this, for they have a plenty to think about. Some are drying their clothes—some are mending theirs—some are wiping and oiling their arms; and some are putting their horse equipage in order. All seem to be engaged in one way or another. It is true their labors are lightened by now and then a dry joke, or quaint saying; and here and there, also, may be heard some able discussion on military affairs, or, it may be on politics—in which many a sage opinion is advanced, that would be the making of such ordinary men as Rochefoucault or Machiavelli. The Black Hussars (our servants) are the most "done up" in a rain of all. They move about, or stand around the fires with that doleful expression which all niggers have when they are shivering with cold, and the wind is blowing the smoke in their faces, and making them of a sort of pepper and salt complexion, by sprinkling the white ashes over them from head to foot. The horses and mules are also, more or less affected by the weather; for they have all left off feeding, and are standing about on three feet and one toe, with their tails to the wind, their ears set back and their eyes dodging; each one, apparently, engaged in some profound metaphysical speculation, that requires a vast deal of real hard horse sense. There is one exception however, to this mode of passing time, in a little bay nag, belonging to one of the officers. He is the most intelligent, and the most volatile piece of horse-flesh that ever a man bestrode. By ten o'clock at night he generally leaves off feeding; he then commences a dance, which he keeps up till broad daylight, accompanying each extra pirouette-caracole and curvette, with a sort of laughing note that is irresistibly ludicrous and comical. *Bob* has an extremely eloquent eye, and a way of laying back his ears and looking fiercely at everybody who approaches him. If he succeeds in frightening the person, he seems almost to laugh in his sleeve at his ruse. A servant who had charge of him used to get alarmed occasionally, at his antics, and in order to appease and conciliate him, especially if upon his back, he would soothingly and affectionately say— "Who-o-o *Robert!*" evidently fearful that if he called him by the nickname *Bob*, the horse would take offence, and become still more restive and unmanageable.

About nine o'clock the Commanding officers' two fine carriage horses were in camp, but all at once they vanished, whither, nobody could tell. Men were sent out in every direction to hunt for them, but without success. Now, this was on a perfectly open prairie, where upon the different summits one could look for miles in every direction, and yet they were never seen again. They became all at once invisible in broad daylight—but how, was a question nobody could answer. Had we been encamped in a dense wood, their absence would not have been so mysterious; but here, in the open grass ground, it was singular in the extreme. There were five full Companies of men present, with the batmen, teamsters and servants attached to the expedition—and yet, not one amongst them all saw them go—but that they went *somewhere* there could be no doubt, as they were never afterwards recovered.

The bridge being completed, we struck our tents at 12 m., and soon arrived at the stream over which it had been built. It was of pure, limpid water, evidently fed by springs, and running to the south. There was a beautiful grove upon it, composed of tall, arching, and solemn elms.

The country on this day's march, has been very high and undulating, with the soil about medium upon the uplands, though exceedingly rich on the water courses. There is also, an abundance of fine timber along the borders of the stream, consisting of elm, oak, hickory, ash, hackberry, black walnut and linden. About two o'clock we came to another large creek, which it took us two hours to bridge. We then took a divide, which ran up between two small water courses, that flowed into the stream we had just crossed from the N.W., and at sundown encamped upon the one on our right. Here we had but very little wood, with which the men were to cook their suppers—in fact, the only fuel that could be found was three small cotton woods growing in a lump, in the edge of the water, and a few dry willow twigs. Besides these, not one tree or shrub could be seen as far as the eye could reach, upon every hand. The men caught a fine lot of fish in this stream. We had seen several deer to-day, and a great many antelopes, one of which Jim had the good fortune to wound. His rifle is daily improving, and it comforts him exceedingly to think of it.

Wednesday, August 21

We were in the saddle and under way this morning before seven o'clock; and, after travelling W.N.W., until nearly noon, over a high and abruptly rolling prairie, with all the water courses inclining to the south—we came to a beautiful stream, also running to our left, and which was finely timbered. Its banks being very steep and miry we were obliged to bridge it, and this caused a delay of two hours. We then went on again, and, before we had marched a league, came to still another stream, filled with quicksands, and which could not be passed by the heavy laden wagons until loads and loads of willows and grass had been cut and matted upon its bottom, to keep the wheels from sinking to their very axle trees, as they otherwise would have done. We encamped at six o'clock on a fine little river that ran into the Blue from the north—probably its largest branch on this side. Its banks being very high and steep, the pioneer party was employed until night in preparing them, so that the wagons could be let down to a ford, which we found about half a mile below the square. Thus, with the constructing of willow fords and bridges, and the digging down of banks of streams, our men were employed nearly one fourth of the time. This part of the service was exceedingly laborious and fatiguing—the dragoons often working in the mud and water up to their waists, and sometimes even swimming, and lifting at the heavy green timber, with which our bridges were built—or exerting themselves to the utmost with their shoulders to the wheels of the wagons, that every now and then would mire down in crossing the soft and marshy places, that here and there lay in our route. All this under a burning August sun, was no child's play, as the reader may well suppose, but the severest kind of labor that could possibly be required of troops under any circumstances. And well did they ever acquit themselves in performing it. No hesitation—no murmuring—no flinching. An obstacle had but to be presented to be overcome, and that too, with a hearty good will, and cheerfulness and alacrity upon *every* occasion, that deserved the highest praise.

Every day, almost, since we started, we have passed peculiar little rings and crescents upon the prairies, which have been the subject of much doubtful speculation as to the cause of their regularity, and as to why the flowers by which they are covered, grow so much more abundantly upon them than upon the soil immediately contiguous. Some of these circles are three or four rods in diameter, and some not over one. The turf and grass in the centre of them is precisely the same as that on the outside. Each circle seems to be generally, about two feet wide, and loosened up around the whole circumference, nearly the same as it would be were it digged with a spade, and then planted by a dozen different kinds of flowers; the prevailing one of which being a species of the sunflower, only much smaller, and with a stalk some three or four feet in height. These stalks are very slender, and, when swayed hither and thither by the wind, and the weight of the blossom upon the top, are extremely graceful and pretty. The plants being so high, and the leaves upon them of such a dark green, these rings upon which they grow are perfectly defined upon the short purple grass of the upland prairies, and can be seen upon the side hills for a long distance. Some were of opinion that the turf may have become loosened, and the soil laid bare by lightning—some that it was originally cut up by buffalo—and, that as soon as the seeds of these plants were thus exposed to the heat, they grew up so luxuriantly as to overshadow and kill out the grass completely. . . . We called them "Fairy Rings."

This evening about eleven o'clock, there came up quite a shower, with lightning and very heavy thunder; the first clap of which was exceedingly startling and loud, and quite unexpected. As soon as its echoes had died away, the horses—who had been unusually still before—began halloing to each other and answering back again, all over the encampment; as if they were alarmed, and wished to reassure themselves that they were not alone—this done, throughout the rest of the shower they were perfectly silent. This cry of theirs, mingling with the noise of the tempest, was as startling as the "all hands on deck" at sea, in a gale of wind.

CHAPTER VII

BAD FORD–MR. JACKSON IN DIFFICULTY–*His Unexpected Flight–His Discomfiture–Arrive at Blue River–Its Character–Its Timber–Our Manner of Crossing it with Ponton Boats–India-rubber boat upsets–It is built on a Bad Plan–Two Wagons sent back–Fires in the Distance–A High Swimming Horse, very!–Strike S.W. Fork of the Blue–Cross again by Pontons–Singular Hills again–One Man dangerously sick–Speculation as to the time we shall reach the Nebraska–Bets thereon–The Doctor and Chaplain, prophets–Chaplain beats the Doctor, on Thunder-storms; the Doctor beats the Chaplain, in suggestions as to Courses–Our nimrod holding up.*

THURSDAY, AUGUST 22

THE baggage train started about 7 o'clock this morning, the ford not having been completed before. The wagons were at first let down into the water by ropes, the banks being still so steep, and one side of the track being so much inclined laterally, that the mules had not power to hold them back, or the drivers to keep them from upsetting. After the wagons were fairly in the stream, they were turned to the right, and driven up its bed some sixty or seventy yards, where the opposite bank was so low, that with but little assistance from the men, the mules could draw them out. It took two hours to get them all over in this way. A party of men was detailed to wade along, to keep the mules in the middle of the stream, as they were continually disposed to get out of it when left by themselves. When Mr. Jackson attempted to cross with his team, his mules got so obstinate after they had entered the water, they would not pull an ounce. One of the leaders—a little black, long-eared, vicious looking donkey—kept cutting up all sorts of antics the moment he got into the river, and was so restive as not to allow the men who were wading beside him, to approach any where near, without danger of coming in contact with his heels. Besides, all the other mules of the team—acting probably from sympathy with the little black—seemed to make a point of getting into as much confusion as possible, and of pulling every way except ahead. The more Mr. Jackson would strike at them with his whip, the less they all seemed inclined to draw, and the little leader got friskier than ever.—"Strike him!—knock him down!—keel him over!" At every ejaculation, he gave a cut at him with his whip, and at every cut, the big saddle-donkey upon which he sat, turned back his ears, and looked blacker and blacker in the face, although the blows were not intended for him, but for his young friend on the lead. Finally, just as Jackson sang out "keel him over!" this mule kicked up, sending poor Jackson himself, like a bomb in the air: he described the arc of a circle—his whip going one way and his hat the other; he himself, meanwhile, turning various cart-wheels and summersets in his flight; illustrating, as he went with his arms and legs spread out, an animated picture of our national bird, done in teamster. When he came down, he struck head foremost into a bank of soft mud and it was some time before he could extricate himself. While he was taking this involuntary aerial excursion, the mules got into beautiful confusion; some completely turned around in their harness, and facing the wagon, and some this way and some that. Jackson, himself, came down like an apparition, in the midst of them, and had hard work to keep clear of their heels when he emerged from the mud, by scrambling away on his hands and feet as fast as he could. When he had got fairly out of their reach, he deliberately raised one hand to his head, and lifting the handkerchief which was bound about it, above his bunged eye, he stood for a moment surveying his team, with the most rueful countenance that ever ornamented the front side of a man's head. That he plainly saw in each of those mutinous and belligerent mules, an elephant, there could be no manner of doubt. The whole command bursted into a perfect roar of laughter, and poor Jackson waded out, a crestfallen, a drenched, and unfortunate teamster; in fact, an altered man; for from that day out, he never smiled again—the shock had been too much for him.

About three miles beyond this ford, we crossed another fine, large stream, also an affluent of the Blue, and which the Pioneers had bridged before the column came up to it. Our course then lay W.N.W., over a high and level table land, with the soil very rich, but with a great lack of water. To-day we saw several clumps of the helicanthus, and also, a small delicate flower similar to the crocus, but with the delightful perfume of the yellow jessamine. About 12 o'clock, M., we struck Blue River. Here a halt was ordered, and the wagons were unloaded, preparatory to crossing it with our ponton boats. This river is about forty yards wide, with semi-transparent water, and running with a swift current. It is very crooked, and is filled with quicksands. In about half an hour a good place was found for crossing, when we immediately commenced getting the property and provisions over. The horses and mules we intended to ford. We had three fine ponton wagons in the train: these were quickly in the water, as was also an India-rubber boat, which had been brought along by the quarter-master.[11] Some lariettes were then tied together, forming ropes long enough to reach across the river, when a man, taking the end of one of them in his teeth, soon swam to the opposite bank with it, and then pulled over a ponton laden with men, precaution being taken to have still another rope fastened into the opposite end of the boat before it went, by which it could be pulled back by the troops on the side. Two or three more boat loads of men were then crossed, in as many minutes, carrying with them the ropes attached to the other boats. In a few moments all the boats were in active operation; taking in their cargoes on this side—flying across, and discharging them on the other—with an alacrity that was really astonishing. One ponton wagon proved to be more serviceable than a dozen such India-rubber boats as the one we had could possibly have been. The companies who had the pontons, crossed over all their property, and had their wagons and mules and horses on the other side in just thirty minutes, by the watch, from the time they commenced. The provisions, hospital stores, and howitzers, then had to be taken across. This took some time; however, the whole command was over by sun an hour and a half high, and before night, was encamped, two miles from this place, up the right bank of the river. The scene, in crossing this stream, was very fine indeed. Each company seemed to vie with the others in its endeavors to be the first over, and there was an activity amongst the men, and boats, and in fact, everything else, that gave the picture the most animated cast. In the midst of all the excitement and bustle, the India-rubber boat, with a common wagon body upon it, filled with property, upset near the middle of the river. Fortunately, nothing of consequence was lost. This boat had only three cylinders of air, and was but little wider than the bed of a wagon. The consequence was that it had no bearings, its whole safety depending upon the just equilibrium of its load. When troops are to cross rivers in a hurry, it is somewhat inconvenient, besides being unsafe for them to stop at every cargo nicely to adjust the balance of an air boat, which from its very construction, admits of no ballast. Had there been four, or even five cylinders, in lieu of three, there would have been one upon each side of the load, bearing no weight at all; and which, after the boat—from its cargo resting entirely upon the middle cylinders—had settled into the water, would have prevented even the possibility of an accident by oversetting, the balance being so completely upon the sides kept by the boat itself. To-night the men caught a great abundance of fine fish.

Two wagons that had been unloaded during the route by issues of provisions to the troops, were sent back to the Fort from this place. It being the last opportunity we should probably have to send letters to our friends from the prairies, the evening was occupied by a great number in writing home. We saw some fires late to-night, off to the southward, which we conjectured must have been at the encampment of some party of Indians. They were probably a hunting party of the Kanzas.

After we had got into camp, one of the gentlemen called our attention to his fine horse, remarking, that amongst his many excellent qualities, he was the *highest swimming* animal he had ever ridden;

for in crossing the Blue, his saddle skirts had hardly got wet. "Why," said one of his listeners, "the water was not over four feet deep, and he must have *touched bottom every foot of the way.*" "Ah! *that* alters the case," said the owner of the horse; "I thought he was swimming all the time, and was delighted at his buoyancy." This mistake went by the name of the "High Swimmer."

FRIDAY, AUGUST 23

This morning we were in the saddle by seven o'clock, and on our way. Our course was about N.W., over a high level prairie, with the Blue parallel with our direction, and distant about two miles on our right. The soil travelled over to-day was very poor indeed, and covered with several kinds of helianthi and artemisia, and also different kinds of flowers, in full bloom, whose names we did not know. They were mostly resinous, and often had large particles of wax concreted upon their stalks and leaves. Amongst them was a species of the sensitive plant, which grew in some places very luxuriantly. It had blossoms of a bright chrome yellow, with dark purple calyx and pistils. They were shaped similar to those of the pea. This plant gave forth a delightful perfume, as it was bruised and trodden down by the hoofs of the horses. At twelve o'clock. M., we struck the south-western fork to be unloaded, when the ponton boats were put into the water, and the operations of yesterday re-enacted. It took us till sundown to pass this stream. Some hundred yards above were the property of the command was crossed in boats, we found a ford with four and a half feet of water, with the banks composed of nothing but quicksand; this, after an immense deal of labor, we prepared with logs, willows, and turf, at the points on each shore where the animals were to make their ingress and egress to and from the water; and by the time all the provisions and wagons were ferried over in the boats, they were gotten across, yet not without much difficulty, dozens and dozens of them miring down, and straining every muscle to get out. The point where the crossing was made was about two miles from the confluence of this fork with the main Blue. As soon as everything was over, we encamped for the night. The country all about this stream is exceedingly broken, especially upon its northern bank. The hills are of that regular formation which characterizes those about Fort Leavenworth, and those at our second encampment. That they serve to mark a former level of the country, which has been swept away, there can be no doubt. One of our men has been failing in health for the last few days, very fast, and tonight the Doctor told us he was afraid we shall be obliged to leave the poor fellow's bones upon the prairie, before we reach the Nebraska.

There is much speculation afloat as to the time we shall probably arrive at that river. Some think we shall see it on the 25th instant;—and from thence up to the 1st proximo, opinions are various; large quantities of wine being at stake on the issue of each man's calculation. The Doctor and the Chaplain, so far, have proved themselves the prophets of the command, whether on time, distances, courses, or the weather. However, on weather, the Chaplain bears the palm entirely alone,—particularly on thunder showers and rain storms. Some of the gentiles of the expedition attributed his accuracy on those points to his direct and frequent communications with the weather office itself; but how far they were correct in such a judgment no one pretended to say; but this we all *did* know, if he said thunder shower, it came sure enough, and that, too, with a vengeance. It was some comfort, though, that he did not say it often. The Doctor, on the other hand, beat the Chaplain in his suggestions as to courses, or which would be the best divide, or how far we had travelled, &c. But on ordinary matters, it was about nip and tie between them. . . .

Our hunter—the owner of the ammunition horse and "Sport," had been very unlucky for the last few days—in fact, ever since we left Wolf River, though yesterday there was a slight change for the better, by his shooting one very small snipe; yet the excitement consequent thereon soon wore off, and things gradually settled down to their wonted level. He however consoled himself and his friends by expecting to retrieve his character as a sportsman when he gets amongst the grouse on the extensive bottoms of the Nebraska; and says the reason why he don't kill more here is because he is holding up for that place. Such probably must be the fact, as he kills nothing here, nor is he likely to, judging the future by the past.

CHAPTER VIII

SCARCITY OF WATER—*Turtle and fish—Wolf chase—Deer chase—Jim put under a quinine regimen, which ruins him as a guide—Botany—Carrying fire-wood on horseback—Soil—Quality of country—Romantic bluffs—Dog town—Bad shooting of our hunter—Description of prairie dog—Death of Private Thompson.*

SATURDAY, AUGUST 24

WE MADE an early start this morning, our course lying N.N.W., with Forks of the Blue upon each hand, and distant severally about five miles. To-day there have been no water courses at all upon our route—which has been over an elevated table-land, composed of thin, gravelly soil. We at one time (about mid-day) came to a sort of shallow basin, which contained a little stagnant water that was standing in the long grass and flags that grew all over it. Here the animals were enabled to quench their thirst, which was very great, owing to the excessive heat. At sundown we struck another affluent of the Blue running to our right, and at a point about three miles from its confluence with the eastern branch, or main river. Here we encamped. This fork is well timbered, but the soil is very indifferent except along the stream. On account of the quicksands of the banks, it will take the Pioneers until late in the evening to prepare a ford which can be crossed by the wagons. Some fine, large, soft shelled turtle were caught here, and quite a quantity of perch, and cat-fish, some of which weighed eight or ten pounds. To-day some of the gentlemen had a very spirited wolf-chase. Having run the animal down, they dismounted, and, at the risk of being badly bitten, seized him; and having tied his legs, and otherwise put him under bonds for his good behaviour, they brought him into camp. He was a savage looking customer indeed, but quite well behaved—however, this was more the result of his fatigue than from any influences his early education may have exercised over him. At times he was a very wolfish sort of a chap.

Just as we were having the horses picketted, two large fawns jumped up out of the grass and galloped off for the hills in the direction from whence we came. Three or four of the officers whose horses were not yet unsaddled, mounted up and started after them. For a mile or so the chase was very beautiful and spirited; each fawn taking a new direction, thereby dividing the pursuers into two parties. They were all finally lost to our view as they disappeared over the distant hills. In a short time the hunters came back, having been unsuccessful; the fawns having secreted themselves in the high weeds of some neighboring ravines after the summits of the hills had been passed. Nine antelopes were also seen to-day by the Pioneers, but none of them were taken. Our prospects for to-morrow are not *very* flattering, for Jim says we shall be on the divide between the Blue and Nebraska, where we can get neither wood nor water. Those who have not yet seen the elephant, having strong suspicions that he will be visible about that time, as they will not be able to have much to eat for some thirty-six hours; that is, if Jim's story is true, which is quite problematical. For a few days he has been persuaded to let the Doctor prescribe for his chills and fever. The consequence has been, that he has been so dosed with quinine, his "ager" has been completely checked; but that awful ringing in the ears, which is sure to result from a free use of this medicine, has supervened, and he has now a new excuse for not knowing the way.

Several times a day, when two divides present themselves directly in our course, the Quarter-master will say, "Well, Jim, which way now?"

"Well, which way you call north?" Jim will ask.

"That way," Looking at the compass.

"Well, which way Pawnees?"

"That way." Pointing north-west.

Jim will then pause a moment, as if in profound thought; finally he will slowly and confusedly answer—"Well, 'spose you take *this* ridge, may-be he take you big divide; 'spose you take *that*, may-be he be better—booh!" whirling his fingers around his ears and imitating a roaring sound—"I can't tell nothing, *no how*. Bad medicine —heap—booh! ugh! bad *medicine*." At the same time shaking his head and shuddering as if he had just drank the bitterest thing in the whole world. This is all we can get out of him as to the direction if there is the least possible doubt which is the best route to pursue. He is certainly an efficient guide, that no one pretends to deny: that is, in his way.

SUNDAY, AUGUST 25

We commenced getting the baggage train and howitzers across the ford very early this morning. This took an hour and a half, at least, as the banks were still very bad indeed. "K" Troop has its wagon broken at this ford, and the one driven by Mr. Jackson was also considerably damaged. He had neglected to water his mules previous to starting, and when they came near the stream they hurried down the steep bank, being entirely unmanageable from their extreme thirst. Poor Thompson, the man who is so dangerously sick, was in this wagon, and was cruelly jostled about by its rapid descent and plunge into the water. However, the whole train was soon over, without further accident, when the column was put in motion, and the day's march fairly commenced. "K" Troop was left behind until new hounds could be made for its wagon, which would probably take some two hours or more. We found upon this stream several beautiful plants, in full blossom. Amongst them was what many of us supposed to be the *Centauria Americana*, spoken of by Dr. Barton, U.S.N.,[12] as indigenous to the valley of the Arkansas and that of the Canadian. I am inclined to think, however, that we were mistaken in our supposition as to this plant, and that it was only a large and luxuriant specimen of the *Carduus Leucegraphus*— a singular species of the thistle common to this climate, and that the Centauria Americana is not found unless in gardens, so far north. We often feel regret that we have no one along with us who is well skilled in Botany. This whole country seems teeming with so much that would be not only highly interesting to those, who, by their study and labor are seeking to advance that science, but with much that would, no doubt, be extremely, useful and valuable in the practice of medicine. To-day each dragoon has a small bundle of faggots tied *en croupe* upon his horse, wherewith to make a little fire to boil a pot of coffee to-night, if we are lucky enough to find water; for Jim says as I before stated—"its all big ridge—heap—all the way clear to Platte—may-be."

"But are you sure, Jim, we shall find neither wood nor water?" asks some one.

"Bad medicine—booh?—(again imitating a roaring noise) can't tell much. May-be wood—may-be no wood—I *can't* tell; head bad—most crazy—booh! ugh!"

As we ascend the dividing ridge which separates the waters running into the Kansas from those running into the Nebraska, the soil upon the uplands is becoming quite indifferent as to fertility though we are inclined to believe it would make good pasturage. It bears a very fair crop of grass and would continue to do so, if less undisturbed by plough. It now has about four inches of dark mould, surmounted by a thin turf and lying upon a coarse, open, gravelly bed, which would be likely to absorb all the manure and dressing that could be put upon it if it were tilled. Along the Blue and its numerous affluents there are extensive intervals that would make as good arable land as any in the west. In richness and fertility they can hardly be surpassed, as they have had all the wash of the uplands incorporated with their own vegetable fatness. If this land is ever occupied by the whites, it will make one of the finest stock-growing countries in the world. Its range for flocks and herds is almost interminable, extending for that matter, to the mountains; and that without any trouble in fencing. There is not rich soil enough to invite many settlers who would depend upon the growth of grains or hemp and tobacco for a living—(setting aside the great distance to a navigable river on which to float their produce to a market)—while there is an abundance along the streams on which the stock grower could raise enough for his home consumption.

His horses and cattle and sheep he could always, at a trifling expense, drive to town upon the Missouri, where he might find a ready
sale for them for shipment. One can hardly ride over these widely
extended plains, which in the hands of the whites, would be made to
produce *so much*, without feeling, that on the grand principle of
"*The greatest good to the greatest number*," and without any reference to
the savage or the civilized, further than considering all of them as
human beings, it would be advancing the cause of human happiness
for the Indians to move *still further west*, and let the shore of that great
sea, which, wave after wave, has driven their doomed race onwards,
and onwards before its wide spreading power—be the shore of the
great western prairie. Those tribes who depend almost entirely on
hunting for subsistence find nothing to kill, comparatively speaking,
on the lands on which they are located, but have to journey out to
the "buffalo country" some two or three *hundred* miles—a toilsome
and dangerous march—to get their food, without no other alternative but to steal from the whites or starve.—I will venture to say,
that along the eastern side of the Great Plain where it borders on the
timber, from Red River to Fort Snelling, there is not game enough
on every five miles square to keep one man in food from one end of
the year to the other.[13]

Our course to-day was N.N.W., and continually ascending, over a
high smooth, table-land, which had a regular inclination to the
southeast. We have a fork of the Blue upon each hand for the most
of to-day, and nearly parallel to our course—distant each, about four
miles. This day has been most delightful, with not a cloud in the
heavens save a cloud of smoke, occasioned by the fires of our last
night's encampment getting into the unburnt grass of last year. We
found some small ponds of water, similar to the one described yesterday, on the levels of this upland, where the animals were enabled to
quench their thirst; but not one living stream has crossed our course
to-day. We have now and then gone over the channels of winter and
spring creeks, but they contained no water. "K." troop overtook us
about 4 o'clock. At 6 P.M., we arrived at another South-western
tributary of the Blue, when we encamped for the night. From this
point to the confluence of this tributary with the main river, is about

two miles. At that place are some very high bluffs, apparently so near the water, that much of the earth of which they are composed has slid off into the stream. The bare places thus formed, as seen through the trees from our encampment, under the strong light of an evening sun, look very beautiful indeed; some of them like houses, and some like vessels lying in the river, with all their sails set. Some pretty good specimens of agate were found to-day. The Pioneers are again obliged to construct a bridge, which it will take until late this evening to complete. Contrary to Jim's prophecy, we find a plenty of wood and water.

Monday, August 26

We took up our line of march this morning, at a quarter before eight, and travelled until noon, over a duplicate of the country of yesterday. We then came to a small stream running to the east, which was very miry indeed, with high banks. This, also, we had to bridge; and from the difficulty of procuring timber—being obliged to haul the most of it from some distance—we were detained upon its banks some three hours. However, the time was not entirely thrown away, as our horses and mules throve wonderfully in that short interval, upon the wild pea-vine, which grew here in great abundance, as did also the wild cucumber. The vines of this latter plant ran entirely over the tops of the bushes in the neighborhood of the stream, completely shading them and filling the air with the delightful fragrance of their millions of flowers. The valley of this creek is nearly two miles wide upon its southern side. About half way from the water to the low bluffs that mark the commencement of the highland, we passed as we came along, by that great curiosity of the prairies, a Dog Town. Our hunter took a few shots at its citizens, but if he failed on grouse and other snail-paced game, how could he be so improvident as to waste his ammunition on animals that are known to be a shade quicker than lightning itself.

Mr. Gregg—somewhat celebrated as a traveller over the great western prairies, says, in a work recently published by him[14]—"The Prairie Dog has been reckoned by some naturalists as a species of the Marmot (*arclomys ludoviciana*); yet it seems to possess scarce any quality in common with this animal, except that of burrowing. This singular quadruped is but little larger than a common squirrel, its body being nearly a foot long, with a tail of three or four inches. The color ranges from a brown to a dirty yellow. The flesh, though often eaten by travellers, is not considered savory. Its yelp, which resembles that of a little toy dog, seems its only canine attribute. It appears to occupy a middle ground between a rabbit and a squirrel: like the former in feeding and burrowing—like the latter in frisking, flirting, sitting erect, and somewhat so in its barking. A collection of their burrows has been termed by travellers, a 'dog town,' which comprises from a dozen or so to some thousands, in the same vicinity, often covering an area of several square miles. They generally locate upon firm dry plains, coated with fine short grass, upon which they feed—for they are no doubt exclusively herbivorous. They must need but little water, if any at all, as their towns are often, indeed generally, found in the midst of the most arid plains. Approaching a village, the little dogs may be observed frisking about the streets, passing from dwelling to dwelling, apparently on visits; sometimes a few clustered together, as though in council: here feeding on the tender herbage, there cleansing their houses or brushing the little hillock about the door—yet all quiet. Upon seeing a stranger, however, each streaks it to its own house, but is apt to stop at the entrance and spread the general alarm by a series of shrill yelps, usually sitting erect at the time. Two other animals are said to live in common with them: the *rattlesnake* and a small *owl*;* but both are no doubt intruders, resorting to these burrows for shelter, and to feed, it is presumed, upon the pups of the inmates."

About a quarter of a mile below the bridge which the Pioneers are building, a small creek comes in from the north-west. Upon its right bank we encamped at sundown, having marched five miles since we passed the one into which it empties itself. Here we find but very little wood, and beyond our encampment, in the direction of our course, there is not a tree in sight, which induces us to be-

*This has been called the *Coquimbo Owl*. Its note, whether imitative or natural much resembles that of the Prairie Dog.

lieve ourselves very near the Nebraska. Poor Thompson died just at *Tattoo*, this evening. He had suffered a great deal, notwithstanding every care had been taken of him which the circumstances of our march would admit. Indeed, Hospital Steward Marsh, who was his constant attendant day and night, watched over him and ministered to his every want, with the solicitude and tenderness of a brother. He knew the hour had come for him to die, and to the last manifested a perfect willingness to commence that fearfully mysterious journey to, it is hoped, a better world, than the one he left behind.

CHAPTER IX

BURIAL OF THOMPSON–*Saw Planet Venus by Sun-light–Mirage–
Out of Sight of Land–Valley of the Nebraska–Great Place for a
Militia Muster–"Capt. Burgwin's Kickapoo Setter"–Soil and General Appearance of River Valley–Jim Rogers Picking Up–Indications
of Buffalo–Wide Bottom–Encamp–Delegation of Pawnees (probably
a couple of Aldermen) Visits Camp with Tickets for Soup (Dog) to-
morrow–Jim holds a Talk with them–Village only Seven Miles off.*

TUESDAY, AUGUST 27

EARLY this morning the funeral of Thompson took place. A grave had been prepared on the summit of a hill, about a quarter of a mile west of the creek upon which we had encamped, and which overlooked much of the fine country towards the south and the east. His remains were wrapped in his blankets and borne upon the shoulders of his comrades, preceded by an escort, and followed by the squadrons dismounted. Next to the corpse, by an escort, the horse of the deceased was led, with his arms hanging beside the empty saddle. It was a sad sight to see the poor animal thus mutely following to his last home, the kind master who had so often fed and caressed him! The troops having formed on three sides of the grave, the remains were lowered into it, and the chaplain read the burial service over them, when the dust was consigned to the dust forever.

The commanding officer named the creek upon which we encamped, for him; and as it is his only monument, may it continue to bear his name.

This soldier was the son of a Baptist clergyman, and had been religiously educated in his youth. The principles then instilled into his mind were those which had sustained him during his illness and suffering, and in the last sad hour of his life. He died far from all who knew and loved him—amid strangers and in a strange land—and yet, he had one great and kind friend ever near him: his religion; this soothed and supported him through that valley, and that shadow, in which the dearest must have deserted him. When the chaplain feelingly and eloquently alluded to these things, as he stood beside that humble grave, many were the eyes that were moistened with a tear. The soldier's last tribute of respect over the grave of a comrade was then fired.

I forgot to mention in the last chapter, that yesterday, about 11 o'clock, A.M., we saw what we believed to be the planet Venus. It was very bright, and so distinctly visible that the eye could catch it at once, when directed to that part of the heavens. At that time of day it bore about 10° west of the meridian, with an apparent altitude of 75° or 80°.

From the time we started this morning, until nearly now, we kept gradually ascending over a poor and sterile prairie, with a few slight water courses upon our right and left, evidently the last fimbrii of the Blue, in this direction. The grass was very short and thin, and filled with artemisia and wild indigo. The country far ahead and still higher, began about ten o'clock to present an uneven surface against the sky. On account of the mirage that seemed to fill the atmosphere to-day, the horizon upon our right, and left, and before us, was uncertain—faintly defined—and trembling to the sight. As far as the eye could see, on every hand, not a tree or shrub of any description was visible; nothing, in fact, but a green prairie and a blue sky. Finally, about half-past 12, M., we ascended a long plain that seemed to terminate in bluffs. When we arrived at its verge we had revealed to our view a scene that can never be forgotten: there, spread out like a map, lay before us the magnificent valley of the Nebraska!

Here we were, then, upon the bank of "the most beautiful and useless of rivers," as Washington Irving calls it. The Nebraska (Shallow Water) is of a grayish muddy color, and runs with a swift current. The bed of the river is but one wide expanse of quicksand, which is formed in bars, and these are continually changing and driving about. On account of the great breadth of the river, the channels are innumerable, but are usually only a foot or so deeper than the surrounding water. The river is filled with beautiful islands. They are all well wooded, but only here and there is there any timber growing upon the main banks. Sometimes we found the channels between some of the islands and shore, entirely dry; presenting to the eye a wide extent of sand, which, as the wind swept over it, was blown about in clouds, as one sometimes may have noticed it upon the barren coast of the ocean. The bottom lands are what would be called high river prairie; nearly beyond the danger of being flooded, though it is said that in the Spring of 1843, the whole valley was covered, from bluff to bluff, by the waters, and presented the appearance of a vast inland sea.

Early this evening, we encamped near the bank of the river, about two miles and a half from the point where we first struck it from the bluffs. There was but little timber upon the shore, and the men went off to the islands with their axes, and brought their nightly supply from thence upon their shoulders. They seemed as if they were walking upon the water, being able to go to any island or part of the river they wished to visit, with apparent ease. To the eye, the Nebraska looks almost as deep and as turbulent as the Missouri itself; it is generally much wider, and it goes boiling, and hissing, and dashing along, with as many important airs as the ass put on when dressed in the skin of a lion; but leap your horse into it, and its true character is known at once.

Here we discovered, upon some dry sand bars, the tracks of sixteen Indians, who had recently passed down, making the bed of the river their highway. That they had gone by within a day or two, there could be no doubt, as we found where they had killed a deer; and other fresh signs, which indicated it.

The principal timber on this river is cotton-wood, elm, a species of poplar,* and one of red willow,† from the bark of which, the

*Populus Monilifera.
†Satix Longifolia.

Indian makes the celebrated *kinicaneek*, which is as indispensable to him as opium to a Chinese. Besides, some of the islands have quite an abundance of red cedar‡ upon them, and to-night our supply of fuel is partly composed of this beautiful wood.

Thus we have encountered every difficulty, and performed so much of the journey with much more ease and despatch than the most sanguine of us anticipated. We know that now, so far as labor is concerned, the worst of our campaign is over, and there is a good deal of comfort in that reflection. Jim says we are below the villages "heap ways," and that we can travel all the way there upon the bottom, without crossing a stream. Now that there is no difficulty at all in finding the way, Jim moves along with an increased importance, making no further complaints of his shakes or the quinine, but on the other hand, assuming a patronizing manner when addressing the quarter-master, as much as to say—"You, of course, have but a faint idea of *this* country."

WEDNESDAY, AUGUST 28

This morning we made a very early start, travelling up the southern bottom of the Nebraska, and keeping about midway between the river and the bluffs, with our course about 10° south of west. The air was quite cool at sunrise; the mercury being down to 42° Fahrenheit. On account of our finding large quantities of *bois de vache*, we were fearful that we were west of the villages. However, Jim was too confident of his locality to make so great a mistake, and we pushed on. The buffalo, from these indications, must have been here within a couple of years. In the summer of '42, they came in much nearer to the settlements than they had done for years before: it is more than probable that then it was that they were here. We saw great numbers of new and beautiful flowers to-day. Some of them were extremely delicate and fragrant. Much to our regret we had not time or means wherewith to press and dry specimens to bring in. We also saw a great many antelopes and sand hill cranes. These birds are very large, and as an article of food are said to

‡The kind used in the manufacture of pencils.

be very delicious. They have a very loud and peculiarly discordant note.

Opposite the point where we struck the Nebraska yesterday, the Loup Fork united with it.[15] The whole Delta for thirty or forty miles up these rivers, is one immense bottom, growing wider and wider as the streams diverge. Consequently the bluffs on the opposite side from us have been receding all day, and now can just be seen like a blue and distant coast, lying close along under the horizon, the whole valley being spread out like a green and (looking eastward) apparently illimitable ocean of grass. After we had marched steadily until past 6 o'clock, P.M., the column was directed to the bank of the river, where we encamped. Our tents had hardly been pitched and our horses picketed out, when one of the guards reported two Indians in sight, coming down the bank of the river. The officer of the day was sent out to meet and being them into camp. They proved to be a delegation sent by the chief of the Grand Pawnees, to bid us welcome to his village. We hailed their arrival with much delight, as we were made sure by it that we were near the end of our journey *up* the river. Each of these Indians carried in his hands ears of green corn, with the husks stripped down about the stalk, in token that we were welcome, also, to their bread. It was truly a beautiful and natural manner of tendering to us the hospitalities of their town. These two Pawnees were splendid specimens of the Prairie Indian, being tall, erect, elegantly proportioned, and with eyes like eagles. They were not of that dingy brown color, like the Tuscarora, Penobscot, or Passamaquoddy Indians, but of that *red*, so peculiar to all the full blooded savages of the West. They had moccasins on, a piece of dressed leather folded about the loins, and over all a large buffalo skin mantle, which they wore like a toga, hanging gracefully from the shoulder.

As we had no one with us who could talk Pawnee, Jim was sent for to converse in the language of signs, which is the *French* of the Indian; a conventional mode of expressing their ideas, common to all the wild tribes. Jim came up, and after having shaken hands with his "brother," the Major told him to ask them how far it was to the village. He went through with a good deal of pantomime, and so did

one of the Pawnees; when they had got done, Jim turned and said—
"He say may be seven mile." But he had not said anything, in fact.

"Ask him if the Pawnees are mostly out hunting."

(Here succeeded about five minutes violent gesticulating on both sides.)

"He say, good many out. Buffalo may be two days off; no more."

The Pawnee then talked a great while to Jim. Whenever he would stop, Jim would turn and tell the Major what he had said, although not a word had been spoken. "He say, he thought dragoons was Shawnees, come to fight, and his people (the Pawnees) had hid everything, in caches. This was last night, when dragoons was great way off—may be thirty miles." (This astonished us; they had seen us approaching, then, for nearly two days.) "He say, he be glad to see you, and that his people will be glad—heap; that's what he say."

CHAPTER X

PAWNEE STRAGGLERS IN QUOD—*Their excitement at our coming—The Village—Pawnee Revolution—The confederacy—Their politics analogous to ours—Charachaush—He gives a great cow feast—His knowledge of drawing maps—A Pawnee Lodge—Western Cupids—Pawnee politicians—Great many children just four years old—"Kickapoo Setter" in a tight place—Pawnee Stable—Manner of curing corn—Plenty of salin in the West—Arms on tripod scaffolds near the doors—Scarcity of wood—They pack it on donkeys the same as three poor brothers in Maine used to pack hoop-poles to market.*

THURSDAY, AUGUST 29

LAST night from *tattoo* until *reveille* the Indians kept coming into camp, and were accommodated as fast as they arrived, with "lodgings upon the cold ground" under charge of the guard. No doubt but they ventured near us in this way in hopes of having fine opportunities for stealing while we were asleep—but the sentinels caught them as they came and held them in durance until day-light. We made a very early start this morning.—Before we had marched far we began to meet dozens of Indians on horseback—armed and painted and decorated with their whole stock of scalps and other valuable trinkets,—They would salute every body from the head to the foot of the column not forgetting the Black Hussars who rode in the rear.—After they had done this they would gallop around us and sometimes take a circle off towards the bluffs and back, evidently with a view of displaying their fine horsemanship—

yet in part, no doubt, from the excess of their excitement at our arrival.—They seemed to regard our coming with more pleasure and curiosity, even, than the boys in the country towns in Maine would the approach of a caravan with real lions and living elephants; and that is saying a great deal.

The bottom upon this side continues of the same character as that described in the last chapter, except that it seems to be more fertile —and is growing narrower every mile in consequence of the approach of the bluffs towards the river; about nine o'clock A.M., we came in sight of the village. At a distance it looked very pretty indeed—the lodges being shaped like domes, from twenty to twenty-five feet in height, and from forty to fifty feet in diameter at the base. They are nestled together under a high bold promontory, which seems to approach within an eighth of a mile of the Nebraska—and extends the whole distance from its foot across the narrow bottom, to the water. This promontory can be seen when you are twenty miles below it. It is one of the highest points of the bluffs; and designating the exact locality of the town, as it does, it must be very useful for the traveller as one of the land marks of the country. When first beheld, at a distance, say, of four or five miles—the village had very much the appearance of the pictures we have of a Hottentot Kraal—only the lodges seemed a great deal larger. We encamped about a mile below it upon the bank of the river—but had hardly got our tents pitched before the square was swarming with Indians. These, however, were the canaille; the aristocracy and *ton* seemed to be delaying their visit until a more fashionable hour.

Before I proceed any farther I wish to inform the reader, that from the best information I could obtain, many years ago the Pawnee Nation became divided into four different parties, from what cause I never learned; probably, however, from internal political dissensions Each party then chose its own chiefs and built a city for itself. In all municipal and domestic affairs they are severally independent and distinct—but for purposes of hunting and war they are as intimate as ever. In each case they form a joint council or Federative Diet, and have one chief elected as the head or president, who has power so long as such an union is necessary—but falling back to his original position whenever the cause for the temporary federation ceases to exist. This chief is *now* Charachaush*; and he is also head chief of the Pawnee Loups.

The village at which we have arrived is that of the Grand Pawnees. The next is that of the Republican Pawnees, and is situated nine miles farther up and upon the same side of the river. Across the immense deltoid that here stretches out like a sea between the Nebraska and Loup, and situated on the northern bank of the latter river, is that of the Pawnee Loups—eighteen miles from this. Then nine miles above that again, on the same side of the Loup is the town of the Pawnees Tepage.

Their different politics bear a faint analogy to our own. The Grand Pawnees are the Federalists of the *ancient regime*. The Republican Pawnees are the Wool Party of the tribe, corresponding with our Abolitionists. The Pawnee Loups are the Locofocos; the real agrarians and levellers;—besides, they are the most numerous, while the Pawnees Tepage are the Whigs. They live at the mouth of the Willow Creek on which, it is said, are found more cows than upon any other stream of its size in the west. They are *all* in favour of encouraging home industry and of protecting the manufacturers of buffalo robes and mocasins, besides of preventing foreign importation of blankets and boots as substitutes. At least we thought so from the fact of not seeing them wear any—which certainly was as strong an argument as they could use against it. If the fact could be ascertained, it is thought the Native American Party is the dominant one amongst them—However, as yet, but little is said on that subject.

The chief of the Grand Pawnees is named *Charachaush*. (The Cunning Chief.) He is about fifty years of age—tall—erect, and finely proportioned. He is quite intelligent—dignified and courteous, and seems to possess a good deal of firmness and strength of character. After our encampment was formed, several of the gentlemen rode up to the town and visited him at his lodge. He gave them a green corn feast. The chaplain and myself soon afterwards went up also—and arrived at the palace just in season to come in for our share of it. The old man was sitting upon a mat with his guests upon

*Whose lodge is the chief one.

each hand—in a circle, and numbering in all say about twenty; for there were several Indians interspersed amongst us, and who like-wise were recipients of the chief's hospitalities. They were probably the members of his cabinet and the heads of Departments. Besides there were a few others who sat near him whom we supposed consisted of his staff. In fact, there was one very fine looking fellow with small feet, that must have been his quarter-master, to say nothing of the tall, thin, lantern jaw'd Indian who saw to the supply of food; him we know to be the commissary from his vocation. In the centre of this circle was the fire, and hanging over it was a big kettle full of corn; which, as fast as it was done was placed in piles and each guest helped himself. Charachaush said something in Indian to us as the corn was taken from the kettle, but we could not understand a word of it. From the fact however, of his having nothing but corn spread before us, we supposed that he was offering an apology for the meagreness of the feast, and expressing his regret that he had been unable to procure a fat dog for our entertainment on account of the scarcity of that animal. After we had all eaten our fill the man whom we took for the quarter-master of the chief, filled an immense stone pipe with a long stem, with *Kinnakaneek*, and after having lighted it, passed it to Charachareesh, who received it with a most reverential air. He then took three slow and solemn puffs—and with the most grave look, passed it to the officer upon his right. He even outdid the old chief himself in seriousness of demeanour—took his three melancholy whiffs and passed it on. So it went the rounds. When it came back to the chief, the quartermaster added another supply of *Kinnakaeek* and around it went as before. In the mean time as soon as the pipe had passed, each individual joined in the lively conversation which had commenced at the time the feast was ended.

It was curious, as Charachaush enquired by signs what route we had come, to see how readily he understood our explanations. He then drew a mark with his finger upon the ground—introducing the Missouri—Kanzas—and Nebraska rivers.—Then he placed a mark for Fort Leavenworth, and afterwards in a manner surprisingly accurate—located the different tribes in their proper places—cutting them off by names as he went along, at the same time touching the exact spot each one occupied, thus: "Shawnee,"" Delaware," "Kick-apoo," "Ioways,"* "Otoes," "Omahas," "Pawnees." All this was done in half the time it has taken me to describe it.

The lodge of a Pawnee family is constructed in this way.—Ten large posts are set in the ground, in a circle say, that is twenty feet in diameter—sometimes more and sometimes less. These posts are crotched at the top and are about twelve or fourteen feet high. In the crotches are laid a corresponding number of large beams, another similar row of posts and beams is then placed about twelve feet outside of the first. These posts are not over seven feet in height. This second row makes the circle forty-four feet in diameter. Then a large quantity of smaller posts are leant against this exterior row of beams. The ends that are on the ground are about four feet outside of the bottoms of the posts that supported the beams against which they rest. This gives them an inclination of nearly seventy degrees. Then long rafters are placed upon both rows of beams, and almost meeting together at a common centre at the top, of which they are the radii. They are fastened firmly to the beams by means of withes made of twisted willows. Then small willow poles are laid laterally from the bottom to the top of this frame and close together—being secured to the rafters the same as the rafters are secured to the beams. Then a thatching nearly a foot thick and made of the long coarse grass of the wet sloughs is put on. This grass is carefully cut with knife and is then tied in bundles in the same way as our husbandmen tie oats—and is not used until it is thoroughly dry. Outside of all is placed a coating of earth nearly three feet thick at the bottom and eighteen inches, or so, at the top. This completes the shell of the lodge. Through one side of this a hole is cut six feet high and four broad;—then a gallery is built from it nearly ten paces in length. This gallery is made of posts, thatching, and earth, the same as the main lodge—at its end a buffalo robe hangs for a door and this is the only entrance to the building. It is lighted through a hole in the top which is about three feet in diameter. This hole serves for window and chimney—the fire being built upon the ground directly beneath it.

*The Indian name of this tribe is *Pa-ha-cae;* literally, Dirty Faces. They neither call themselves Ioways, nor are they called so by their neighbours.

All around the lodge, and perpendicular from the lower row of beams, is a wall of mats, and the space in rear of it is divided off into berths or cuddies—six or seven feet long by four broad at the bottom. These berths are nicely fitted up with mats and skins, and are quite private. The entrance to each of them, is about four feet high by two broad;—so as you stand near the middle of the lodge you find yourself surrounded by a circular wall of mats filled with these apertures like a row of port holes. This wall is decorated in the interior between three doors with bows—Spears—Shields—Antlers— Medicine bags—Medicine birds†—and sometimes with scalps—and finery for decorating the person on state occasions.

If a party of strangers enters a lodge (say for instance when we were there)—these state rooms and cuddies are filled with squaws and little children; peeping out when not noticed and watching your every movement with curious eyes—but if you look suddenly toward them they draw back into the darkness of the interior of their retreat like tortoises.

When you enter a lodge a mat is generally spread down for you to sit on—and if the head man of the lodge is at home, he invariably offers you the best he has got to eat. If he is not there, the squaws are so timid they will hardly speak;—and seldom ask you to sit down —or show you any hospitality;—apparently afraid you might construe it into a freedom on their part with a stranger. Probably after a little acquaintance they might become more sociable.

These lodges are capable of holding an hundred or an hundred and fifty people. While we were at Charachaush's, I counted seventy souls present at the same time, setting aside the unknown members in the cuddies. About thirty of them, however, were boys —and probably belonged to poor neighbours, at least we judged so from the scantiness of their apparel—which, by the way was the most natural costume we had ever seen before—and, notwithstanding it was made in the Pawnee country, fitted them like a glove— these little fellows filled the gallery and portal, and if one of us made a demonstration to go out—the way they would run—the little fatties—was beautiful. If they found we still staid, they would timor-

†Stuffed birds skins which are kept as amulets. *Rev. Mr. Irvine.*

ously venture back and stand there and gaze at us as silent and mo-
tionless as a group of antique cupids—with bows and arrows—and
in fact, everything but the wings; but these they didn't need—for—
to use a sporting phrase "they had both the heels and the bottom"
for all necessary purposes of locomotion, as each of us could testify.
On every lodge on the opposite side of the circle from the entrance
and facing towards it, we invariably found a buffalo skull with the
horns on. Some of them were gradually painted and decorated. This
we afterwards learned was a "great medicine" and served to give the
hunters good luck, and to draw the game nearer their village. As I
before stated the only light they have comes through the aperture in
the centre of the lodge overhead, and Mr. Deas said it was the most
glorious light for a painter he had ever seen. As he was making a
drawing of the old chief's lodge and myself writing this description
of it, one of the Indians thinking it was too dark where we sat for us
to see conveniently—went and took down a white shield made of
buffalo-bull's scalp, and held it just in the sunlight that came streaming through from above; in a moment the lodge was as bright as day
from the reflected rays. This man was probably the Sire Isaac Newton
of the tribe.

These lodges during the day are swarming with children on their
outsides; and ofttimes the old people may be seen sitting up there,
and chatting and deliberating with all the gravity of parish beadles,
when discussing so important a subject as the adding of a half a
pound more of meat to a soup for sixty paupers. I noticed two old
codgers of them on a house top, evidently in fierce debate; probably
on some political subject; and the way they gesticulated and laid
down their arguments, giving a *vim* to each word with the four fingers, reminded me very much of similarly profound reasoners which
one will often hear brawling in the bar rooms of country taverns as
the stage stops to change horses, when the question of bank or no
bank is at its height, or that of the annexation of Texas. As you ride
into this village on horseback, the little children will run up on to
the lodges to get out of the way, and the damsels will make a dive
for the cuddies. After you have entered a house, the children will
come around to the gallery and peep in, and the damsels from the

cuddies, will peep out, as I before described. Once in a while, some timid little fellow, who is afraid to approach so near, takes a look at you down the chimney, meanwhile getting punished for his curiosity by the smoke that compels him to make up ugly faces as he endeavours to peer through it with his tearful eyes. The Grand Pawnee village contains fifty-eight such lodges as I have described. They are clustered together without reference to order. Each one, however, is entered from the east, and here and there, is a public square or Plaza. Where they put all the men, women, and children, of nights was more than I could tell, for it seemed to me if they filled the cuddies, and then stacked the children, and spread the balance on the floor, they would have had hard work to house the whole of them. This town is said to contain two thousand souls. Of all people to own children and most of them about four years old, commend me to the Pawnees. You see them everywhere; on the lodges, in the lodges, on the *plazas*, in the cornfields, on the bluffs; besides shoals of them swimming in the river, boys and girls together, but all about four years old, and just three feet high. It's true we did see a few smaller and lashed in little cribs like coffins without covers, and here and there stood up against posts, or sometimes hanging on a peg, little black fellows with eyes glistening like checker-men cut out of patent leather, but they were scarce, and so were the boys and girls from twelve to twenty. The whole population seemed to be made up of grown warriors and squaws, who had become mothers, or the little three footers I have named. The exceptions of this rule were very few indeed.

If a Pawnee honours you with a feast, you must expect to be regaled on dog meat as a matter of course, besides you must eat out of the same ladle with all the other guests—taking a mouthful of meat and a drink of broth, and then passing it around on the same principle as the pipe—Dog Soup is the favourite dish of the Pawnees, Sioux, Crows, Blackfeet, and Cheyennes. The Indian who gives a feast does not touch a mouthful until all his guests are done. He then eats, and after him, his family. It was said Capt. B's Kickapoo Setter happened to follow some one up to the village, and he was looked upon with those greedy eyes and watering mouths, with which a gourmand would behold a fine green turtle. If the Pawnees could get near enough to lay their hands upon him, they would feel through his skin to ascertain his condition, the same as sportsmen would through the feathers of a grouse when they are fat in August and September. Troops of hungry dogs would follow and gaze at him with wishful eyes, as one sometimes sees white children in cities, looking through baker's windows at cakes. He seemed to suspect their heathenish looks, and started back to camp. If they could have done so unobserved, they would have had him in a pot in two minutes, and then sent his master an invitation to dinner—the scoundrels!

Near each lodge is a pound, or fold, for the horses and mules of the inmates. These folds are made by planting pickets in the ground, the same as we do in building a stockade; are circular, with a hole on one side for the ingress and egress of the animals, which is securely fastened with bars tied by thongs. Evey morning the horses of each lodge, guarded by one of the Indians belonging to it, are taken across the river on to the wide bottom where they are allowed to graze until night, when they are driven home and put in the fold again. They dare not leave them unguarded for fear other tribes would come and steal them.

On the great plains the horse to the Indian is invaluable. By it he traverses the broad ocean that surrounds him in quest of food and clothing, or to punish those who have injured his tribe. In his estimation the greatest feat he can perform after taking a scalp, is to steal a horse!

While we were in town the women were employed in cutting corn for the winter. As soon as the corn is well filled, and has just begun to turn a little hard, they pluck it, boil it well while on the ear, then shell it off and dry it thoroughly, by spreading it on skins in the open air. By doing this they can cook it much easier than they could if they let it get ripe. They seldom, if ever, make it into bread, but boil it, making a kind of soup by adding a bit of dried buffalo or elk meat. If this is a great day with them, a real Fourth of July, they may put in a fat pup, or a kitten, just to give a fine relish to the dish, but extravagances of that kind are never indulged in, except on some really grand or joyful occasion. When corn has been cured in this way it preserves its original flavor for a great while, besides, is very tender and digestible, and void of the hull which is so difficult to separate from the ripe kernel. The prairie Indians seldom use salt with their food, it is so much labour to transport it from the Salt Plains, or to make it by evaporation at the various salines found in the West. There is no country in the world, except perhaps, some parts of Siberia, where salt is found so abundantly as upon the plains just named. Capt. Nathan Boone* 1st Dragoons, who visited them in '43,[16] says: "The most wonderful saline is the *Great Salt Rock*, which I found on the Red Fork of the Arkansas. The whole cave on the right of the two forks of the river appeared to be one immense salt spring of water, so much concentrated that as soon as it reaches the point of breaking forth, it begins depositing its salt. In this way a large crust, or rock is formed all over the bottom, for perhaps 160 acres. Digging through the sand for a few inches anywhere in this space, we could find the solid salt, so hard that there were no means in our power of getting up a block of it. In many places through this rock salt crust, the water boiled up clear as crystal but so salty that our hands after being immersed in it and suffered to dry, became as white as snow. Thrusting the arm down into their holes they appeared to be walled with salt as far as one could reach."

The Nebraska at this village is nearly a mile wide, if not quite, and filled with islands. According to Lieut. Fremont's calculation, made twenty miles below the head of the Grand Island, (which lies above the Republican village), its bed at *this* point is 2000 feet above the level of the sea; and the Latitude 40° 45'—the Longitude about 99°. Some idea of the velocity of this river above here may be had, by considering that at St. Vrain's Fort on the South Fork, in lon. 105°45'13" the elevation of the river is 5400 feet above the Gulf of Mexico, therefore in 6°45'13" of longitude, with their diminished length in such a high latitude, (say 40° to 41°) the river falls *three thousand four hundred feet* before it gets to this village from that post, which by the way, is far this side the base of the mountains.

*Son of the celebrated Daniel Boone.

Before the entrance of several of the lodges, and indeed, sometimes upon the tops of them, would be fixed a frame, something
like a painter's easel, generally made of three peeled willow poles, to
which would be attached a spear and shield, sometimes bows, and
quivers, filled with beautifully wrought arrows. These arms were invariably bright and clean; the shields as white and stainless as the
virgin snow. How much they reminded us of those days of chivalry
and feudalism, when each gallant knight, or feoffee, placed in a
similar manner *his* arrows before his tent, ready to spring forth and
meet in mortal combat, whoever should touch them with sword or
lance. Those, we were afterwards told, indicated the lodge of the
chiefs and principal warriors. No man was allowed to hang his weapons in such conspicuous places, unless he had taken a given number
of scalps or stolen a prescribed quantity of horses. (!)

There being no wood upon this side of the river, the Indians are
all obliged to get their whole supply from the islands and opposite
shore some ways below. This labour is performed entirely by the
women, with the help of donkeys and Jackasses. These animals are
procured by stealing them from the inhabitants of New Mexico, or
from other tribes, who did steal them there from the Texans.
"*Honor amongst thieves!*" don't hold good amongst Indians—not it;
—they steal all they can from everybody else, and then as much as
possible from each other. Property changes hands with them without any such troublesome ceremonies, as *bills of sale*, and *receipts in
full*. They have rude pack saddles fastened upon the animals' backs,
with places upon the sides made of raw hide, like those into which
fills are put in our harnesses. Into these they place the tops of the
poles cut for firewood, and compel the animals to drag them along,
trailling on the ground like Camanche tent poles on a dog. All the
wood is not hauled in this way. The fine branches are cut and tied in
large bundles like faggots, and packed one on each side of the saddle. At almost any time of day, you can see troops of these animals
crossing the river with their burthens, followed by their squaw
drivers, with long switches to touch them up, when they lag in the
quicksands. Seeing the donkeys packing wood in this way, reminded
me very much of three poor brothers, who lived in Maine and were

compelled to gain a livelihood by cutting hoop poles, and taking them to market for sale. They were not able to buy a cart, and so they were obliged to fit a frame upon the back of an old horse they had inherited, into which they would stow a thousand or so of poles and proceed on their long and toilsome journey. The eldest brother generally trudged on ahead leading the old nag by a rope halter, while the other two brought up the rear, with crotchel sticks to trig him when the road went over steep hills, to keep him from running back as he would stop half way up for breath. Their business was finally broken up, by a farmer suing them for injury done to an old filly which grazed by the road sides, at a time when their animal was loaded down with hoop-poles and had become entirely unmanageable as he was passing along. After this accident (for the horse had to be sold to pay the damage) they were obliged to take to making chairs.

Last night the news of our coming having reached the village of the Pawnee Loups, to-day there have been many arrivals from there. The interpreter, who also lives at that place, is expected over this evening. This afternoon the old chief will visit us in state; but as I have arrived at the foot of this sheet, I will reserve for the next chapter the account of that and fifty other things, I have not room to speak of here. Reader, as Toney Lumpkin used to say, "we are now getting into the cream of the correspondence" and may therefore expect a "concatenation accordingly."

CHAPTER XI

THE MANNER OF BURYING THEIR DEAD—*Their Sentinels—Sun-flower Fences—Not so very much romance in living with Indians—Women ugly—Men handsome—Their wardrobe—Manner of dressing their hair—"Iowas"—Indian traders—Arrival of the Chief—Whole Deputation embrace the Major—Marriage Ceremonies—Descendants of Lost Tribes—Mode of warfare with spy glass—Old Chief sups with Commanding Officer—Calls for Chowder—Offers to sleep with him—Gets angry and clears out—Rockets.*

THE Pawnee bury their dead upon the summits of the bluffs, and for two or three miles above and below this town, the top of each hill is covered with graves. Those who have died recently they suffer no grass to grow over, until two summers have passed away. This custom prevails to a great extent amongst many of the other western tribes, particularly with the Pottawatamies and Ottawas. They say they do this as an evidence that, like the earth that rests on them, so is their memory for the dead—fresh, and uncovered by the springing up of new ties and new affections. It is a very simple, yet touching and eloquent custom, and shows more feeling and less stoicism, than many are willing to accord to the poor Indians.

This tribe—being at war with many of its neighbors, and living as it does upon a vast prairie, where it is liable to attack at any moment, from the hordes of Camanches and Sioux, who lead a sort of nomadic life, like the Arabs, and are continually moving from place to place, making war indiscriminately with all whom they may meet, and subsisting entirely upon the buffalo, which they follow from one spot to another—is obliged continually to guard itself from surprise by keeping sentinels posted on the high bluffs for miles and miles on every side of its town. In summer and winter, day and night, storm and sunshine, still are they there and watching out in every direction, with the eyes of eagles. Unseen themselves, they see everything that moves between them and the horizon. Where we should be unable hardly to distinguish a moving speck in the distance, they would at once recognise, for instance, a band of horsemen, or a herd of buffalo. Trained up to this duty from childhood, and being naturally quick and far-sighted, no doubt they are the best sentries in the world. As I before stated, they discovered our column, as they said, when we were thirty miles off, which will give the reader some idea of their watchfulness.

For one or two miles above and below this town the corn fields are planted. They are generally upon the rich little patches of land that stretch across the bottom and are irrigated by small springs in the bluffs. These fields were literally fenced in by sunflowers curiously woven together. Here and there a few slight stakes and withes served to support them, but the body and bulk of the fences were composed of the stout stalks of this plant. At this time, when we are here, they are all in full bloom, and are very beautiful indeed. The main street from our encampment to the town is, for nearly half the way, fenced in on each side in this manner; and as you ride along, with these flowers at different heights from the ground, to an elevation above your head, you cannot but feel that the natives *for savages*, have shown a great deal of taste in the decoration of the principal promenade of their city—literally the Boulevard and Broadway of the Pawnee exquisites. However, I should mention that the streets are *not* so clean as I have seen streets, and the city generally is not redolent particularly of incense or choice perfumes; and on the whole, unless a man had a sort of idiosyncrasy for Indians and a morbid taste for their way of living, he would be extremely liable to get a little of the romance with which, *at a distance*, and through the medium of overwrought and unnatural descriptions, he had invested them, rubbed off in, say about a month; more especially if he took *pot luck* (!) with them every day, and slept in one of their cribs every night. The Hon. Charles Augustus Murray, during his tour, visited the Pawnees, and stayed some time with them. They were then in a summer encampment near the Kanzas. He went in for romance, but judging from present appearances, he must have found a great many lively realities spiced in with it.

The women do all the work in and about town, except to stand guard and take care of the horses; consequently, they are very ugly and masculine in their appearance. It is their business to plant and gather corn, get wood and water, build lodges, dress skins, cure meat, cook, make mats, and take care of the babies; while all that the men do is to make and repair their arms, go to war, steal horses, and hunt. Go to the village at any time of day, and you will find the men entirely idle; there may be here and there one who will be making a bow or sharpening a lance, but the majority are either lounging about, smoking, or talking politics, while *all* the women will be seen engaged at *something*. The men are finely formed; indeed, and most of them are perfect models of manly beauty. The majority dress as the two I described as having come into camp last night. Generally, however, the poorer classes of them go barefooted during the summer and have no clothing except the centre cloth—which is similar to a pair of trunk hose without any legs—and the buffalo mantle. The latter is the grand *sine qua non* of their wardrobe, it being their bed, "Sunday-go-to-meeting," and every day dress, all in one. They are of that clear pure red, when clean, which characterizes all unadulterated Indians—a complexion which does not wholly hide a blush or veil the crimson of anger, or pride, or of excitement. They have small and delicately formed hands and feet, which, according to Lord Byron's belief, are sure indications of an aristocratic and noble birth and breeding. Their hair is shaved close to their heads; when I say close I mean it is *all* shaved off except a strip about two inches wide, extending from the forehead to the back of the neck. At the crown of the head, a tuft of this is allowed to grow some two feet in length. This pig-tail is kept carefully braided and greased, for it is the celebrated scalplock, which a man would be a coward not to wear, as he would leave his enemy no chance to "skin him," having nothing to pull by. The hair on the rest of this strip is cut about two inches in length, and is so dressed as to stand normal to the surface. This hirsute fringe, stiffened up with grease and vermilion, looks something like the red wool crest on the old leather caps of the Revolutionary Dragoons; in fact, when a demure Pawnee is at a little distance, with his side towards you, the *tout ensemble* of his head is very much like that of a Grecian helmet. The wearing of the hair shaved in this way, is the most cleanly habit of which they are ever guilty.

Many of the Pawnees have suffered very severely from the ravages of the smallpox. We noticed a great number with but one eye each, having lost the other by that disease. Upon seeing these unfortunate creatures, one of the gentlemen told the commanding officer that we must have made a mistake, and got amongst the I-aways instead of the Pawnees. Such, however, was not the case.

At 2 o'clock to-day a very large deputation, headed by the principal Chief, Charachaush, paid a visit of ceremony to the commanding officer. This deputation was well mounted. Following it came a great number of the commoners, on foot. They were laden with divers articles of merchandise, consisting in part of dried buffalo meat, buffalo robes, moccasins, hair lariettes beautifully braided, green corn, leggins, &c., &c., &c. They soon struck up a brisk trade with the men, and generally got the best end of the bargain, by stealing twice as much as they bought. One of the men purchased a fine robe for a pound plug of tobacco, but when the Pawnee with whom he had traded had gone, I believe he missed his knife, both his spurs, and sundry other articles, which he strongly suspected were keeping company with the tobacco.

If old Fagin, the Jew, had got a Pawnee boy in room of Oliver Twist, he never would have been compelled to teach him how to steal as he did "Work' us," as Noah Claypole used to call Oliver. A Pawnee would have stolen Fagin's shirt off his back, and cheated such common fellows as the Artful Dodger and Charley Bates, out of their eye teeth. They take to it more naturally than beavers to water. "Boz" never saw Pawnees.

When the Chief and his suite arrived, they rode directly up to the commanding officer's tent, and as each one dismounted, he sprang forward and immediately threw his huge and greasy arms around the precise and fastidious Major, and gave him a hug which for vim and power might well have rivalled that of a Greenland bear. It was their emblem of courtesy and etiquette, the welcome being proportioned in each man's case to the vigor and duration of the squeeze. When the Major reflected upon the habits of his last night's guests, can it be wondered at that during the slackening up of each hug, (the force of it not being continuous, but periodical), and when he could catch a half breath, he naturally put on a look which was rather as if he did not relish this part of the ceremony *so well* as a man with less imagination and less refinement might have done? But by virtue of his office—being the Ka-he-ka (Chief)—all these were little extras and emoluments, which we were not honored with—sort of double rations of hugs, accruing particularly, as an appurtenance, to his office. After this ceremony was through with, (and it did not end in a hurry, Indian after Indian coming up, many no doubt who did not belong to the Staff of the Chief, but who "roped in"* for a hug on such an especial occasion, real Ka-he-ka Majors not coming along every day), the commanding officer held a sort of colloquial sub-council with them, which was void of any parliamentary restraints of forms whatever. The hugging part of the visit was too fatiguing to all parties to admit of much profound thought or finished declamation. No doubt the Major would gladly have had the ceremony performed by proxy; that is, on the part of the government; but he was not so fortunate as to have any one volunteer for the service, as Jack Downing did to shake hands for General Jackson, and he was obliged, therefore, to go through with it alone. He sacrificed all personal feelings in the matter, of course, and now and then, as a part of his duty as a public officer, faintly reciprocated the embrace; but as an individual in a private capacity, I've no doubt he looks back upon that part of his visit to the Pawnees as one of the most unpleasant occurrences of his life. It was a very hot day, and that made the whole ceremony infinitely more disagreeable.

*The term "roped in," in the West means the coming to entertainments, &c., where the individual is neither expected or invited. If in New York three gentlemen were going to a Cafe for an oyster supper, and a fourth, unsolicited, should join them, he would "rope in."

As with all the other tribes of Western Indians, polygamy is common with the Pawnees. Every man has as many wives as he is able to procure. This custom is not so objectionable with such a people as it might at first appear to be. The male part of the population being so continually exposed to danger, there would soon be a surplus of females without adequate protection. Besides, as the women of a household do all the work, an increase of their number makes a corresponding division of the labor—hence, they themselves are rejoiced at every new addition their husband may be so fortunate as to make to his family circle.

The manner of courting and of marrying, with this people, is rather curious. When a warrior sees a squaw he would like to have for his wife, he takes a fine horse and ties it to the door of her father's wigwam. If the old folks are willing to part with her for that amount, her father sends one of his own horses, and has him tied to the door of the proposer's lodge; if not, he sends the horse of the lover back again. In that event he does not despair, but takes over two horses; if these are not accepted, he will go as high as three, and throw in a jackass or two, for good count. Such an offer is sure to be successful. The marriage is then celebrated in due form—i.e.: the girl goes to her lover's lodge, and makes herself at home with as little ceremony as can be imagined. Mr. Gregg says—"The eldest daughter is the heiress apparent, and when she gets married she becomes absolute owner of the entire property and household of her parents—family and all. While single she has no authority, but is herself held as a piece of merchantable property, estimated somewhat as in civilized life, in proportion to her charms, and the value of her hereditaments. The fortunate lover who may get her is fully indemnified for his heavy disbursement in the purchase of his bride, for he at once becomes possessor of the entire wealth of his father-in-law—master of the family lodge, and all the household: if there are a dozen younger daughters, they are all his, *de droit*—his wives or slaves, as he may choose to consider them. In fact, the heiress herself seems to be in the same predicament; and the wife among them all who may have the tact to gain the husband's affection, generally becomes mistress of the lodge. From the refuse of this estate of fair ones, the indigent

warriors and inferior Indians, who are not able to purchase an heiress, are apt to supply themselves with wives upon a cheaper scale;
the second-handed ones being, generally, decidedly *low*. Wives can
be got on an average for a horse a-piece; some range as high as four
horses, and some go as low as a jackass. When there has been a big
war, and the market is over-stocked with young widows, and such
like, a mule will buy one from fair to middling. In fact, a very passable and handy wife can be got most any time for a good sized donkey." There is not much romance in all this, I must confess, and yet
it is true. If a person had just read one of Cooper's beautiful Indian
novels, or Murray's Prairie-Bird, and then looked into the old Logbook, he would see a vast difference between the way the Natives
make love in the one, and the way they are said to make it in the
other. One is truth, the other fiction. If the parties are well to do in
the world, after the marriage they give a feast to all their relations,
and send round bits of dog to their neighbors as we do cake; but if
those animals are scarce, this part of the ceremony is omitted.
Amongst the Otoes and Oneakas, there is less ceremony, even, than
that. If they see a girl they like, they just take her home and that ends
the whole matter. They give a horse in payment, if they have one;
but if not, it's all the same.

If one should be curious enough amongst the Indians for evidence
of their having descended from the Ten Lost Tribes, he could find
much which would go to sanction the probability of such a theory
in many of their customs. The Mosaic Law is in force with them to
considerable extent. It is said the statute, as laid down in the XV
chapter of Leviticus, is still in full force amongst the Pawnees, Sioux,
Crows, Blackfeet, Chippeways, Winnebagoes and Menomonies.

The Pawnees seemed to express more curiosity about our negroes
than about anything else they saw in camp. They would look at
them and watch their every movement with wonder and astonishment. Once in a while they would come up to one of the servants
and without saying a word to him, put their hands on his head and
feel of his woolly hair with the most puzzled and perplexed expression that could be imagined. How a human being *could* be so black
as that, was a good ways past their comprehension. Knots of them

would sometimes get together near a fire where one of the boys would be cooking, when they would discuss the subject amongst themselves—eyeing him all the time with the utmost interest. This manifestation of curiosity towards them, the negroes did not seem to relish at all; but if they looked angry about it the Indians laughed, and that only made matters worse.

One of the officers showed them a spy-glass, and let several of them look through it at some horses that were feeding on the bottom, on the opposite side of the river. This nearly beat their wonder about the negroes. The glass was a very fine one, and seemed to bring the animals to within a few yards of where they stood. He then took one of Colt's revolving pistols, and having explained to them how many times it could be fired without loading—just to hoax them—he made signs as if he could bring Indians who would be at a great distance, close to him with the spyglass, and then shoot them down by scores with the pistol. This put their pipes out entirely. That gun that brought horses which were a mile off to within thirty yards, was the "*biggest medicine*" they had seen yet. It was one spat over them—that was—to a certainty.

The Commanding officer invited Charachaush to sup with him this evening. All his suite had gone except five, and the old Sachem said he would be happy to do so provided they might be permitted to partake of the meal also. The major objected to such an arrangement, as Cleggett (his servant) had not made the necessary arrangements for that number of guests. This was all carried on by signs. The old Chief hesitated sometime whether to eat or not unless they did; at last his appetite turned the scale, and after explaining to his staff that so far as they were concerned 'twas "no go," he commenced.

The Pawnees generally are not bad trencher men, and as they advance in rank and years they seem to improve in appetite and power of doing justice to the good things set before them. The head Chief therefore, was a man few would beat at a table and live. He went on the system established by Sir Dugald Dalgetty, as related by Sir Walter Scott, in the Legend of Montrose. He made it a rule at *every* meal to lay in provent enough to last him three days, so in case of a siege he would have something of a stock on hand. In all Sir Dugald's service with Gustavus Adolphus, he never met with a man who could carry out his doctrine with more ease to himself than this same Charachaush. The old fellow drank three pints of hot coffee, (he was fond of coffee) ate all the major's nice corn-cakes, (and cakes too) and all his meat, (he liked meat also) and was about to commence an onslaught on a big chowder that Cleggett had taken much pains to prepare, when the major peremptorily moved an adjournment. The sapient Sancho, after having been installed as governor of the island, and had set himself down to his first banquet, could not have been more thunderstruck when the old doctor touched dish after dish with his wand, and it vanished before he could get a taste, than Charachaush when the chowder disappeared. This dish Cleggett had been at much pains to prepare, having made it *secundem artem*, with first a layer of pork, then a layer of catfish, then a layer of bread, and then a layer of potatoes, then *vice versa* until the pot was full; this being the rule as laid down by the head cook of the Mammoth Cod Association. The major had no idea that this chowder should go the way of all the flesh, but refrained from expressing himself on the subject so long as it was not in immediate danger. When Cleggett took it away Charachaush sat for nearly a minute in almost speechless astonishment, with his eyes on the mouth of the tent through which it had vanished. He then made three or four asthmatic attempts to call for it, saying the Pawnee for "*Big Chowder!*" but Cleggett not understanding the language, never came back.

The staff all this while stood looking on. Charachaush finding the supper was *really* over, begged the major would give them all some tobacco, which he did so, out of a quantity he had brought along for such a purpose. The major then said they (the five) must clear out as he was getting tired of them. Charachaush remained behind. After having filled and lighted his pipe, he said in Pawnee, and as if conferring a great favor at the same time, "*Now I sleep with you all night!*" This was one point farther than the major could go. He could stand the hugging, and all the other things pretty well, but when it came to the sleeping part he demurred. Charachaush at this arose, and, thinking his host was "d—d inhospitable," (this also in Pawnee) left camp for his own village, puffing the smoke spitefully, as he went, as if in high dudgeon. At sun-down the town crier proclaimed in a loud voice that every Indian who should be found in the camp after dark would be kept there till morning. This was told them in their own language, and they left immediately for their town. At tattoo several rockets were sent up. This was a new thing to them also, and at each explosion in the air we could hear them shout in their astonishment at the noise and the shower of stars which would succeed it.

To-morrow we are to have a Council.

CHAPTER XII

STOICISM OF THE INDIANS—*Charachaush and the green spectacles—The Indian dandy's attempt to imitate Mr. Oldbuck in "turning over a new leaf"—A Council—Preliminary measures ending in a smoke—Synopsis of the Major's speech—Charachaush's reply, Indian eloquence—"Wild Warrior"—His speech—His wig, of scalps and Battle Robe—Big Greasy's attempt to "Unaccustomed to public speaking as I am"—Sudden adjournment of Council—We take up our line of march for the Loup villages—Passage of the Nebraska—Terrible night march—Big Greasy's race for a ride—Buffalo close by.*

FRIDAY, AUGUST 30

ONCE in a while an Indian will manifest much curiosity and wonder about those things which are novel and strange; but as a general rule, show him what you please, and however much it may be past his comprehension, he will look upon it with as much apparent indifference as he would had he invented and constructed it himself. This coolness and complete control over their feelings is entirely a matter of education. The Indians are as curious, and can *feel* as much surprise as any people in the world—but they keep such a perfect guard over themselves, that it must be only on an extremely rare occasion—such for instance as the complicated one of the spy-glass and pistol, that they can be betrayed into the least expression of wonder at all.

We were much amused at a remarkable instance of coolness on the part of Charachaush, at the time we were at his lodge and enjoying his green corn feast. Our Chaplain, who was then with us, had on a pair of green spectacles with four glasses—there being two additional ones upon the sides to protect the eyes from the wind. These he presented to the old chief. He received them with a most profound bow, and, having looked at them a moment, as if to get "the hang of them," he put them upon his own nose with the gravity of a judge. Fortunately for him he got them wrong side up, and from that cause they afforded him no obstruction to his sight. It was amusing to see him looking out from under them at his various guests, with a face as solemn as a tombstone, more particularly after we had done eating and the old man had commenced upon the corn himself; then to look at him holding a long ear of it in his hands, as a man would a flute, and eating the corn without removing it from his mouth—at the same time paying profound attention to some one who might be talking to him, and grunting frequent acquiescence, was ludicrous in the extreme. All this time the parson's old glasses were not only upside down upon his nose, but out of all sorts of a level; one end being tilted up to an angle of 30°.

An Indian dandy, who visited our camp, was so fortunate as to purchase a calico shirt from one of the dragoons, and in order to create a sensation in the village upon his return, he concluded he would put it on before he went up. For an individual who never before had had any experience in such matters, this was much more easily thought of than done. At first he commenced with the lower end up, but getting his arms caught in attempting to introduce them into the sleeves, he naturally concluded he was wrong, and after much labor, extricated himself, when he endeavored to get into it by pulling it on over his legs like pantaloons. His good sense, however, soon taught him that that course was decidedly the worst one he could pursue. All this time he betrayed not the least impatience or embarrassment; on the contrary, he seemed as collected as if he was working by the day. Finally, distrusting his own judgment in the matter, he paused in the middle of his labors and looked steadily for about a minute at a soldier who was standing near him, in his shirt sleeves; he then went to work with much better success. After a deal of straining and tugging, the shirt not being half large enough for a man of his size, he made out to get into it. But, unfortunately, it was wrong side before, with the bosom opening down his back and the collar in front. However, this he did not mind; and with all the airs of an empty headed exquisite, he strutted off with his new garment, occasionally looking slyly to the right and left, as he walked along, at the various Indians whom he passed, in order to see if he attracted the additional attention and admiration, which such address was so wonderfully calculated to inspire. We watched his movements with much interest, and could not conceal a smile at the resemblance which was naturally presented to our minds, between his action and those of individuals belonging to *his* school who reside amongst ourselves. Human nature is the same everywhere.

By nine o'clock this forenoon the Indians began to arrive at our encampment from the village, in great numbers. Charachaush seemed to have forgotten all about his last night's ill humor, and shook hands with the Major with as much cordiality as if nothing had happened to interrupt their friendly relations. Had he been permitted to eat all the chowder and then to have shared the "Kahekas" bed, he could not have looked more smiling and happy than he did upon the present occasion. The Pawnee interpreter, Mr. Cleghorn, came down with the old chief, having arrived from the Loup villages last night. There were also with him, representatives from the other three bands of the tribe, who were all introduced in due form. After this ceremony was ended, the Commanding officer informed the Indians that he was then ready to communicate to them the wishes of their Great Father, the President. Mr. Cleghorn was a Canadian Frenchman, and understood English very imperfectly. It therefore, became necessary to employ one of the dragoons as an assistant. This man rendered the Major's speech into French to Cleghorn, who translated it into Pawnee for the Indians. In this way every sentence had to be uttered in three different languages before it could be understood by the party addressed, either when the Major spoke to the Indians or the Indians replied to him. The Indians, at this intimation, formed themselves in a circle, by sitting down cross-legged upon the grass. Charachaush sat next to the Major on the right. From him they were arranged according to precedence of rank all the way around—the inferior chiefs and braves occupying the front row. The next succeeding rows were composed of the next successive grades, until all were seated in their proper places. In the outside rows the Indians were very common indeed. The officers occupied the interior of the circle, immediately opposite the chiefs, while the troops were gathered around outside of all. As a matter of course, before any business whatever could be transacted pipes had to be filled, and everybody obliged to take a good smoke. For this purpose the Major presented the Indians with a large quantity of tobacco, which he had brought along for such occasions. In a few moments clouds and clouds of smoke began to ascend from the ring—each Indian evidently striving to beat all the others in the length and volume of his whiffs, at the same time putting on an air as if his mind could hardly contain the profound thoughts with which it was weighed down. All this was really wise just to look at. After the pipes were lighted not a word was spoken for some minutes. Nothing could be heard but the countless puff, puff, puffs of hundreds of smokers, in full blast. The Commanding officer then arose, and made known to them the objects of our visit. Amongst other things, he told them that we came amongst them with friendly purposes. That although we had come a long ways to see them, we had come very quickly; and that notwithstanding it was our business to fight, our errand there was one of peace. He also explained to them the ability of the Government to protect them so long as they conducted themselves properly, and lived amicably with their white brethren; and likewise its power to punish the aggressors. He alluded to their manner of procuring doubtful subsistence, and enjoined upon them the necessity of cultivating the soil, and of endeavoring to learn other of the primary arts of civilization. He explained to them how much happier they would live by pursuing such a course, than they now do. He deprecated the long and bloody war, which still continued between them and the "*Suhaws* or Sioux"—and contrasted its consequent horrors and distresses with the inestimable blessings of peace. He enjoined upon them to bury the hatchet, not only with their enemies the *Suhaws* or Sioux, but with all other tribes with which they were, unhappily, at variance. Above all things

he told them to be sure to avoid all causes of war—such as the stealing of the horses and peltry of their neighbors, and the occasional
robbing their red brethren of their scalps. That notwithstanding
these things were mere trifles in themselves, still they were calculated at times, to provoke a spirit of retaliation, which might eventu-
ally produce unpleasant consequences. There was an enemy more
dangerous than the *Suhaws*, of which he would warn them to beware. That enemy was whiskey or *fire water*. He told them "so sure
as the dry grass upon the prairies would be consumed, and vanish
before the flame which they applied to it, so sure would they, as a
people, be destroyed, and pass away before this powerful enemy."
Finally, he told them that whenever they met any of their white
brethren upon the great plains, to treat them kindly; and if they
were hungry and in distress, to assist them all in their power. And
particularly, when bands of weary and travel-worn pale-faces should
pass their lands for the great country that lies by the big water, under
the setting sun, to afford them every relief, and by their kindness to
lighten their hearts on their long and comfortless route.

I have only given the outline of this speech. It was a very good
one indeed, and contained several happy figures illustrative of its
various important points and which were calculated to give the Indians at once a forcible and proper understanding of the subject.

Charachaush rose in reply, and having shaken hands with all the
officers, a custom invariably observed by Indian orators previous to
the commencement of their speeches, he said in substance as
follows:—

"Our Father,* we have heard what you have said, and it shall not
pass out of our ears. We are glad you have come amongst us, for you
see with your own eyes that we are very poor. Our great father in
Washington promised us many things which we have not yet received, although we are sorely in want of them. You will tell him of
this, and he will send them to us. We look to the time when we first
knew our white brethren with much pleasure. Before, we were

*All public officers they address as "*Our Father*"—the President they call their
"*Great Father.*" When speaking to one another, or to white men generally, they
invariably say "*Our Brother.*"

obliged to use flint for arrow heads and our lances, and likewise, vessels made of clay. We are now blest with iron spears, and with kettles in which to cook our food. When I went to Washington to see my great father, he gave me this medal as a pledge of his friendship. Then I saw ships, and rode in houses drawn by an iron horse. Wherever I went I was treated well, as were those of my people who were with me. By that we shall always be kind to our white brethren. What you have said of the fire-water is true. It will ruin my people if they do not put it from them. I have repeatedly told my young men they must not steal, and that they must avoid taking the scalps of their neighbors; but the Sioux having come amongst us and burnt our villages, and murdered our women and our children—they will not hearken to my council. I hope you will see the Sioux and compel them to cease molesting us; likewise, to make them give us back our brethren whom they have with them as prisoners."

This speech was delivered with that natural eloquence and grace of action, for which the Indian is so celebrated. There was no foolish clap-trap, or ridiculous intonation of voice, or unnecessary ranting about it. It was spoken in a deliberate and dignified manner; and with an ease and self possession, which would be worthy the imitation of ninety-nine men out of a hundred amongst us, who would really make great pretensions toward being considered fine speakers. What he wished to say was condensed and to the point; and besides, there were no words thrown away in a struggle for effect. All was simple and straight forward. Every idea seemed to be perfectly defined in his own mind before he commenced speaking upon it. He then clothed it in as few and expressive words as possible. We were all forcibly struck with his truly beautiful delivery. Every writer, at all familiar with the habits of the North American Indians, has spoken of the decorum invariably characterising their public meetings and discussions. The Hon. C. A. Murray,[17] who visited the Pawnees when he was in this country, says:—"There is not a public body in Europe, from the British Parliament down to the smallest Burgh meeting, that might not study to advantage the proceedings of an Indian Council—whether as described in the faithful pages of the German missionaries, or, as it may still be seen by any one who has leisure and inclination to visit these remote regions, where Indian character is least changed and contaminated by intercourse with the whites. Such an observer would find his attention attracted to two remarkable facts: first, that no speaker is ever interrupted; and, secondly, that only those speak who from age, rank, and deeds, are entitled to be listened to."

Charachaush was followed by several other chiefs. Their speeches were generally short, and contained nearly the same sentiments as those expressed by the old man himself.

There was a man whom they called the Wild Warrior, a Republican Brave, who then stepped into the circle and delivered himself of the following sentiments:—

"Our Father, we have heard your advice about our living at peace with our red brethren. It is good. Our ears are closed upon it. We wished peace—we wished to meet our brethren with our hands unstained with blood. But the Sioux came down upon us and murdered our fathers, our mothers, our wives and our little ones; and the lodges in which they dwelt were burned to the ground. What could we do? It is true, some of our chiefs advised us to sue for peace, and not retaliate. But *I* could not agree to that while my people's bones lay unburned and unrevenged. I thirsted for the blood of my enemies. Alone I pursued them—I followed them through heat and through cold—through storm and sunshine, and when hungering; still, still I followed them! One by one they felt the edge of my tomahawk, until all there fell.† I have revenged my people. Others may be advised to peace, but I was born to slay my enemies. *Wa-con-dah*‡ made me a great warrior. He decreed that I should be successful in procuring furs for my white brethren, and scalps for my self, and I have done so. Here, upon this Battle-robe, is a history of the exploits of Wild Warrior. Take it to your home, that your people may know of his deeds!"

†On saying this he pointed to the number of scalps drawn upon his mantle.

‡As the Great Spirit was designated by the Indians who resided upon the east side of the Mississippi river by the name of "*Manitou*," so is he known among the Osages, Omahas, Ioways, Pawnees, and other Missouri tribes by that of *Wa-con-dah*, or "*Master of Life*"—Murray.

There is a beautiful prairie opposite Lexington, Mo., about which there is an Indian legend, that goes by the name of Wacondah Prairie to this day.

At this he spread his robe upon the grass in front of the major, and retired from the ring. This robe was covered with hieroglyphics, indicating his many successes, both in the taking of scalps and the stealing of horses. He was dressed in the most fantastic manner that could be imagined. His hair was all shaved off except his scalp-lock; and covering his whole head was a wig, composed entirely§ of the scalps he had taken. Besides, his buckskin coat and leggins were fringed from head to foot with these horrible trophies.

As soon as he had sat down, a Tepage chief, named Stede-le-we-it* came forward and shook hands preparatory to making a speech. He was the drollest looking old chap we ever saw, being nothing but a great ball of animated fat; and besides, he had the smallest legs that ever before had the temerity to attempt to support such an unwieldy globe of flesh, as the one that rested upon them. Some of the officers named him *"Big Greasy"* for short. He had hardly begun his exordium before a tremendous alarm seemed to pervade the whole body of Indians, from, as they said, a report which had just arrived, that the Sioux had cut off one of their hunting parties. The consequence was, the whole Council was broken up, and Big Greasy's speech cut short by the noise and panic that ensued. Big Greasy himself seemed to understand it all perfectly well, and said, colloquially to the Major, "Never mind, I'll tell you what I wanted to say, at the next village." It seems that the old fellow was unpopular on this side of the Nebraska Valley, and that the alarm was only a *ruse* to prevent him from speaking.

Thus ended our Council with the Grand Pawnees. I should have been pleased to have given copies of all the speeches that were made upon the occasion—but a fear that they would not be generally interesting, decided me against transcribing them for publication. After this tumultuous adjournment the Major issued to the Indians a large quantity of flour and pork, that they might have one good feast to commemorate our visit. This done, the tents were struck, and the baggage train took up its line of march for the Loup village,

§It is a frequent custom among the Indians west of the Missouri, to sketch upon the interior of a buffalo robe the various battles in which they have fought and conquered.

*He who has killed many.

directly north across the valley, and distant about twenty miles, following the trail they were obliged to travel. As soon as they had started, the Squadrons were manoeuvred on the plain, in front of the whole town, and several of the divisions were "*charged as foragers*," to give the Indians some idea of our mode of fighting. In order to cross the Nebraska at the best ford, we were obliged to pass directly through the village with the whole column. Every lodge was covered with men, women, and the little four-year-old children. Look which way you might, you could see crowds and crowds of them clustered upon every prominent point, to get a last look at us as we passed. The passage of the river was a beautiful sight. The water was hardly up to the bellies of the horses in any place, and the river was wide enough to have the whole column marching in sight between its banks at the same time. After the howitzers had descended to the water, several shells were fired down the river. The report of the pieces, and the roar and splash of the shot as they went ricocheting along, seemed to astonish the Indians very much. Previous to witnessing the effect of these pieces, they had, in fact, no idea of the execution that could be done with them. They saw at once that even their lodges, which are built with a view to protection from their enemies, as well as from the weather, would be no defence at all against such terrible engines. Leaving them with such impressions of our power still fresh in their minds, I have no doubt, as they saw us gradually fading away in the distance from their sight, they secretly wished us and our means of destruction, any where else but in their neighborhood. We were decidedly Bad Medicine, thought they.

The interpreter, Cleghorn, had told us that the two villages were not over ten miles apart, and that the road was excellent. We therefore, hoped to arrive at the Loup Fork by sundown. What was our surprise when night came on, to find ourselves just getting amongst a series of lagoons and quagmires, where five or six wagons would be stalled at once, and which would take the men, in some cases, hours to extricate. We shall never forget that awful march. Men and mules were, in some cases, mingled together in their labors; all struggling to force the heavily laden vehicles through the mire, which some times would be twenty or thirty yards across, and so soft and deep, the wheels would cut through to the axletree at every step. To make matters a thousand times worse, myriads and myriads of mosquitoes swarmed upon us, covering every spot where a drop of blood could be drawn. A man could not strike his horse *anywhere* with the flat of his hand without killing, absolutely, hundreds of them at a blow. It was twelve o'clock at night before we reached the bank of Loup River. A more tired and worn down set of men and animals can hardly be imagined, than we were at the conclusion of this march. The tents, however, were soon pitched, the horses picketed out, and supper got as usual. Reader, coffee and bread, and fried pork, didn't relish badly *that* night, you may depend. It was one o'clock that night when the bugles waked the scared echoes with the tattoo. While Big Greasy was attending the council just described, some mischievous Indian had turned his horse loose. The animal finding himself at liberty, deliberately trotted off for his own village, leaving his master to get home the best way he could. Fortunately, the teams had not gone when Big Greasy ascertained these facts, and he was enabled to persuade a driver to haul his saddle and bridle on one of the wagons, though not one of them could be induced to do as much for the old man himself. He was too fat for that. However, they told him, through Cleghorn, that one of the officers, who was sick, had gone on ahead in a light Jersey wagon, and if he hurried he might overtake him and get a ride for the rest of the way in that. The idea of his running with his ton of fat was not exactly obsolete, for no sooner said, than off the old man started, at a rapid pace, to overtake the carriage alluded to. When he was half a mile off, this gentleman saw him coming with long strides over the tall grass, and heard him calling—"Hallo-o-o-o!" in Pawnee. He knew at once who it was, and the object of the chase, and was determined to try the old fellow's bottom, by keeping him at his speed as long as he could hold out. So when he had almost caught up with the carriage, this officer would slyly touch up the horses, when off they would start, bringing Big Greasy down to his utmost speed, with his *"Hallo-o-o-o!"* to a mere quinzical squeak, from his want of breath. At last the carriage was stopped, and the old fellow allowed to get in. Lord, how the water rolled off of him! In running he had cast off every garment except his leggings and a blue calico shirt, and these were reeking with perspiration. His buffalo robe and several other articles were rolled up in a wad under his arms, in such a way as not to interfere with his action. He never before had been in a wagon, and its motion seemed to produce that sensation upon him which one feels when moving rapidly in a large swing, for every time the horses would make a quick start he would catch his breath, and in a sort of ecstacy sigh out, "Eh-hep! good! heap! eh-oo!" But if by accident the wheels dropped suddenly into a hollow, so as to produce an unpleasant jolt, he would make up the most horrible face, and exclaim—"Ugh! bad-heap! eh! oh!" It was his first ride, and no doubt his sensations were as novel as could well be imagined. Mr. Deas made a very spirited sketch of the old fellow's race, in which, at a glance, a better description of his appearance and character is conveyed, than could possibly be given by words.

To-morrow we are to cross the Loup Fork, and hold a Council with this branch of the tribe. I forgot to mention that this afternoon, as we were crossing the bottom, we met a great number of Pawnees with their horses literally loaded down with fresh buffalo meat. They told us there was a plenty of this kind of game within two short days' ride of the village. Many of the officers are in hopes yet to get amongst them before we return home. *Au revoir!*

CHAPTER XIII

LOUP RIVER—*Mr. Dunbar—Extract from our Chaplain's Journal, in relation to his conduct—Big Greasy makes a speech—A windy oration ending in "pork and tobacco"—Loup village—Indian fortification—Mr. Deas finding the Indians at fault in English, plays the agreeable to them in French—The two little princesses—Dressed a la Cracovienne, with hair braided a la the Misses Kenwigs'—Little dears—Indian war-song chanted in the distance, and procession by moonlight—Song in the distance swells upon the ear like that chanted by the boatmen to Roderic vich Alpine—Night scene in real life—War dance—Indians costume—They recount their exploits—Pawnee clown—Heir apparent enacts a Bashaw of one tail—Intelligent horses—The various dances—They understood animal magnetism long before we did, same as the Chinese did the daguerreotype and the election of Mr. Polk.*

SATURDAY, AUGUST 31

THE Loup Fork of the Nebraska is a very beautiful river—it is about six or seven hundred yards wide, and runs with a very swift current. The water is as clear as chrystal, and although flowing over a quicksand bed, is entirely free from the detritus which renders the waters of the Missouri and Nebraska so turbid and opaque. At least it is so now, though in the spring, when the heavy rains have swollen its various tributaries, it may be as muddy as either of the rivers just named. The Loup village is situated on its northern bank, and about half a mile above our last night's encampment. This morning several hours were consumed in endeavoring to find a suitable ford for the crossing of the wagons. There being a Missionary Station but a short distance below the village, the Commanding officer was in hopes that some knowledge as to the best place for the passage of the river, and the most desirable spot for an encampment, could be gained from the people residing there; consequently, at a very early hour he wrote a note to the Rev. Mr. Dunbar—the Missionary who had been stationed longest in the country[18]—inviting him over to our camp, with a view of obtaining information on these points. The whole conduct of this reverend gentleman while we were in the country, was such as to merit the unqualified censure of every individual belonging to the Expedition. I will here make an extract from the Journal of our Chaplain, Mr. Ker, in which the Rev. Mr. Dunbar's course toward us seems to be spoken of in very plain, though in very just terms.

"The Major stated to him (Mr. D.) the objects of this military visit to the Pawnees; that it was entirely pacific and friendly both to the Indians and to the missionaries; that being unpleasantly and inconveniently encamped, he was desirous of crossing the river, but not being able to find a proper ford, and having no guides upon whom he could depend, he politely requested Mr. D. to have the kindness to send him one, and also oblige him by coming over himself and conduct us to a suitable place for encampment. But strange as it may appear, although his letter was promptly and safely delivered into his hands by a trusty Indian, no answer was returned and no notice taken of it whatever. After waiting a long while for the return of the messenger, and ascertaining the fruitlessness of his errand, the Major determined to cross the Loup at all hazards, and select his camp where best he could. In pursuance of his resolution the troops were put in motion, and the column descended into the river. The greatest danger to be apprehended was from the treacherous and bottomless quicksands, into which, though apparently solid ground, a horse and his rider might instantly sink, and totally disappear. The ford is very hard to keep on account of the rapidity of the current, and its zig-zag course. It crosses the river in a diagonal direction, and is followed with the utmost difficulty. It was well known to all the missionaries, who, with the Indians, often cross it;

and to those acquainted with its many sinuosities; it can be passed with perfect ease, more especially when the water is low, as was the case when we were there. Some of these missionaries, with Mr. Dunbar among them, were assembled on the opposite bank, and had a full view of our situation and difficulties, and yet, not one of them offered the slightest assistance. The Indians were much more considerate and kind, for numbers of them came down from the village, and dashed like waterfowl into the river, as if it was their proper element; men, women and children; some on ponies and donkeys, some swimming, and some wading along the shoals. All were shouting and yelling as for dear life. But though these volunteer guides came to direct us, their number and noise defeated their kind intentions, and increased the existing difficulties. Solomon tells us that in a multitude of counsellors there is safety, but had he been with us, he could not have affirmed, that in a multitude of Indian pilots there was a corresponding degree of sure guidance. However, we all got safely across. Some of the dragoons were dismounted by their horses sinking into and floundering through the beds of quicksands, greatly to the amusement of their more fortunate comrades. After the Squadrons had crossed, the wagons followed—many of them sank up to their axletrees in the sands. Unless they were kept in rapid motion all the time, they would immediately go down. For the purpose of preventing the possibility of losing them, fifty men were detailed and placed under charge of an officer, to assist in getting them over. These men had a long picket-rope, which they tied in the chain of the lead mules, when at a word off, they would start through the water, pulling mules, wagons, and everything else over with a run. The Indians, by scores, volunteered for this kind of labor, and laid hold of the ropes and wagons with a will and a vigor which rendered us much service. In this way, in a couple of hours, everything was safely over. But query?—which need civilization most, the Indians or the missionaries? The former, who dashed into the water to render us what assistance they could, or the latter, who stood snug and dry upon the banks, looking on with stoical apathy? On ascertaining that Mr. Dunbar was amongst them, I approached him and announced my name and calling. At the same time, I extended to him my hand, which he received slowly and apparently with a good deal of reluctance, and replied to my salutation in the briefest and most distant manner, immediately stepping back into his company of missionary friends and declining all conversation and further intercourse, as if he had already proceeded too far. This I thought was what might be considered rather cool, by the most charitable. To the rest of the officers he was quite as distant. Indeed, his manner and conduct, and that of most of the missionaries seemed to indicate that they looked upon our visit to the people among which they lived, as an uncalled for intrusion. They were neither communicative, nor would they give a satisfactory reply to the questions addressed to them, either by the Commanding officer, or by any of the other gentlemen. This we all regretted exceedingly, as we expected to obtain much interesting information from them, in relation to the Pawnees, respecting whom so little is known. Mr. Dunbar had not even the courtesy to visit the Commanding officer, to whom an apology at least, was due for the unusual manner in which he had treated his letter. On the contrary, he seemed disposed to shun him altogether, and would have done so entirely, even had not one of the officers (the Adjutant) almost compelled him to call. The Major held a Council with this band this afternoon. This Mr. Dunbar attended, but as soon as it was over he started off to his home without showing the slightest civility or hospitality whatever, to any of us. Whatever may be thought to the contrary in civil life, and amongst religious people, there are no men that more highly respect Christianity and its ministers, than a great majority of the officers of the army; but they require the former to be exhibited without cavil, bigotry, sectarian stiffness, coldness; and the latter to be simple in their manners, pure in their morals, and sincere but unostentatious in their piety; and they know that religion generates kindness, courtesy and hospitality, and that Christian ministers ought to be an example and pattern of these things. We found an unhappy state of affairs among the missionaries at this village. Small as their number is, they are divided into two factions, as are the Indians also. The former are doing the latter but little good, if any. I am constrained to declare, from personal observation, that the money which is annually expended on many of these missionary enterprises could be laid out much more profitably at home, on more needy and pressing objects, of both moral and physical destitution. There is an ultra feeling of religious sentimentalism pervading a numerous class of citizens that can sympathise with no species of destitution and want, unless associated with a black or yellow skin, and dwells far away from the abode of this Quixotic philanthropy. While around it, daily and hourly, may be seen the living embodiments of ignorance, vice, poverty and want, in all their total abandonment, wending on their melancholy way unheeded, unpitied and unaided."

The Council[19] referred to in the above extract, did not differ materially from that held with the Grand Pawnees yesterday. Big Greasy succeeded in making his speech, (and a very good one it was,) much to his own satisfaction and to ours too, for we all began to take quite an interest in the fat old fellow. He was followed by a chief who seemed to talk a great deal more for grandeur than to any given point. We often see such orators among the pale-faces. He began by saying that "Wa-con-dah made both the white and red man—they should be brothers. He had been in Washington—had seen his Great Father, and his Great Father was good. As for hunting buffalo, that was something he loved to do, for the Great Spirit had made the buffalo for him to hunt—he had; and he liked his white brethren, and never had stolen their donkeys. And (said he in conclusion) we are very poor, our father; and hope you will give us a great deal to eat, cause we are very hungry—and some tobacco."

The speech was very long, but as disjointed as the above specimen, and ended in the same manner. The fact was, all he wanted was to get the provisions, and so forth; but he felt fearful that if he just asked for them in so many words his wishes would not be gratified, hence the long and windy argument, with the brief and pithy peroration of "pork and tobacco."

After the adjournment of the council, the head chief Charachaush* told the commanding officer that in the evening his young men would entertain us with a war-dance. The Indians then left the camp for their village to arrange their toilette for the occasion. At

*"Whose lodge is the chief one."

"retreat" (sunset) the whole command was mustered and inspected —it being the last day of the month. The Loup village is about a mile above our encampment and immediately upon the bank of the river. This bank at that place is some twenty-five feet higher than the water and is nearly perpendicular. The village is twice as large as that of the Grand Pawnees, and the lodges are much more commodious, and are all quite new. It is nearly square, having the high bank of the Loup on its south side, and is protected by a wall of turf and earth on the west, north, and east. This wall is about five feet high and, say, four feet thick at the base by three at the top. There is a dry ditch upon its outside all the way round. This ditch is no larger than the supply of turf and soil of which the wall is constructed— originally made it. The wall itself is perforated every eight or ten feet by rude loop holes of a sufficient size for the discharge of arrows or rifles. The Chaplain, Mr. Deas, and myself rode up to this town, and were struck with the extreme beauty of its location. To the Southward, the vast plain, over which we had wended our weary way the night before, lay spread out like a summer sea covered with green and inlaid with beautiful flowers, the mosaic work of nature. Eastward the foliage bordering upon the Loup, seemed in the distance like a rich embossing of velvet interlaced here and there with silver, as glimpses of clear and joyous river might be caught as it danced onward in gladness as its union with the Nebraska.

Mr. Deas seemed to possess the whole secret of winning the good graces of the Indians. Whenever he entered a lodge it was with a grand flourish and a mock bow that would put even an Ottoman in ecstasies. And, as he said he was sure they did not understand English, he always gave his salutations in French and with a tone and gestures *so irresistibly comic that, generally, the whole lodge would burst into a roar of laughter*, though not the shadow of a smile could be seen on his face.

"Bonjour Messieurs"—(with a low bow to the old men).

"Bonjour Mesdames"—(a slide—a long wink with one eye—and a still lower bow to the old squaws).

"Bonjour Mesdemoiselles"—(two slides—a sentimental look up sideways—with one hand laid impressively upon his heart, and a gentle inclination of the body towards the girls). Then standing bolt upright, he would ask with all the gravity of an undertaker, "Comment se porte *toute* la famille?" By this time he would be on easy terms with the whole of them, when he would take out his portfolio and commence sketching; all the while rattling away at them in French to keep them quiet, though not a word of it did they understand. Every now and then his conversation to them would be interrupted by some remark to himself as a new idea of the subject he would be drawing would strike him.

The women in this town appeared to be prettier than those of the other village. I saw two or three beautiful little girls. They were daughters of the chief, and were dressed with much taste. Their hair was very long and glossy, and braided in two parts like the Misses Kenwigs' in Nicholas Nickleby. They had on pretty calico frocks and neat little moccasins, worked with porcupine quills, with cunning little leggings made of scarlet cloth, decorated with ribbon. They seemed not to be at all afraid of us—on the contrary, they would take hold of our hands, and walk with us from lodge to lodge, chatting to us all the time in Pawnee, and apparently as delighted as they would have been had we been their brothers. I can never forget their sweet expressive faces and eloquent eyes—those pretty children—they reminded me so much of a dear little cousin—a little brunette—whom I may never see again.

After "tattoo," we heard the Indians coming toward our camp from their village. It was a still, calm, beautiful moonlight night, and, as the procession advanced, the war-song, chanted by hundreds of voices, swelled gradually upon the ear, with its wild accompaniments of flutes and drums. At times, when the road wound around some point of woods or bluff, it would sink almost to a murmur, when again it would burst forth with increased power, as some new turn in the path brought them nearer to us. The effect was really enchanting. If there was ever any romance in real life, this was a specimen of it. To stand in a military camp, with all those fine touches to the scene which the moonlight gives to armed men, and horses, and tents; to have the broad prairie around you—a beautiful river in front, with its waters sparkling like silver,—with its long dark fringe of woods casting here and there deep shadows over the glassy mirror in which they are reflected—and to be away, *so far* from the noise of the big world, is in itself a near approach to those pictures which fancy will sometimes create as its ideals of the beautiful; but when she adds to it the long procession of warriors dressed in their battle garb—the Children of the Desert—with all their arms, and decorations, and war songs, the same as they were *how long ago!*— gradually approaching on such a night,—the song growing louder as they advance, and the frequent war whoop more distinct, it is making the drawing almost too extravagant for nature—and yet, it was just as it is here painted as to outline, with the addition of that indescribable effect which is borrowed from a thousand local circumstances, and thoughts, and feelings, which no one can delineate, and yet which go to give a coloring and tone to the whole subject.

An immense pile of logs had been collected before dark, and, as soon as the Indians were heard advancing, it was set on fire. As they arrived, they formed about it, in a large circle, with those who were to dance on the inside. All this was without our chain of sentinels, yet all were present from our camp who had any desire to be. The officers occupied a place in the interior of the ring, opposite the dancers. At a signal given by the Chief a song was commenced by a choir of a dozen or more warriors, accompanied in perfect time by four or five drums, and the wailing of some half dozen Indian flutes. This song had not continued over a minute, before first one warrior sprang into the area near the fire, and commenced his dance, brandishing his tomahawk and knife, and singing his war song, pausing every now and then to yell his most unearthly and terrific battle cry—then another, and another, until the whole blazing fire was surrounded by these dancing savages—springing this way and that, as the song went on, and going through with all their movements of attack and defence with a fearful truth to nature.

Their dresses were most beautiful. The most of them had caps made of war-eagle feathers, which gave a splendid contour to their heads. They also wore necklaces, formed of the huge claws of the grizzly bear, and mantles of the white wolf skin—or buffalo robes worked with the stained quills of the porcupine, and painted with views of their battles. After dancing in this way some eight or ten minutes, a signal would be given when every dancer would instantly stop, give his war whoop, and retire to the circle. Then some Chief or brave would step into the ring and recount his exploits in war, and his successes in stealing horses.* This part of the entertainment was very interesting, as it presented to us some fine specimens of their oratory on subjects calculated to call them out. There are no people, in my opinion, so graceful and eloquent in their gestures and actions, as the Indians of the West. Their voices are flexible and of great compass, and their manner of delivery bold, impassioned, and earnest. Of course we were not capable of judging of their reasoning powers, or of the logical structure of their arguments; but to the eye and to the ear, so far as action and tone went, they were infinitely more eloquent than the best among us. As soon as the speaker had got through, the singers and players upon the drums and flutes would strike up, when the dance would again begin. Thus, with first a dance and then an oration, the night was spent, until the "wee short hour ayont the twal." They now and then enlivened the entertainment by little comic touches that were ludicrous in the extreme. For instance—there was a lad, say about eighteen, who had his face and body entirely muffled up in a robe, and every once in a while he would dart into the ring and take off, with a burlesque imitation, the various warriors who were dancing. This occasioned an immense deal of fun. In fact we all admitted that, as a clown, he beat anything we had ever seen.

There were three or four others who were decorated with feathers, and had the horns of the buffalo upon their heads, and something fixed to their hips like tails. Among these was the Heir Apparent himself. They only danced now and then, but their style was so vigorous, and so unique withal, that they would have forced a laugh from even a tomb stone. They were the real Aegipanes of the West.

After all the ceremonies were completed, a large quantity of flour and pork were distributed to them by order of our commanding

*An Osage once made a boast at a similar dance in his tribe—"that he had been cast an hundred times on foot, but always returned on horseback." Meaning that he had stolen that number of horses from the whites.

officer. For this they joined in what is called the Dance of Thanks, which was entirely different from the war dance. This over, the heads of the barrels were knocked in, and the old Chief distributed the provisions equally to all.

While the dancing was going on, we were struck with the curiosity the horses of the Indians manifested. They stood outside the whole ring, yet looked over the shoulders of the Indians in front, and with their ears pointed forward, seemed to regard the whole affair with an interest as intense as that exhibited by any one in the crowd. And once in a while, as a dance ended, or at the conclusion of an oration, they turned their heads around to each other, and with a nod and a wink seemed slyly to say—"*They'll pass!*" "*He'll do,—he will!*"—or expressions of that kind, indicating the satisfaction they experienced at the performance.

A war dance is the most important of any of their ceremonies. Next to it is their great Medicine Dance, which is a kind of religious reel, in which all take a hand.

They have a great many charms and snake skins, and amulets which, when darted at each other, had the extraordinary effect of knocking the dart*ee* over,—when he lays in a *mesmeric* state until relieved by the dart*or*. They also have what is called the Green Corn Dance, and the Scalp Dance. We noticed that the *common* Indians—those who had not distinguished themselves in any way—were not admitted inside the ring at all. During the entertainment, one of them happened to creep in by accident, but he was no sooner discovered than he was kicked out. After he had got away, and the warrior who had driven him had returned, he put on a great many savage scowls, and shook his fist threateningly, but this he only ventured to do when there was no danger at hand.

After the provisions were all distributed, the Indians departed for their village as they had come. To-morrow we shall take up our line of march for the Otoe Towns, near Council Bluffs.

CHAPTER XIV

COMICAL SCENE WITH A COCK OF HAY—*Loup sentinels—Population of the tribe—Battle between the Sioux and the Pawnees—Death of Capote-Bleu—"Kickapoo setter" sold into captivity—Beaver Creek—The Surgeon does not kill an Elk—Game in abundance—Unhappy reflections thereon—Looking Glass Creek—Army life.*

SUNDAY, SEPTEMBER 1

IT THREATENED to be a rainy day from "reveille" until "guard mounting." About nine o'clock, however, it cleared up, and the Commanding officer concluded to commence the march for Council Bluffs. This encampment lays, as I before stated, about a mile below the town—and is immediately in the great road that leads down to the Lower Mission—say two miles from us. This road is travelled a great deal by the Indians, as they have large fields of corn below; and besides, they get much of their wood, and nearly all of their thatching from the bottom lands further down the river. This morning, while we were yet remaining in camp, undecided whether to move or not, one of the most amusing incidents I ever witnessed occurred. It is impossible even to attempt to describe it as it really was—though from a rough outline, perhaps the reader can imagine something of the ludicrousness of the effect. The squaws were continually passing our camp with their donkeys laden with faggots, as I described them in a former chapter. One old woman had loaded down a jackass with hay cured for thatching, and attempted likewise to drive it to the village. The load was so piled up on the animal's back, and hung down around him so low, that nothing could be seen except his feet underneath, his long ears projecting through in front, and his short tail sticking out behind. In all else he seemed only a locomotive cock of hay. As he drew near our encampment the horses began to prick up their ears and snort, evidently very much alarmed. Some of the officers fearful that there might be a *stampede*, called to the men to stand by the lariettes. The cock of hay heard all that was going on, and getting frightened itself, ran away from the squaw, and came down through the line of sentinels in full blast, right into the middle of the square. There never before was such a tumult as it occasioned for about five minutes. Horses broke loose—men ran this way and that to catch them—some dashed at the hay to drive it out; but it seemed to get so confused, that sometimes it would run backwards until it struck a tent, or something of the kind, when it would rally and charge this way and that, scaring the horses in the neighborhood, as if the old Harry himself was after them with a sharp stick. At last it made a dash towards the river. The bank was about fifteen feet perpendicular height; the lower level being covered with a growth of small willows, the water having receded and left them high and dry. Over this he went like a streak. We saw the shape of a couple of pairs of hoofs when the hay became inverted, as it turned a summerset over the bank, when in an instant all was out of sight. He struck the bottom with the hay first; the consequence was, his fall was completely broken, besides the ropes which were used to bind it upon his back, slackened up, and he absolutely slid out from under them, and dashed off for the village like mad, with the old squaw after him as hard as she could run. It was sometime before the horses got quiet, many of them continuing to keep their eyes steadily fixed upon the point where the hay went out of sight, as if expecting it to come back every moment, to renew the charge.

The Loups are equally as vigilant as the Grand Pawnees, and keep up the same system of guard duty, day and night. In addition to corn, we noticed that they cultivate pumpkins, squashes, potatoes and beans with considerable success; though not in a quantity sufficient to sustain themselves as a people, for any length of time. If the men could be induced to work, they could raise enough to last the whole population the year round with all ease, but they will not lift a hand in any labour except hunting and stealing, to save themselves from famishing.

According to the official statement, the whole nation of Pawnees —(that is, including the Republicans, Grand Pawnees, Loups and Tepage)—numbers 12,500 souls; but that estimate is undoubtedly a great deal too large. Several men who have traded with them for many years, and have had every opportunity of knowing nearly their exact population, informed us that they did not exceed 6,500, with 1000 warriors. Such probably is a very correct estimate of their force. They are said to have descended from the same stock with the Rickarees of the North, and the Wacoes, Wichitas, Towockanoes, Towyash and Keechyes of Red River; all of whom speak languages still traceable to the same origin, and have customs and observances nearly alike.

In the month of June, 1843, a band of the Dahcotahs (throat cutters,) or Sioux, made a descent upon a village of the Pawnees, (the site of which is immediately upon the road, and not more than a mile and a half below our encampment,) and after a most sanguinary conflict succeeded in burning the most of the lodges which it contained. This village occupied one of those beautiful parterres that lay between the bluffs and the Loup, and had upon its western side a fine clear stream of water, that passed near it on its way from the high prairie to the river. A similar stream came in between the village and the houses of the Missionary, Farmer, and Blacksmith of the tribe, which are situated half a mile further down. The Sioux numbered some three or four hundred warriors, approached the town in the night by sending large bodies of men down the channels of these two streams to the river, under the several banks of which they were to lie concealed until a signal from the chief, who stayed back in the hills with the main part of his force, should be given, when a simultaneous attack was to be made from every side. This approach had been conducted so adroitly that the eagle-eyed sentinels upon the hills had never taken the least alarm. Day at length began to dawn in the east. Just as everything was completed for the attack, one of the women of the town went to the stream for water, where she discovered the concealed enemies, and gave the alarm. In a moment all the Sioux who were occupying positions along these two water courses and under the bank of the river, darted from their cover and closed in upon three sides of the village, shouting their terrible battle cry as they ran. The Chief of the Dahcotahs, finding the parties who were laying in ambush had been discovered, gave his war whoop, and at the head of his mounted men broke through the line of sentinels upon the hills, and charged down upon the devoted town with the thunder of an avalanche. For a few moments the poor Pawnees were panic stricken, but their gallant chief—the celebrated Capote-Bleu —soon aroused them to a spirited resistance, by yelling back to the clouds of advancing enemies his shout of defiance, and with his long lance and tomahawk engaging hand to hand with the foremost of them. The battle soon became general. The Sioux finding that they could not draw the Pawnees from their town by a feigned retreat, which they made, returned to the combat with renewed fury. Here the Pawnees had them for a time at an advantage, as they shot them down from the galleries of their lodges as they charged through the streets. The Sioux at last sprang upon the wigwams, and tearing the earth away set fire to the straw thatching within. In a moment the interior of several of them was in a blaze, and as the men, women and children rushed from the fire, they were brained by their implacable enemies without, and their mangled bodies thrown back into the flames. The battle continued from about five o'clock until half past ten in the forenoon. Over half of the lodges were burned, and from sixty to eighty of the Pawnees slain. It was impossible to determine how many the Sioux lost in this attack. We were told that those of them who were dead, or those who were wounded past recovery, they threw into the burning lodges, to prevent the Pawnees from getting their scalps, or of tormenting them. Poor Capote-Bleu fell early in the battle, his body pierced by a dozen bullets. It was but the September previously that I met this gallant old Chief at Council Bluffs, where he gave me his bow and arrows; the latter encased in a rich quiver of otter skin, and in return, I presented him with a fine gun, and a quantity of powder and lead. I little dreamed then that he was so soon to fall in defence of his people. Had he lived with us and fought as he fought there, and have fallen, his name would have been immortal. I conversed with a lady whose husband is employed in the country as (I believe,) a school teacher, about this battle. She lived the nearest to the village of any of the whites. She told me that the Sioux would sometimes be driven entirely out of the town, when again they would rally, to hand, with knives, tomahawks, lances and war-clubs, both parties would be indiscriminately mingled, pell-mell, in the work of death, and filling the air with the most fiendish yells and shrieks. Sometimes, as a warrior upon the outside of the melee would fall, his antagonist would spring forward, and cutting around his head with his knife, would place one foot upon his back, and with both hands clenched in his hair, tear the reeking scalp from the skull; when giving his war whoop, and waving the bloody trophy in the air, he would again spring forward like an infuriated devil, to the fight. I asked her if she was not afraid the Sioux would kill her? She said at first she was, but a party of them came down and entered the house of the blacksmith nearby, and, without touching him, killed his wife (a Pawnee woman,) before his eyes, when they returned to the battle without molesting any one else. From this she said she knew they did not wish to harm the whites, and afterwards she had no fears.

We started about nine o'clock, and soon passed the scene of this battle. The burnt timbers and a few remaining lodges indicated the spot. The rank grass and luxuriant helianthi filled the desolate streets, and no sound or sign of life could be seen, where so short a time since had been so much animation and tumult, and strife. The survivors had all moved away, and the band which embraced the fortunes of Capote-Bleu, became scattered, by mingling with the other branches of the tribe. They could not bear, they said, to sleep upon the ground which had drunk the blood of their beloved chief, their brothers, their wives and their little ones! I have given the account of this fight as I gathered it from people who were on the ground, and who saw everything that transpired, from the first charge to the retreat of the Sioux. From it the reader can gather a faint idea of the conflicts which frequently take place between different tribes of the natives, out here upon the Great Prairies, and which, with all their

acts of daring—their heroism—their individual and collective brav-
ery, pass down the stream of time forgotten forever! With us how
different it would be. Palafox, at the seige of Saragossa, with his battle cry of "*War to the knife!*" exhibited no more valour, or dauntless
and indomitable courage in the defence of that ancient city, (he
Cesarea Augusta of the Romans,) than did the humble and obscure
Pawnee Chief, Capote-Bleu, in resisting the attack of the warlike and
bloody Dahcotahs. One will be known to posterity as a hero—the
other is already nearly forgotten, even by the little band who fought
side by side with him, and in whose defence he so gallantly fell.

Capt. B.'s "Kickapoo setter" met with an unhappy fate to-day.
Notwithstanding he "took on" for the campaign voluntarily, and
had followed his master's fortunes through thick and thin; and notwithstanding his zealous attempts to assist the Quarter-master in the
capture of that buck, and the risk consequent thereon, one of the
boys had the cruelty to-day, to *swap* him off for a half bushel of potatoes and two water melons! What a dog's life he must lead in the
state of captivity to which he was thus unexpectedly and treacher-
ously sold. The last we saw of him was his ineffectual struggles to
get out of the identical bag, that but a few minutes before had held
the paltry sum of two water melons and the potatoes—the ignomin-
ious price of his liberty. How unfeeling and immeasurably base it
was to put him in that bag. But, as the Latins say—"*sic waggit
worlduni?*" About two o'clock we reached Beaver Creek,* where a
halt for an hour was ordered. The old Chief of the Loups had accompanied us nearly to this place, on our march from his village. This
stream is about thirty yards wide, and is of the same character of the
Blue—with quicksand bed and banks, and a swift current. We found
no difficulty in fording it, as at this season of the year it is very low.
A few miles back a large elk came dashing down the bluffs, and
crossed the road but a short distance in advance of the column. The
Surgeon, who was ahead, was unfortunately without *his* gun, so the
animal escaped; and that has been our luck: if our hunter saw grouse
and deer in abundance, it did us no good; the grouse flew away, and
the deer ran for all *he* could do to stop them. Jim never could get his

*Quitpisatontch.

gun off in season, and the Surgeon never carried his with him. All the gentlemen, who by permission, occasionally rode a mile or two in advance of the troops, would come back at night and tell us of the vast quantities of game they had seen.

At sun an hour high we crossed and encamped upon Looking Glass Creek.† This is a beautiful tributary of the Loup, from the north. It is about three or four rods wide, and is as clear as crystal, and abounding with fish. The soil upon this side of the river is much richer and deeper than that upon the other, though resting upon the same bed of quicksand. The health of the Command is most excellent, and everybody seems in the best of spirits. I was just thinking as I lay here in front of my tent, waiting for the "Keystone of night's arch"—twelve o'clock—so that I can visit my guard, whether this kind of life has not more to make one enamoured with it than any other. Gentlemen in civil life, who meet officers of the army and navy in cities, where they are on flying visits to their friends, are apt to suppose that they are paid well and have nothing to do. They forget the years of toil and confinement they have had to undergo for the two or three month's furloughs that come like angel visits. They have no idea of the sleepless nights in storm and tempest, that are incident alike to the sailor and the soldier. The responsibility, the labor and exposure they have to go through with, or the dangers they have to encounter. These are all forgotten. They see the man light hearted, generous, joyous and full of happiness, and think he never could have a care. They forget that he is like a prisoner set at liberty—like an uncaged bird.

†*Quitooquataleri.*

CHAPTER XV

OUR MARCH DOWN THE VALLEY OF THE NEBRASKA—*Buffalo not seen—New flower—Sentinel blows his hand off—"Fortress Bluffs"—Beds of sand—Elk Horn River—Its character—Suggestion to Ole Bull—Not in striking distance of Sioux—A tempest at night—Passage of the river and farewell to the valley—Papillon—Splendid colors of landscape ending in the Surgeon's hobby—A Turf fence—Arrive at Council Bluffs—Suffering of the troops there in "auld lang syne"—New pill for the cure of consumption—Wonder if the Chinese knew of its efficacy before we did?—Council with Otoes and Missouries to-morrow—Letters from home.*

MONDAY, SEPTEMBER 2

TOOK up our line of march at 7 o'clock, keeping down the Loup River. After marching sixteen miles we came to its confluence with the Nebraska. From hence down to where we encamped for the night, the river bottom upon *this* side was very wide; sometimes the bluffs to the northward were so far away that they looked low—blue—and undulating, like a coast of sandhills from out at sea. About noon, some of the gentlemen thought they discovered a herd of buffalo on their distant summits, and a great excitement in the column was the consequence, until the glasses were got out, when it turned out to be the dark green tops of a skirt of timber just showing themselves over the horizon. We found several new flowers to-day. One—the most beautiful—had corollules of the most delicate purple, with clusters of pods just beneath, filled with seeds of the size of a grain of mustard. Its perfume was precisely like that of the vanilla. The soil passed over on to-day's march has been rather poor. Nothing worthy of further note occurred.

Tuesday, September 3

An early start was made by the column this morning. One of the sentinels on post last night accidentally wounded himself by shooting the whole of the contents of his carbine through his hand. Such accidents are very common with this weapon. No less than five men have been wounded in this way, in the companies stationed at Fort Leavenworth, within a twelvemonth. Our course for the day has been directed close along the bank of the river. About eleven o'clock we crossed Shell Creek, a tributary of the Nebraska from the north. It had been bridged by the Indian traders, and we were therefore enabled to pass it without loss of time. Upon the southern side of the river the bluffs have been gradually growing higher and higher, as we descended the valley—and have been approaching nearer to the shore. Besides, many of them are clad with timber, while upon the northern side they have apparently receded further and further away. This evening we had to march until nearly dark before we could find any wood, or water that was fit to drink. A long lagoon lay between us and the river, which we were unable to cross, and not a stick of timber grew upon the prairie side of it; though between it and the Nebraska, there was an abundance of fuel. So we had to keep marching until we had arrived at its foot, when we struck into the edge of a fine large cotton-wood grove and encamped. Just opposite of where we now are, the huge bluffs are washed along their base by the river. As the water is continually wearing them away beneath, the earth is all the time sliding down from their very tops—say three or four hundred feet; thus, for miles, forming an almost perpendicular wall, facing towards the north. In some places this singular embankment is worn into bastions—with long curtains between, and with here and there, buttresses, turrets, and battlements, which, as the slant rays of the evening sun shines upon them—bringing the prominent points into a strong light and throwing the retreating portions into deep shadow—appear very beautiful indeed.

Northeast from this encampment the Elk Horn River† breaks through the hills and enters the valley. This river has a heavy growth of timber along its banks, which is just discernable from our camp from the great distance. The Nebraska from the Loup River to this point has run nearly an east course, but here it begins to incline more toward the south. By calculation these hills upon the opposite side of the river are about eighty miles east of the Grand Pawnee Villages. They are called the "*Yellow Bluffs*," from their color. Our march to-day has been extremely fatiguing and monotonous, being all the time over a perfectly dead level. Besides, we have suffered a good deal from thirst.[20]

Wednesday, September 4

The column was under way this morning by half past six o'clock. For about four miles our course lay over an immense plain of sand, which, being very dry, the wind was blowing it about in clouds. We supposed it was deposited there last year, as the Nebraska then broke over this bank and ran across toward the Elk-Horn upon the opposite side of the valley, where the soil was very fine indeed. At this point—our route being due east—we began to leave the Nebraska, which, as I before stated, inclined more to the southward, and to approach the Elk-Horn, which ran in a semi circle; commencing an easterly course when it first entered the valley, then sweeping around and crossing our direction at right angles. This river hugs well in the bluffs all the way; decreasing the breadth of the bottom, until it is not over a mile in width at its confluence with the Nebraska. We arrived at its bank about four o'clock P.M. when we encamped for the night. This is a beautiful river. It is three or four hundred miles long (rising in the Sioux country near the head waters of L'Eau Qui Court, a tributary of the Missouri) and, at the point where we crossed it, a few miles from its mouth—it is seventy yards wide. Its depth is about four and a half feet—and its current is from four to five miles the hour—even at this season of the year. Of course, in the Spring, it could not be crossed without boats, on account of its increased ra-

†Qui-gitic.

pidity and depth. It is a quicksand river and consequently has no eddies. Its depth is uniform, and its current runs all the way alike from bank to bank. On the valley side, there are numerous lagoons, and bayous, which have been formed by the river having once run through them in its serpentine course—and then afterwards cutting off, here and there, its own sinuosities. Opposite, its banks are the bluffs themselves. They are finely timbered, and are composed almost entirely of fossiliferous limestone, and also of a ferruginous sandstone that would be very useful as a material for building.

Not having heard of the whereabouts of the nearest bands of Sioux (*or Sahaws*) and fearing that it will be impossible to get within "striking distance" of them—the commanding officer has concluded to push on directly for Council Bluffs.

THURSDAY, SEPTEMBER 5

About twelve o'clock last night we were visited by a tremendous shower. The rain poured down in torrents, and the wind blew almost a hurricane. I never before witnessed such prolonged and vivid flashes of lightning or such terrific and continuous thunder. A great many tents were blown down, and the inmates, in a twinkling, were left to "Bide the peltings of the pitiless storm."

It took us an hour and a half to cross this river. We then ascended the bluffs by a zig-zag road, and immediately found ourselves upon the high prairie which stretches off to the Missouri on the east, and northward, to an illimitable extent. Here we were then, say, two hundred and fifty, or three hundred feet, above the great valley we had been travelling over for so many days. And, although we had all got heartily tired of its continuous level, and had longed for some ups and downs to our marches—we involuntarily paused to take one last good look at its magnificent beauty. It was the next morning after a shower, and the brisk north wind seemed pure and invigorating. The trees looked greener than usual—the atmosphere was more transparent—there were no clouds in the heavens—and, as we looked back upon the course we had travelled—there lay the valley like a sweet picture, with the Nebraska and Elk Horn plainly visible through the scattered groves that fringed their sides—coming on from so far away, and drawing nearer and nearer, until like two brothers who had long been separated, they run into each others arms and joyously rushed forward to meet the Missouri and accompany her home to the "Father of Waters." Far off to the west, under the clear cold sky, the scene faded away—dimmer and dimmer in the distance, until the horizon alone arrested the view. The word "*Forward*" was given, and in a few moments we had looked our last upon this boudoir of Nature.

Our course was now due east—and lay over one of the most beautiful and fertile prairies in the country. Almost every mile we came to a fine spring branch of as pure and limped water as a man ever drank. At ten o'clock we struck some of the head branches of the "Papillon."[21] We followed down on a dividing ridge between two of them, and crossed the main stream by a bridge about one o'clock. Here in a beautiful grove of walnut, hickory, oak, and ash, we halted for an hour. In this grove we saw myriads and myriads of butterflies. Every tree was literally swarming with these winged flowers. I really believe that there were more in sight, at any one moment, than I had seen in all the rest of my life. On account of the multitudes of them which have been found in the groves along this river, ever since it was discovered the French have given it their name.

As we ascended the high lands again, we could see along the whole eastern horizon, a dark line of foliage which we knew bordered upon the Missouri itself; and by 5 P.M. the distant bluffs upon its opposite sides were distinctly visible. Near the "Papillon" we passed two new graves;—and, upon riding up to them, saw a large hole at both ends of each, where the wolves had digged down to their horrible repast.

This afternoon we have experienced a great deal of difficulty in crossing even the smallest water courses. There was no wood upon them of which to make bridges, and the pioneers were obliged to cut with their knives immense quantities of grass and weeds to form a matting sufficiently thick to withstand the weight of the loads as they passed over. This was very slow and toilsome work. Every Prairie Expedition should have amongst its other pioneer-utensils, at least, three scythes; for with them and half the labor, a grass causeway could be built in fifteen minutes, that it would take four times the number of men an hour to complete, with nothing but knives to work with.

The colors of the uplands at this season of the year are very rich, and, in some places, beautiful beyond description. The fine warm tints and glorious purple of Claude Lorraine[22] are here met with in perfection. They are caused by the tops of the grasses that are now just ripening. As the wind sweeps over the prairie in a clear bright day—giving through the opening waves, a view of the green and yellow hues nearer the ground—the effect is extremely fine. In the afternoon when the sun was sinking low in the west, and the mellow rays lay over the land like a flood of light—the eye in looking back toward the Elk Horn from the high ridges near Bellevue, was delighted with the magnificence of the picture, as swell after swell of the grass lands rose like huge waves of the sea—each one farther and farther away—bluer and bluer, as they receded, until at last they seemed almost to mingle with the sky itself. The land is gently undulating and with as rich a soil as can be found in the United States. If ever this country is vacated by the Indians it must fill up with a fine population in a very short time. As soon as the turf fences become in vogue—and they are as cheap, and I believe more durable, than those made of rails—every section of this land will find purchasers. Speaking of turf fences—if they are laid up, say, three feet thick at the bottom, eighteen inches at the top, and four feet high, with the grass side of the turf out, and the interior filled up with earth taken from a ditch all along the *outside* of the wall, I will warrant that nothing will go over them without wings. There will be, necessarily, enough earth taken from the ditch to fill in between the sods as they are laid up, to make it (the ditch) two feet and a half wide, and two feet and a half, or three feet deep. Thus the wall, measuring from the bottom on the outside, will be from six to seven feet high, and everybody knows that a fence composed of part ditch and part wall, is as bad to get over, if not worse, than one that is all wall. Besides the ditch upon the outside will keep the cattle from tearing it to pieces with their horns before the grass has knit it well together by its firm web of roots. I know of one field that was fenced in this way in 41—and it is infinitely stronger now than when it was first made, and there appears to be no earthy reason why it may not be as good fifty years hence as it is now, for it is covered every year by a fine crop of grass, with as firm and well knit turf as that which grows upon the surrounding prairie. Where a prairie country is very rich, and wood is scarce, this kind of protection to fields, or else hedges, must be adopted. To procure and set out the holly would be three times as expensive, and then not so durable as the turf fence. This little digression may be of some use, and if so, I am gratified in having made it.

Encamped near a fine grove upon the northern bank of the Papillon at sundown. We are delighted at getting so near the Missouri once more. Having been stationed so many years upon its banks, we have learned almost to love the mighty river. How natural it is to feel an affection for even the inanimate objects that have for a long while surrounded us. Like loadstone to the steel that has lain beside it for any length of time, when after a long absence we return to their neighborhood, our hearts are attracted toward them with an affection with which we never before dreamed they had inspired us.

Friday, September 6

Made an early start this morning, and having marched only a mile or two, came to the north fork of the Papillon, which being very deep and mirey, detained us all of two hours in the crossing. From thence, in to the Missouri, we met with no further obstructions. We arrived at Bellevue (a trading post of the American Fur Company)[23] at twelve o'clock, and encamped upon a beautiful tableland about a half mile below the Otoe and Omaha Agency. This is what is now called *Council Bluffs*—though the point of hills designated by that name by Lewis and Clarke, is (by land) twenty-five miles further up the river. At that place a large military post was established in 1819, 20—by the Rifle Regiment and the 6th Infantry. The companies of the latter Regiment left Plattsburgh, N. Y. in March 1819; and were upon the journey until the 14th of November the same year—when,

after the most persevering exertions they reached their destination—
having paddled their keel boats against the torrent of the Missouri,
and its many dangers and difficulties, nearly one thousand miles.—
The Riflemen left Belle Fontaine on the 15th June the same year, and
arrived at the Bluffs on the 2d of October.[24] The post they erected
was called Fort Calhoun. The first year the troops suffered almost
incredibly from scurvy. In order that the reader may have some idea
of their hardship and sickness I will make a short extract from the
report of Surgeon Gall to the Surgeon General, the late Dr. Lovell.—
"It will not surprise you to learn that the fatigue endured in transporting loaded boats such a distance in the peculiarly laborious manner of navigating the Missouri, and exposure to the meridian sun,
the dews of evening, and the chill air of night, were productive of
disease. Nearly every man had suffered severely from sickness, and
many experienced relapses, before arriving at our point of destination; nor did we then cease to suffer from dysentary, catarrh, and
rheumatism. * * * * With every exertion, our buildings were not
completed until the first of January, (1820.) At this period from ac-
cumulated suffering, a disposition to despondence was manifest.
Nearly all seemed to be reduced by protracted sickness and long continued labour. The sutler's supplies were exhausted, the fresh provisions nearly all issued, and the Hospital stores were inadequate to
an emergency. In this situation, when the most nutritive diet was
requisite to restore our exhausted energies, the men were compelled
to subsist on salted or smoke-dried meats, without vegetables of any
description. To add to our list of sufferings, the weather in January
became excessively severe; the mercury at different periods for several days in succession, did not rise above zero, and once fell 22 deg.
below that point. Under these circumstances, about the 20th of
January the scurvy made its appearance, to which all other diseases
soon yielded precedence: but it proved fatal in few cases until February—when nearly the whole regiment sunk beneath its influence.—
The disease continued unabated until the 7th of April, when wild
vegetables appeared. After this period no new cases occurred and
those already affected began to recover. Of the riflemen, alone,
eighty fell victims to it." Probably as many more died in the 6th.

Surgeon Mower, U.S.A. who also was there and made a special report of the sickness that winter, and who had several times witnessed
smallpox and epidemic cholera in their most malignant forms, avers
that neither is as dreadful as the endemic described therein. It is not
the sight of pale forms encircled by bloody bandages, that blanches
the soldier's cheek, for he knows that such is the chance of battle.
Even when the Surgeon tells his wounded patient that he must look
for help beyond the grave—the transition from time to eternity is
borne with calmness and resignation, soothed by the consciousness of
having fallen in the discharge of his duty and in his country's cause.
But when the wards of an hospital become crowded with ghastly,
and attenuated frames; victims to a baneful climate, or a loathsome
pestilence; living skeletons—slowly sinking, and doomed—

> —"to feel
> The icy worm around them steal,
> Without the power to scare away
> The cold consumers of their clay,"

how appalling to the living is the spectacle of the dead and dying?—
When those, who but a few days previously bore their comrades to
the grave, are in turn stretched upon the same bier, then it is that the
bravest heart quails.* Such was the suffering at the early establishing
of this Post;—and yet, after it was completed, and the troops began
to have good gardens and fruit about them, it was considered one of
the most healthy and delightful of any in the country. It was abandoned I believe, in 1828. They used to have fine times at this post.
At one period, duelling seemed to be the order of the day. There was
an officer stationed there then, who belonged to the Riflemen, a very
excellent shot;—Captain Marryatt speaks of him in his Journal;—by
the by, he *now* belongs to the 5th Infantry, and if I mistake not, is in
command at Fort Mackinaw—well, from *not* "joining in the dissipa-
tions" of the Post, he became very unpopular. Hardly an officer
spoke to him unless on duty. It was finally agreed by all of them to
run him out of the regiment. To do this they intended to challenge

*STATISTICAL REPORT of the sickness and mortality in the army of the
United States, pp. 17, 18.

him in turn, and *if he fought*, to take a shot at him in succession. However, they did not think the matter would come to such an issue as that. The first gentleman that sent him a message was at that time in a consumption, and it was thought, that at best, he couldn't live long, his disease making rapid inroads upon his constitution. His wishes were met by the challenged party by referring him to the sutler of the post for "necessary arrangements." The sutler told his friend it was the intention of the officers to *keep calling upon him* until their purpose was effected, and that he had better try to hit each one as he went along. He said at first that he would fire in the air, but his friend insisted so hard upon his not doing so, that he finally abandoned the idea, by saying—"Well if you think it necessary, I will fire at him and hit just exactly at the second button on his coat."— The parties went upon the ground, and it so happened that most of the officers were present. Each man took his post, the weapons (pistols) were placed in their hands, and the word was given. Both fired at once. The consumptive gentleman fell, shot directly through the lungs. He had hardly touched the ground when the sutler advanced towards him, not with feelings of pity or commiseration, *but to see what kind of a shot his friend had made.* When he saw where the bullet had struck he exclaimed—"Plump through the second button by—!" The other gentleman then turned to the crowd of officers and said— "I have understood it was your intention to force me out of the regiment in this way. Will you, sir, take a shot?"—addressing the first in rank—"Or you? Or you? Or you?" speaking to each one of them. They all thought they wouldn't *take* one; at least *then*, and left the ground. Strange as it may seem the consumptive gentleman recovered, not only from his wound, (and he was shot directly through the body) but from his disease. It was rather a harsh and somewhat dangerous remedy it is true—the taking of lead pills for consumption, but it proved most efficacious, not only to the shoot*ee* but to the shoot*er;* for after that the balance of the gentlemen let him alone, and he soon became as popular, as his antagonist did healthy. So there is one argument in favour of duelling. I have writtten this story just as I heard it. It was told to me by the best authority, and is no doubt perfectly true in every particular.

Such was Council Bluffs in the olden time. To-morrow we are to have a Council with the Otoes and Missouries. These tribes have been united for many years and live upon the north and south side of the Nebraska near its mouth, (nine miles below Bellevue). They are considered the most rascally Indians in the whole West. We shall probably remain here two or three days in order to let the animals recruit themselves after their protracted fatigues. We found here a supply of provisions that had been sent up by steamboat for our use by the Assistant Commissary at Leavenworth; and the most of us also received letters from our far-off homes, which had been kindly forwarded by Mr. Rich, the Postmaster at the Fork. When one is away in the Indian country so far away from those he loves, a letter from a dear mother or an affectionate sister comes to him like a little winged messenger, with words of comfort, a blessing from the heart, and a prayer. Our mother and sisters never forget us! They alone love us with a home love!—God bless them!

CHAPTER XVI

COUNCIL WITH THE OTOES AND MISSOURIES—*Uniform of the field officers of those tribes—Major's difficulty in making the interpreter appreciate his sentiments—War dance—Decide upon going down on the east side of the Missouri—Begin to cross that river—200 Pawnees arrive at Bellevue—Big Greasy re-appears—Continue the passage of the river—Sudden council with Pawnee Delegation, from learning of their attempt to murder Lieut. Fremont and his party—New method of illustrating our manner of fighting for the edification of the red skins—Complete the passage of the river—Some remarks upon the Pottawattamies.*

SATURDAY, SEPTEMBER 7

ABOUT nine o'clock this forenoon, the Chiefs and principal men of the Otoes[25] and Missouries came into camp. They were soon after followed by the warriors of these united tribes, on foot. The latter were well armed, and marched in regular order, keeping a cadenced step to a war song which they chanted. They were marshalled by two of their people, mounted upon horseback. These men cut the most singular figure that could well be imagined —not having the first article of clothing on, save a wreath of pea-vines about the loins, and another wreath composed of the wild grapevine, hanging diagonally across, from the shoulder down to the sides of their horses. Each one was painted with a kind of ochre, *a bright sky blue*, and carried in his hand a lance some ten feet long. Perhaps the reader can imagine from this, the singular appearance they made. They were the Colonel and Lieut. Colonel of the regiment of painted and bedizened braves who followed them on foot! I believe it is a part of the Indian tactics to sing when on duty—at least it seemed so in this case—and if discordant yells, prolonged and horrid whoops, together with a continual repetition of "*Me-ahu!-ha! ha!* Me-ahu!—ha! ha!*" are any indications of valor, they certainly were the bravest people we had seen. Cromwell's troops, commanded by Col. Moses-in-the-Bullrushes Barebones, although in their way excellent singers of psalms and spiritual songs, could not compete at all with these savages, in point of volume of tone and of harsh and jarring discords. As soon as they had all arrived the Major distributed a plenty of tobacco amongst them, when they seated themselves in a large circle upon the grass, and commenced smoking. When all the pipes were well under way, the commanding officer informed them why he had visited their country and called them together in Council. The interpreter was a half-bred Otoe, and understood only English enough to express his ideas on the most common subjects; the consequence was, that when the Major expatiated upon a favorite simile, or figure of speech, by way of illustration, Morang (the interpreter) was entirely at a loss to render it in Otoe, until it was simplified by words with which he was familiar; hence, the Major having addressed himself to the Council in a loud tone, with the necessary inflections and gestures to give his speech effect, would have to turn around and reduce the whole thing down to Morang's limited capacity; thus carrying on two expressions of the same ideas before any interpretations could take place; the first, as I before said, for Buncombe, to the tribe—the last, *sotto voce*, for Morang. The effect of this was sometimes amusing in the extreme. Here is a sample:—

Major (for Buncombe).—Let me enjoin upon you to abandon the precarious method you are now pursuing to procure a doubtful subsistence by the uncertainties of the chase, and at the same time seriously to urge upon your attention the necessity of cultivating the soil; by which, with less risk and a moiety of the labor, you would be compensated with an abundant supply of food for home consumption, and a surplus sufficient to be adequate to the cost of your other wants.

Morang.—That's most too hard— (after a long pause)—I don't *adzactly* understand.

Major (sotto voce).—Tell them to leave off hunting, and plant corn —then they would always have plenty.

Here Morang would occupy about five minutes in explaining this, in Otoe.

Major (for Buncombe).—It is with extreme pain that your Great Father, the President, has learned of the misdeeds of the Otoes and Missouries, more particularly of their having fired into boats, when they passed down the river, and wounded those who were in them.*

Morang managed this pretty well, without explanation.

Major (for Buncombe).—If you continue to behave in this manner, all the people will entertain an animosity towards you. You will be like a lone tree upon the prairie that has stood the shock of many a storm, until at last a tempest comes more powerful than the rest, and prostrates it forever.

Morang paused for a long time, with the most puzzled and per- plexed expression upon his face.

Major (sotto voce).—Go on.

Morang—Don't *adzactly* understand.

Major—Tell them everybody will hate them, if they don't quit acting in this way.

Morang.—Yes—but the tree: don't *adzactly* get the hang of him.

Major.—Oh, never mind the tree; just go on with the other.

Thus all the figures were thrown away, being so much dead loss to the Indians, from the obtusity of Morang's comprehension, and a cruel waste of very fair poetry on the part of the Major. Morang could only understand the plain matter of fact: the embellishments were one grade farther than he had advanced. I have given the above only as examples of the difficulty the Major had to encounter, in communicating with these tribes. He gave them the best of advice,

*Two of the Otoes who fired upon the boats to which the Major referred, were arrested and taken to Fort Leavenworth and put in the guard house. In attempting to escape the sentinel on duty shot one of them dead.

and warned them to beware how they ever again molested the whites; as the next time, the aggressions of the few would be visited upon the heads of the whole. This council, no doubt, will have the greatest effect upon these rascally Indians. The presence of the troops, and the firm and decided tone assumed towards them by the commanding officer, gave them to understand very plainly, that in troubling the traders or the citizens, they were in reality meddling with edged tools. In substance, the Council was of a similar character to those held with the Pawnees, and was ended by giving the Indians like quantities of provisions for a feast upon the occasion.

In the evening, these tribes gave us a war dance. It was so like the one we witnessed at the Pawnee village, that a separate description is unnecessary. However, the Otoes and Missouries are more agile and graceful in their movements than the Pawnees, and their whoop is infinitely more terrific. The reader must know that the war-whoop of every tribe is different. A Pawnee can at once tell the whoop of the Camanche or Sioux, or Blackfoot, or any other tribe with whom he had ever come in contact: so can the warriors of every tribe. Sometimes, to deceive, they adopt the dress and whoop of each other to carry a point, but unless as a dernier resort to save life, or gain an end of unusual magnitude and brilliancy, such a course is esteemed the most cowardly that could be pursued. It is equivalent to sailing under each other's colors, by the men of war of civilized nations, when they would not dare to hoist their own.

SUNDAY, SEPTEMBER 8

To-day, the commanding officer ascertained that the bottoms of the Nebraska and Nemaha rivers, are so miry near their mouths that it would be next to impossible to cross them; he therefore has determined to pass the Missouri at this point, to the Pottawattamie Nation in Iowa Territory, and then pass down on the eastern side, until we shall be opposite the Sacs and Foxes, and Iowas, who live on Wolf River; then to re-cross again, and visit these tribes on our way to our post. By taking this route, we shall avoid the passage of not only the above-named rivers, but of several other very bad streams of smaller size. Nothing was done in camp to-day. The animals were allowed the whole time to rest and recuperate. Corn having been sent up on a steamboat, from Fort Leavenworth to this point, they are supplied with as much as they can eat of it while we stay here. When horses and mules have been kept entirely upon grass, during several weeks' hard marching, one can hardly imagine how much vigor even a bushel of corn or oats a-piece, will give them. It is like giving meat, now and then, to a laboring man who has been kept for a long time upon bread and water.

Monday, September 9

This morning, early, a large detail of men commenced ferrying across the Missouri the wagons and teams of the Quarter-master's Department. This was an exceedingly slow and laborious operation, as we could procure only one flat boat, and that was old and leaky; besides, a heavy sea was running, from a high wind blowing directly up the river. It took until 2 o'clock, P.M., to get them all over. In the evening, "K." Troop made its passage. It was impossible to induce the horses and mules to swim, on account of the high waves. From the size of the boat only eight or ten animals could go over at a time; hence, it was after night before this troop got across and had its tents pitched.

Two hundred Pawnees arrived here to-day, from the same villages we visited, having followed in our trail. They have come to the Agency which is established at this place for the purpose of getting their annuities, which the Government supplies them with, in kind. These annuities consist of blankets, guns, powder, lead, hoes, axes, tomahawks, knives, strouding, looking-glasses, paints, beads, and tobacco. They have encamped just under the bluffs from us. Even at a long distance, we discovered amongst them some of our old acquaintances. Charorakareek is in command, assisted by the heir-apparent—Cleghorn—and Big Greasy. For a mile, we could pick out Big Greasy from all the rest: the old, round, oily fellow, with his fat, jolly face, and his little legs.

TUESDAY, SEPTEMBER 10

During the night the wind changed to the N.E., and to-day it blows almost a gale down the river, accompanied occasionally by a cold drizzly rain and mist, which to the "ager" patients, seems to penetrate almost to the bone. With the greatest exertions, "G." and "C." troops were crossed, leaving only "F." and "A." upon the western side. It is much more labor than people residing in the North would imagine, to cross a whole troop of horse, with all its appointments, over such a river as the *Missouri*, with nothing but an old leaky scow to work with; especially when the reader takes into consideration a five mile current, with a ten knot breeze blowing *down* the stream. The last load went over just at retreat.

As the sun was going down, it burst from the dark leaden clouds which for the whole day had covered the heavens, and for a moment lit up the sky, and covered the distant bluffs with a beautiful purple; but, like the bright hopes which will occasionally gleam through the chill storms of every man's life's-sky, that light as quickly faded away, leaving to us nothing but gloom, and coldness, and the dark night.

WEDNESDAY, SEPTEMBER 11

This morning the weather was comparatively fine, and the remaining troops were gotten over by noon, leaving only the guard and howitzers, together with the "field and staff," to be crossed. The commanding officer, by a mere accident, learned to-day that when Lieut. Fremont came in from his mountain expedition this summer, the Grand Pawnees conspired together to cut him and his whole party off, and were only prevented from doing so, by a small number of Loup warriors who happened to be present at the time. As the principal actors on both sides (that is, so far as the Indians were concerned) were present—having come in with the delegation for the annuities—he immediately summoned them together in Council, to ascertain if such a report was true. The Loup Pawnees corroborated it in every particular, as did the Grand Pawnees. One of the Indians who had been foremost in proposing, and attempting to carry out the massacre of that officer and his men, soon as he learned what the Council was being called for, ran away and concealed himself until we were gone. The commanding officer upbraided the aggressors in the severest manner, for their contemplated treachery, and gave them distinctly to understand that had they carried their purpose into execution, not one of them would have been left alive; and that should they, or any of their people, ever molest, or in any way disturb the whites while pursuing their journeys, or while transacting business in their country, their whole tribe should be held fearfully responsible for it. To those who had so nobly prevented the committal of so horrid a butchery, he gave some handsome presents which he purchased at the expense of the Government, as a reward for their fidelity, and as an evidence that the country was as ready and as able to reward good deeds, as it was to punish the bad. It is believed that our having learned these facts, and having taken the course adopted by the commanding officer toward both parties, (the Grand and Loup Pawnees), will be conducive of the utmost good; more particularly as the Pawnees live directly upon the great thoroughfare of the hundreds of emigrants who annually cross the country, for Oregon.

After this Council was over a large quantity of shells were fired, to impress upon the hundreds of Indians present, (and there were representatives of the following tribes upon the ground, viz.: Pawnees, Otoes, Omahas, Missouries, Shawnees, Pottawattamies, Chippewas, Ottowas, Iowas, Miamies, Menomonies, and Poncas), some idea of the power of these destructive missiles. There was a little incident which occurred at this time, which, though trifling in itself, occasioned not little amusement. The Indians had all been informed through the various interpreters, that they were to see a specimen of the manner in which we combatted our enemies, by repairing to the bank of the river where the howitzers were placed. Hundreds of them immediately assembled around the pieces, to witness whatever belligerent performance we might see fit to volunteer for their especial edification and entertainment.

One of the gentlemen present was blessed with the possession of that worst of evils on a campaign—a stubborn and sulky negro. I have once before said that the Indians seemed to manifest more curiosity about the blacks who were with us, than about anything else they saw. Wherever one of these might go, or whatever he might do, all his motions were watched by these wandering savages, with an interest that was sometimes really amusing. Knowing these facts, some of the servants, whenever the natives were present, would assume airs of consequence, evidently with the vain intention of impressing their unsophisticated audience with the belief that they occupied a station among the armed crowd with which they so fearlessly moved, which was by no means contemptible. But there were none amongst them so impudent as the one belonging to the gentleman alluded to above. He had deserved a half-dozen severe whippings for his insolence upon various occasions, but his master had humanely put up with it all, in hopes to get back to our post without being obliged to resort to coercive measures to make him respectful and obedient. Another reason why he wished to avoid any violent arguments which should teach his servant his duty, was, that during the summer he had sprained his leg very severely, and he knew if he commenced punishing Charles, (the servant), ten chances to one if in hopping about during the exercise, all the tender granulations which had commenced the union of the muscles, would break away, and cause the limb to be more lame than ever. While the pieces were being loaded, and the fuses of the shells adjusted to the proper length, down came Charles through the crowd of Indians, with a most important swagger. He was leading his master's horse with the intention of watering him. As soon as he made his appearance, he attracted the general attention of every savage upon the ground; not only on account of his color, but from a belief that he was about to enact an important part in the operations which they had been told were about to take place.

While we were at Bellevue we received many little kindnesses from the traders residing there. Mr. Peter Sarpy,[26] of the American Fur Company, was extremely hospitable and obliging to us. About five o'clock the rear guard and howitzers were all crossed, and "retreat" found us all encamped three miles from Bellevue, upon the Merangoin (*Musquito*) a small river of about eighty miles in length, which empties into the Missouri nearly opposite the mouth of the Papillon.—This evening the commanding officer held an informal council, or rather a friendly talk, "with the Pottawattamie and Chippewa Indians. These people are generally called the *Pottawatamies:* though they are partly composed of Chippewas, and Otawas. The whole of the United Tribe does not live at Council Bluffs (here); one half of them having moved on to the Osage and Marais de Cigne, near Fort Scott, which is one hundred miles south of Leavenworth, upon a small river called the Marmiton. They number, in all, about four thousand. Two thousand live here. They are a very peaceable, quiet and inoffensive people, having grown very effeminate by their intercourse with the whites. Thirty-four years ago, when they fought at Tippecanoe with the Kickapoos, Shawnees, and Delawares, against General Harrison, they were a much hardier and braver race than now. Some of that old stock still remains. Wabonset (the war chief) and Chabona, who was aide to Tecumseh when he fell, are still living, and distinguished for their integrity, their high-toned courage and firmness. They are splendid specimens of that dauntless race which used to hold our best troops in check in real hand to hand hard fighting. Such an emotion as *fear*, has ever been as foreign to their bosoms as to that of General Jackson.

It does a man good at times to see the surviving representatives of those brave enemies who so long ago showed our fathers such elegant play upon the battle field. They are fast passing away, and giving place to a degenerate and dissipated race, who from their habits are fast getting into their blood the insidious and sure cause of their ultimate extermination. It is melancholy to reflect that the wretchedness which one sees amongst *all* Indians who live contiguous to our settlements, has been caused in a great measure by ourselves.

Wherever their race has come in contact with ours it has begun to wither like those native plants which are overshadowed and blighted by the more vigorous growth of some hardy exotic—until drooping, they have perished, and passed away forever. *These* Pottawattamies have, I believe, 2,000,000 of acres of the very best land in the West. But they cannot be induced to cultivate it to any extent, from their habits of idleness and their apparent recklessness of the wants of to-morrow. These two thousand people the Government pays annually some fifty thousand dollars or thereabouts. What do they do with this money? The whole north line of Missouri is dotted with houses, where they are supplied for the year with any quantity of whiskey they may wish *on trust;* and to these places they resort until the amount of their anticipated annuities is run up, when they will sell their horses, rifles, blankets, and everything else to get liquor. Weeks and weeks at a time are often spent by these poor wretches in drunken rows—while their families are perhaps starving for bread, or shivering with the cold. That is the way the money goes. In the winter time the men go out in the lands and spend a couple of months or so hunting. The peltry they thus obtain is in value worth about half the amount of their annuities. This the traders get for blankets and gew-gaws, at about one hundred per cent. profit. Now how can any people, surrounded by any such influences be expected to *improve.* Can it be wondered that their race vanishes before the flood of whiskey, with all its attendant evils, that is, and has been constantly setting upon them from every side? Let no man, or set of men, dream of making them "good citizens," unless he or they can eradicate these causes of their idleness, wretchedness, and want. These things *are just so*, however much they may be glossed over by those, perhaps, who have an interest in perpetuating the misery they have been instrumental in occasioning. I could not but give a glance at them as I went along, although it may be considered out of place. This is not the case with the Pottawattamies alone, but of all the Indians who live upon the line from Red River to Lake Superior. I do really believe if the Government would not give them one cent of money they would be infinitely better off. If the $50,000 dollars which is paid annually to *this* people could be placed at the disposal of some *trusty* agents, who would expend it in the making of elegant farms, and in the purchase and rearing of stock, how long would it take, in a land unequalled for fertility, *and where the soil costs nothing*, to raise enough to support these two thousand men, women, and children, without requiring even one hour's labor from them? Every dollar expended in the improvement of grounds, in the building of fences, and the planting of fruit trees, would be, of itself, a profitable investment as more than the original sum was worth. Imagine how many beautiful farms could thus in a few years be established with this amount *properly* laid out. *Now* it vanishes almost as quick as a flash of lightning, as soon as they receive it, and like that flash, leave ruin, and desolation, and death in its tracks. I merely suggest the building of farms; there may be better ways to expend this money—but it would be a blessing to this poor people if it were even thrown into the river rather than that they should be allowed to use it the way they now do. Reader, the Log Book is nearly completed. Pleasant dreams.

CHAPTER XVII

BATTLE BETWEEN THE POTTAWATTAMIES AND SIOUX–
*Cannibals–Battle between the Sioux and Delawares–Establishment
of Fort Croghan–Great Flood of '43–Horse-marine tactics–The biter
bit–Iowa–Its soil and capabilities on the Missouri–Arrive at the
Nishne bottom—at English Grove—at Jeffrey's Point–The effects of
the Great Flood of '43–The poor bees.*

ENCAMPMENT near Council Bluffs, Iowa, Sept. 12th. The Pottawattamies removed to this country from near Chicago, Illinois, some eight or nine years ago. They have had other evils to contend with besides those enumerated in the last chapter. In the year 1840, the Sioux began to waylay and attack their small hunting parties; and finally were so bold that they came into their settlements and killed and scalped them in sight of their houses.

The country from Vermillion (Floyd's) River down to the Little Sioux, had been ceded by the Dahcotahs to the United States,[27] and lay as a debateable land between them and the Pottawattamies. This unoccupied ground extends from the Missouri on the west to the head waters of the Des Moines having the two above named rivers for its northern and southern boundaries. Here the most of the fighting took place. On account of the danger there was to either party hunting upon it, they seldom visited it for anything but scalps—and hence the game seemed to gather in upon it from every quarter, as a place of refuge. In the summer of 1841 a large band of the Pottawattamies got upon the trail of a small war-party of the Sioux very near Council Bluffs (they having been lurking around in hopes to cut off whatever stragglers they might find outside their settlement,) and followed it up for nearly a hundred miles. As soon as the Sioux found there could be no escape from them, they got in a little hollow, and placing bushes about themselves to avoid the certain aim of their pursuers' rifles, determined to sell their lives as dearly as they could. The Pottawattamies came on as warily as possible, circling stealthily around the hollow occupied by the Sioux, in hopes to get a chance to aim upon them with a certainty through the veil of bushes by which they were surrounded. The Sioux lay perfectly quiet until their enemies were within a sure distance, when they began to pick them off with a most fatal rapidity. The Pottawattamies immediately retired without the range of their adversaries' bullets for the purpose of devising some way to get at them without suffering so much. The Sioux meantime would show themselves, and by the most insulting gestures dare them to return. This maddened the Pottawattamies, and they determined to make a rush at their enemies from all sides at once, and despatch them with their tomahawks. This they did do, but several bit the dust before they arrived at the hole in which the Sioux had so valiantly defended themselves. Ten—fifteen—twenty of the Pottawattamies gave their deadly warwhoop and sprang in upon them. The work was quickly over then. The moment—and their hearts, still palpitating, were torn from their bosoms and eaten by their infuriated enemies.* The Pottawattamies then cut off their hands and feet—scalped them, and returned to the bluffs, singing their war-song, and bringing these bloody evidences of their success dangling at their saddle bows. For a week, dancing and rejoicing over the death of this handful of Sioux was kept up; the mutilated limbs were then dried, powdered, and put away in the medicine bags for luck. We may talk of the Anthropophagi of Scythia, who fed on human flesh, as a fabulous race—but even amongst ourselves in the nineteenth century, we have a people, who, under certain circumstances, are equally as barbarous as they are said to have been.

*The next summer I was upon the ground with a large party of the Pottawattamies, and I asked one of them—a half breed named La Frombois—why his people were so brutal as to devour the hearts of their enemies? "Ah!" said he "Great Medicine, is hearts of brave men. Make strong-heap—great deal; and brave, too." "But did you eat any?" "Oh, yes. I like him very much, cause he's *great* medicine."

In the fall of that year sixteen Delawares came to the Bluffs for the purpose of making a winter's hunt upon this debateable land. The eastern reader must know that the Delawares are considered the bravest Indians upon the Continent. Small parties of eight or ten of them will go *anywhere* upon the prairie, and through every valley and defile about the Rocky Mountains, totally regardless of any numbers, or people, whom they may meet. *All* tribes fear them; and although they never molest others unless with cause, still they are said to be the terror of the Plains. When the sixteen above named arrived at the Bluffs they were fitted out with a full supply of ammunition, blankets, traps, &c., by Mr. Sarpy, who was to receive their peltry in the spring. Only one Pottawattamie accompanied them— a son of Half Day, the orator of the tribe—a brave young fellow of about twenty-one years of age. They fixed their encampment upon the Racoon Fork of the Des Moines, near its source, and soon began a very successful hunt. This encampment was on a little triangular point of intervale, around two sides of which ran the stream, heavily fringed with willows; the other side being entirely cut off from a view of the high prairie beyond by a crescent shaped bluff, which stretched across the point they occupied from the water upon one side, to where it came around upon the other. A large band of some two hundred Sioux had come down into this country, determined to cut off every Pottawattamie they could find, in revenge for the five whom they had killed during the summer. One morning about daybreak, some of the spies of this band discovered the smoke of the Delaware camp, and believing it proceeded from the fires of the Pottawattamies, immediately communicated with the main body, which, keeping down along the stream to the bluffs I have spoken of, was soon enabled to occupy it from one end to the other without being perceived by the Delawares, who were quietly eating their breakfasts on the point, which lay like the arena of an amphitheatre directly below, and within a hundred yards. At a given signal the Sioux fired their fusees upon this little party, who were first made aware of their proximity by the shower of bullets that came hurtling down upon them. Five Delawares fell dead, leaving only eleven alive and the young Pottawattamie; and some of them were severely wounded.

They immediately sprang upon their feet and gave their war-whoop. The Sioux were thunderstruck. They thought they had attacked the effeminate Pottawattamies, but the terrific battle-cry of the Lenno Lenape—so dreaded and so well known—told them the fearful mistake they had committed. But they had gone too far then to recede. The Delawares looked toward the bluff and its whole summit was *beaded* by the heads of the Sioux as they lay upon their bellies, peering over to the valley they occupied. A volley from this cool and skilful little band, told fearfully among the Dahcotahs. Not a bullet came from the unerring rifles of the Delawares, but brought death with it to whomever its flight was directed. The Sioux immediately drew back from the crown of the hill, and only crept up occasionally to deliver a desultory fire, but hardly one could show his head over the edge without receiving a ball through his brain. The Delawares were entirely exposed—and what was worse, their bullets began to be scarce. The wounded, however, soon remedied this evil, by creeping up to the fire, and with their remaining strength casting a supply for their gallant brethren, who were standing between them and the bluffs. There was no retreat. The stream, it is true, could have been crossed, but all was an open prairie beyond; besides, whoever knew a Delaware to run from death! The odds were so great that the Delawares knew if they ran up the hill they would be instantly cut to pieces, and they were becoming every minute weaker and weaker, both from wounds and from five more of their band having fallen during the prolonged fight. The young Pottawattamie had received a shot through the ankle, another through his arm, and one through his neck; and at this stage of the battle he crept down to the stream to get a draught of water to cool his intolerable thirst. He says while he lay there, too weak to move, he heard the Sioux give their war-whoop and rush down the hill upon the six surviving Delawares. That he heard that little band shout back in defiance—and soon heard the death grapple, and shrieks, and the dull, heavy blows of the tomahawks, as the combatants closed in one horrible melee. He then fainted from loss of blood and fell into the rushes and water, by the side of which he had crawled. When he came to, all was still, and the sun was high in the heavens. With much exertion he crept to where his comrades had so gallantly stood, and there they lay—the whole sixteen, dead and scalped. Not one inch of ground had they yielded, but had fallen, each man, where he had fought. Wounded as he was, he started on foot for the Bluffs, an hundred and fifty miles off, with nothing to eat upon the journey except what few roots he could procure as he went along, or anything to protect him from the cold, (and it was late in the autumn,) save what clothes he had on, and the uncertain chance of his arriving upon wooded water courses at night, where he could build himself a little fire. When he came home he was so emaciated from famine and fatigue, and the three wounds he had received, that hardly a soul knew him. He told his people of the fight. Soon after a large party was raised to visit the ground—and there they found the combatants where they had fallen. *Sixty-five* Sioux lay dead upon that bluff and in the hollow where the last charge was made. The Sioux, who returned to their village high up the Missouri, told the traders there of the fight, and acknowledged they had lost that number. They said that so sure as they exposed themselves in the least over the bluff, they were certain to be struck by a bullet. The Delaware tribe never wished to revenge the loss of their men, they proudly say when alluding to the fight— "*They revenged themselves!*" None of these Indians ever bury those who fall in battle. I asked one of the Chiefs when near one of their battle grounds, where the bones were still to be seen, why they had not buried them? Said he—"When a brave man falls in a good fight, why give him to the worms? Better let the wolves and vultures eat him; then he will still be carried over the land he loved so well.*" "But," said I, "you buried one of your men whom the Sioux killed close to your town."

"Yes," answered he, "but they shot him down like a dog. He never saw them. If he had fought them bravely we would have let him lie where he fell, as we did these."

On account of this continued war between the Sioux and Potta-wattamies a Company of U.S. Dragoons, under Captain Burgwin,

---

*How much that thought is like the one expressed by Fergus McIvor when he desired that his head might be placed where ever after death he could look out on his own blue hills.

was ordered to Council Bluffs from Fort Leavenworth, in May, 1842, to prevent further hostilities. As soon as this force arrived in the country, that band of the Sioux who lived upon Vermillion river, (nearest the Pottawattamies) removed two or three hundred miles further up the Missouri—and from that time to the present no fighting has taken place between them. He found the Pottawattamies almost starving for food, being fearful to go out in the lands for game lest the Sioux should cut them off, and having nothing in the whole country to eat except a little corn. In order to relieve them all in his power, he sent an officer and twenty dragoons, with a party of one hundred Indians, men and women, (the women went along to cure the meat,) on to Sioux river, where game was said to be abundant. In sixteen days that party came back with every animal loaded down with dried buffalo, elk, and deer meat.† This kind of duty, with that of adjusting quarrels between the tribes on the western side of the Missouri, and preventing the smuggling of whiskey into the country, together with the building of FORT CROGHAN[28]—a new post Capt. Burgwin was directed to establish—kept the troops under his command forever on the move. However, by the latter part of November every building was completely finished—fine storehouses erected, and excellent stables built for the horses. This post was built near the Missouri, upon a high bottom land. It was just five miles back to the bluffs—all the way a beautiful and perfectly level prairie, save one little ridge which was elevated above the surrounding surface six or eight feet, and extending from the hills to the river. The troops had the pleasure of enjoying their new homes but a little while—for in April, '43, came the great flood, covering the whole bottom like a lake—the first time it had been flooded since '27. The provisions were hauled to the bluffs as soon as the river had filled its banks—but the Fort was occupied until the water began to run between it and the bluffs, (five miles off!) when the command was given to mount, and the whole garrison took up its march for higher ground. Before it could reach the little ridge I

†See an account of that hunt published Sept. 12th and 17th, '42, in the "Spirit of the Times." The game killed was 57 Buffalo, 20 Elk, 104 deer. The Indians to this day refer to it as the "*Big Hunt.*"

spoke of, it had to pass over a hollow about a quarter of a mile in breadth. In this the water was belly deep, and running like a mill-tail, with big rafts of driftwood booming through it at a killing pace. Here the captain had to abandon the *French system* of conducting Cavalry, and adopt in its stead a little of the Horse-marine drill. Every man at length reached the ridge, when all danger was passed. In thirty-six hours the water was running over the eves of the houses at Fort Croghan.

There is a little joke they tell on one of the officers who served there during this time, which is most too good to be lost. This is the way it goes, and if true, is an excellent thing. He was sent out with the party of Dragoons which was to protect the Pottawattamies while hunting—from the Sioux. One of the Indians who was along with him was an exceedingly ugly fellow, with a face that was out of all sorts of proportion, and which had that singularly hideous expression as if he was continually standing in a smoke. The officer alluded to was no beauty either. In fact, even in Maine where the men have not a *great deal* to boast of in the way of good looks, he would have broken up a town meeting, which certainly *is* equivalent to saying that he was not particularly handsome. One day when the Indians were all together, he thought he would have a good joke at the ugly old fellow's expense. So he got up and in a very pompous manner made a speech. He told them that in his country it had been a time honoured custom for the homeliest man in every community to be presented with an immense *Jacknife*, which he was to carry until some one more ugly than himself should have an undoubted title to it. That he had regretted that amongst the other usages they (the Indians) had received and adopted from their white brethren, this should have been so entirely forgotten. It pained him, it did, to reflect upon it. But he felt proud he said to be the first who should introduce such an ancient observance to the notice of a new race. He felt sure that they would properly appreciate it—and that seeing its utility, and the great and lasting benefits which they as a people, and their children, and their children's children, would derive from it, they would *perpetuate* that observance to time's latest day. He felt sure of it, "blow'd if he didn't." He then turned to the old Indian, "to you belongs this emblem of ugliness," (handing a huge jacknife to him). "Take it as a gift you so richly merit, and if, what would now appear to be impossible, you ever meet with an individual with better claims to its ownership, based upon such grounds, than you have —*then*, and not till then, you may part with it."

The old fellow received the gift with many manifestations of deference and respect, and rose as the officer supposed, to make suitable acknowledgments for the distinguished honour that had been conferred upon him. His reply when rendered in English was as follows:—

"I am very old man. I have seen a great deal peoples. Folks, heap. Some very pretty—some awful. My son—he's dam *bad* ugly—chip of the old block. But I must not give it him. Old as I am I have never seen anybody who should have it better than *you*. So spose I keep it, I *rob* you of your right. Take him back; I shall no more see anybody so ugly again, that's *certain*."

This morning we made a very early start, intending to keep the bottom road, but before we had marched over seven miles we came to an immense slough through which it took us two hours to force our wagons. Finding from this that it would be better at once to strike across through the hills to the "old Ioway trace," we left the valley, and after a hard day's march reached a new road that lead to it, and encamped near old Wabonset's at dark, the wagons being unable to get up until nine o'clock at night. It may be interesting to some of the readers of these "rough notes" to know what kind of a country this part of Ioway which borders upon the Missouri, is. I have been over it considerably from near the head of Sioux river to the north line of Missouri, and so far as my judgment goes, I do not believe there is any better land in the United States. The soil is a light, rich mould, free from stone, and from two to three feet thick upon the bottom lands, and on the intervales, while upon the uplands it is nearly, if not quite, as fertile, though not so deep by, say a foot. It would be years before it could possibly require any dressing. I know of one farm at Council Bluffs that grows everything which can be cultivated at all in this climate, without any manure at all, and in the utmost profusion. Garden vegetables, corn, wheat, rye, oats.

or potatoes, will yield as much here as anywhere, I will venture to say. The potatoes are infinitely better than they are in Missouri in latitude 38°, and 39°. I believe if the Pottawattamies could be induced to cede their lands in Ioway to the whites, that portion of the Territory would fill up with a first rate population. The land is so fine either to cultivate or for stock that it would immediately invite the best kind of settlers. The uplands are greatly undulating, laying generally in large swells, with fine spring branches in almost every hollow. I am persuaded there is not a country that is better watered than this is, in the west. It rests upon a limestone base, though it is only here and there that this foundation makes its appearance. The seasons are a little shorter than in Missouri, (the latitude being from 40 deg. 44 min. 6sec. upward) though not enough so to interfere with the ripening of crops, except now and then (as happens everywhere) an unusually early frost sets in. The river valley seldom overflows *above* the mouth of the Nebraska. For instance this year (1844) when what is called the Lower Missouri, has been higher than it was ever known to be before, *above* the mouth of the Nebraska it was not out of its banks. This is a great consideration where one remembers what an immense bottom this is, with all its advantages in point of soil, its abundant supply of wood, its rushes for wintering stock, and its being immediately upon the finest river in the world. If Ioway ever becomes a State I have no doubt she will be very anxious to have this Pottawattamie Country as soon as possible. I believe it would be the garden of her territory.

Friday, September 13

This morning we were on the march by half past six o'clock. It was difficult to tell exactly the course to steer in order to strike the highlands we were aiming for, on account of a dense fog that set in from the south. However, by keeping an Indian trail which seemed *understandingly* to thread the intricate mazes of the various ravines and water-courses that ran toward the west, by nine o'clock we found ourselves upon the "Ioway Trace." After we had struck this we had a high and well beaten road for the rest of the day. The fog cleared up by ten, and by two P.M. we struck the north line of Missouri and immediately found ourselves in quite a densely populated country. One of the gentlemen who belonged to the Medical Staff, and who bestrode a tidy bit of horse flesh in the shape of a real iron nerved, grey Canadian, rode on a mile or two ahead of the column in order that he could get a better look at the country, and now and then make a leisurely examination of the soil. As I said in a previous chapter, the population nearest to, and along the line, is that which in a great measure floods the Pottawattamie country with liquor. Hence the very first house this gentleman arrived at was a notorious whiskey establishment situated exactly on the line.

At sundown we encamped upon the Nishnebottona at Hunseker's Ferry. Here we procured a fine supply of oats for our horses and mules. This night our squadrons were all encamped in one line along the river, which at this point made a beautiful bend, giving the row of tents the form of a crescent. After dark, and when the fires were all lighted, the effect of this scene was magnificent. The fires, and tents, and men, and horses, were all reflected in the water: while back were the deep woods and the obscurity. Mr. Deas made a splendid drawing of it. To give the reader some idea of how this country has filled up, we were told that in the grove which extends from the river up towards the line, some seven miles, there were *seventy* families.

SATURDAY, SEPTEMBER 14

We got across the Nishnebottona by 9 A.M., and after a fine day's march through a country unsurpassed for the beauty of its scenery, or the fertility of its soil, encamped at a place called the "English Grove" at sundown.

SUNDAY, MONDAY, AND TUESDAY, SEPTEMBER 15, 16, 17[29]

During these three days we were marching, over a fine road, and as nothing out of the ordinary routine occurred in that period, I have brought both the column and the reader, again to the Missouri river, and here we have encamped at Jeffrie's Point on the evening of the 17th. To-morrow we shall cross the river to the Sac, and Fox, and Ioway country, which lies directly opposite. To-night is the time when three of us had only one snipe for supper. The Lord only knows what the others had; our messing has not only got a little short, but *the* hunter continues in bad luck. However, stock in him rose a shade to-day, from the unhappy death of this poor snipe!

For the last ten miles of our march to-day, our route has been across a portion of the Bottom that was flooded last spring. From here to St. Louis, a distance of seven hundred miles by water, the farms along the river were nearly all ruined, by being covered with the sand, which was deposited by the water while they were inundated. Houses, stock, fences, crops and everything else, were in hundreds of instances swept away; the poor families flying to the highlands, and saving hardly anything but life. As the traveller passes along he sees projecting through this desolate waste, perhaps part of a chimney where was the cheerful fireside, and the comfort, and the happy hearts. They have all gone, and a deep and lonely silence settles over everything like a pall. It is never disturbed now by the silvery ringing laugh of children, and their noisy whoop and halloo, the barking of the faithful dog, the lowing of cattle, or any of the glad sounds that were wont to be heard; but instead, from morning till night, the singing of the wind, or the rushing sound of the sand as it blows about in drifts, is all that breaks its melancholy and desolate repose.

CHAPTER XVIII

PASSAGE OF THE MISSOURI—*Iowa Village—Manner of burying their dead—Groves of the Dead—Missionaries—Printing Press upon the Prairies—Little Iowa girl—Council—Charge—Flight of Natives—Howitzer's fired—Major Richardson—Falls again—We get home—Everybody glad—General reflections on the Indians—Roads Fork—End.*

WEDNESDAY, SEPTEMBER 18

WE COMMENCED the passage of the Missouri this morning by six o'clock.[30] By procuring a skiff, and having two men to row, with one to set in the stern to lead a horse which had been driven into the water, and then letting the other horses and mules follow in, one at a time, we soon got every animal over. There was just a single file of them extending from one shore to the other. It looked like a string of beads—every bead being a horse, or a donkey with his long ears—laying upon the water, and swayed down stream in the centre, where the current was strongest. There was a great deal of snorting, and blowing—and the shaking of themselves after they had got out, like big Newfoundlanders, was very amusing. The equipage, men, wagons, and howitzers, were all crossed in a fine flat-boat which is kept at this place. We were not three days and better, as at Bellevue, but got everything over snug and dry by ten o'clock, A.M.: we then took up our line of march, and after travelling through the *Iowa* country about seven miles, we arrived at the Great Nemaha Agency, where we encamped in order to hold a Council, to-morrow, with the Sacs and Foxes, and Iowas.

On our way from the river to this place, we passed the Iowa village. It is built entirely of bark, and the houses are not near so comfortable as the lodges of the Pawnees. In front of the town were several poles set in the ground. They were some thirty or forty feet high, with the bark peeled off, and here and there ornamented with vermillion. These were scalp-poles, and had been erected on the occasion of the Iowas having killed eight Pawnees, this summer, who had been in and stolen their horses. For two or three days there was a great rejoicing in town—the scalps of the Pawnees were hung dangling from the tops of these poles, and the celebrated Scalp Dance was performed by the warriors, around them.

We noticed in passing their burying-ground, flag-staffs set up at the head of some of the graves, on the top of which were fluttering several little white flags. Upon enquiry, we learned that these were to distinguish the graves of deceased warriors. The Iowas do not always bury their dead; the Sacs and Foxes hardly ever do. They dig a trough out of a cottonwood tree, large enough to lay the corpse in; they then place a piece of buffalo robe over it, and cover the whole with a piece of raw-hide. Having done this, they plant four posts in the ground, which shall be eight feet high; upon these they build a little scaffold, and place the trough upon it, fastening it firmly down to the cross-poles with leather thongs. Here it is left to decay and drop to the ground by piece-meal. We passed one of these scaffolds, and I rode up and examined it carefully: it had been there some four or five years, but the frame—upon which the remains were still resting—seemed to be as sound as ever. In room of placing the bodies upon scaffolds in this way, it is more common to put them in the forks of trees. Near some of the populous villages on the Mississippi, and even with many of the tribes high up the Missouri, where there are a great many deaths during the summer season, it is extremely disagreeable to approach anywhere near these Groves of the Dead.

Near the Agency there is a Presbyterian Missionary station. The missionaries are the Rev. Mr. Hamilton and the Rev. Mr. Irvine;[31] their families are with them. They have succeeded in building some very comfortable dwellings, and have gardens, and fields, in which they raise enough to supply themselves with nearly everything they need in the way of vegetables and bread. They have cows, bees, and a fine little orchard, which is beginning to bear very well. I never saw any people so contented as they appeared to be. They manifested the greatest zeal for both the spiritual and temporal welfare of the poor, ignorant, and wretched Indians by whom they are surrounded, and every moment of their time seemed to be occupied in trying to win them over to religion and happiness. When the reader reflects that the missionary, in going to reside amongst a savage race, has so *many* difficulties to encounter before he can be at all useful to them—has gently yet steadily to combat their prejudices—to win their confidence—to study their customs—*to learn their language* —to endure privations and exposure—often in danger—*always* cut off entirely from the dear associations of life—surely, there is everything in their patience, perseverance, courage, untiring industry, and disinterestedness, to call forth his esteem and admiration. These gentlemen have gone through with all this. They are exceedingly intelligent, well educated, hospitable, and unassuming; and, together with their estimable families, endeavored by every means in their power to make our short stay with them as pleasant as possible. It will probably astonish the people in the East, to learn that away out here in the Great Western Prairie, is a *Printing Press*, which is telling to a band of rude savages, with its thousand little mute, yet eloquent tongues, that *eighteen hundred years ago* a child was born in a manger —that he grew up—that God's voice from heaven said —"This is my beloved son, in whom I am well pleased!"—that he preached to humble people like them—was persecuted—had no where to lay his head— and finally was crucified—and all that they might be happy. Such is the fact—Mr. Hamilton and Mr. Irvine have learned the language, and printed with their own hands a little book, in *Iowa*, which contains St. Matthew, the first eleven chapters of Genesis, and the Commandments; besides a primary book for children to begin to read from: this also contains several beautiful hymns, translated into the language. Such industry and labor needs but to be known to be appreciated and admired. Let any man think one moment on the subject, and what a crowd of interesting thoughts will come up in his heart!—I will venture to say that more real poetry will visit it in that moment, than he would have dreamed could have invested such a subject. The Gospel has been the Pioneer of the Pioneers of the Anglo-Saxon race, and ever preceded it in all its glorious advancement upon this continent. Long before the axe has been heard, or the plough has turned a furrow, in however remote the place, the patient Missionary has been there, teaching the true God.

These gentlemen have a school of Iowa boys and girls—of, say about sixty—on the rolls, though it is very difficult to get half of that number together, on account of the apathy of the parents, who do not seem to care whether their children improve or not. I saw one little Iowa girl at the Rev. Mr. Irvine's, aged about eight years. He asked her to read for me: she took down the Bible and read off half the chapter of Christ's temptation, with as clear an enunciation as any child of her age amongst ourselves. She seemed to be exceedingly intelligent. It was truly touching to hear this little Indian girl read from the history of our Saviour—and that, too, in our own language—there, in the midst of a wild and savage tribe, and far beyond even the boundaries of civilization. If the Iowa Indians do not improve, it will not be the fault of these two gentlemen, whose whole lives seem to be devoted to their instruction.

To-night a large number of rockets were sent up, for the particular benefit of these tribes. They don't like the idea of fighting an enemy that uses such fearful weapons as those "fire-hawks."

THURSDAY, SEPTEMBER 19

This morning, the Major held a Council with both the Iowas and Sacs and Foxes, at the same time, having two interpreters who rendered his speech into each language, sentence by sentence, as he went along. This Council did not differ materially from those he held with the other tribes whom we have visited, except that the replies of the several Chiefs were much more brief and condensed than those we had heard in previous Councils. The Sacs and Foxes have a most musical language. It seems to flow from their mouths like a chant, with every word a soft note; besides, their voices seemed sweeter and more flute-toned than that of any other Indians we were acquainted with. They are a much better people than the Iowas. After the Council was over, the troops were mounted, and four Divisions executed a "charge." As they came over the plain, almost like so many living thunder-bolts, a hundred or so of the warriors who were mounted began to fear the movement was a serious one against them. So, just as the Divisions came up in a cloud of dust, with their sabres raised, these warriors put spurs to their horses, and away they went, with the dragoons after them. It was the most laughable sight in the world, to see those painted and ornamented savages frightened half out of their wits, pounding their ponies down to a run, and all flying in the most splendid steeple-chase order, long after the compact masses of cavalry had halted, or returned to the column. This done, a great number of shells were fired, to show them their effect. Many of these shells were so arranged as to explode in the air, and some after they had struck. *How* this was all brought about was past their comprehension. No sooner had the firing ceased, than clouds of them galloped off, and gazed with astonishment at the places where they had torn up the earth, and had scattered their iron fragments in every direction.

Major (W. P.) Richardson, from Kentucky, is the U.S. Agent for these tribes. He is a gentleman of the old school, and when I say that he treated us with Kentucky hospitality, it is paying him the highest compliment I am capable of expressing.

At 2 o'clock, P.M., we bid good-bye to the kind friends we had met here, sprang into our saddles, and were soon "out of sight of land" again, steering by compass S.S.W., in order to strike Wolf River, which we did do at sundown, and encamped.

Two days more of steady marching brought us back to our post.[32] We were met by the Band, and the whole column entered the square from the North-west sally-port, and wheeled into line upon the exact spot where, forty-one days before, it had taken up its march for the prairies. Like a ship's coming home from sea, the first fifteen minutes were nothing but shaking of hands and how-d'-doing, right and left. Everybody glad—everybody smiling—all happy. Ah, it's fun to come home from a campaign. "Why, how are you?"—"Bless my soul! why how *do* you do?"—"How did you leave the Paw-

nees?" "All well, I thank you."—"How have you been, old fellow?"
—"Why, is it possible!"—"Come, it's dusty!"—"Hallo! got back?
why, how d'*do?*"—"Bless my *soul!*"—and that's the way. I hold that
such are among the really happiest moments that one ever experi-
ences.

This has been, on the whole, an extremely pleasant campaign.
Every object for which we went has been attained; besides, we all
received that great benefit which such practice has given us as soldiers. We have had innumerable rivers to cross, morasses to traverse,
bridges to build, &c., all of which has been of profit to us. It is a
species of information that can only be gained by absolute labor and
experience. In all the fatigues attending such labors, cheerfulness
and alacrity have invariably characterized the movements of the
men. They performed every duty with a promptness, and a good
will, which was remarked with the most complimentary satisfaction
by every officer of the command, from the highest down.

Thus, reader, I have performed my promise to you, by taking you
along on this campaign, and showing you both the serious and glad
sides of the little events which occurred to us. I have now brought
you back to the starting point. There is one question which you
would probably like to ask—especially if you live east of the Mississippi—and that is, "What is the character of the Indians along the
frontier." I will try to answer that to the best of my belief. With the
exception of the Chickasaws, Choctaws, Cherokees, Creeks, Shawnees, and Delawares, they are a poor, drunken, dishonest, and miserable race. They will get drunk if they can buy, or beg, or steal
liquor to do it with, and will keep so as long as possible. They will
steal everything they can lay their hands on. They are idle, cowardly, and treacherous, with but very few exceptions, and filthy to
the most disgusting extreme. These are the Indians along the frontier. The farther you get from the influence of the whites, the better
they become. The Pawnees are just what I described them to be.
Beyond them, the Crows, and Blackfeet, and Sioux, are better still.
All these upper Indians steal as a profession, except the Pottawattamies: they are generally honest. There is one other thing which I
will mention: it is said that no good, in fact, has been obtained by

the education which has been given to hundreds of Indian children. I know several Indians who have been educated at Col. R. M. Johnson's celebrated school, and I believe it is notorious that all those who have been taught there, as elsewhere, have turned out to be worse men and more adroit scoundrels than those who have stayed at home. It is next to impossible to win an Indian from his natural freedom, independence, filth, and idleness. Take him from home, he learns more readily our vices than anything else, and all the additional knowledge he may receive, seems to be employed by him upon his return, to cheat and impose upon his more fortunate though more ignorant brethren. I know of several instances of this kind, myself; and the officers who have lived longest in the country, and the citizens, invariably declare that educated Indians, and half-breeds, are the most rascally part of the population of almost every tribe. They are not only eternally getting into difficulties themselves, but are ever seeming to do their utmost to keep everybody else in trouble.

Missionaries may devote their whole lives to their instruction, and try by every means in their power to make them happier, yet if hundreds of white men upon our borders, are continually awakening their worst attributes, and ruining all their energies by keeping their country filled with liquor, what good does it all do? Besides, in every tribe can be found a set of idle and worthless *white* scoundrels, who by their laziness and villainy could not have lived with us, but who go there and marry squaws so as to incorporate themselves with the tribe. They teach the Indians all *their* vices; well, now to combat all these influences, does not the poor Missionary row against the current to attempt even to better their condition? It is a crying shame that some determined step is not taken by the Government to effectually correct these evils. Keep these abandoned white men from settling in the country at all. Let the States contiguous, pass laws, making it a Penitentiary offence for any individual to sell or give an Indian a drop of liquor within their boundaries. Let the United States pass a similar one regulating the Indian country, and then the Indians may be improved, but not till then, reader, you may depend. Nearly all the broils, and murders, and disturbances along the whole line of the country from North to South, are occasioned by these causes. There is no denying or getting around it. Pass efficient laws, *and see them executed*, and these evils will cease; until that is done, they will continue.

Reader, if in all these chapters I have given you any information which has been interesting or useful—if I have ever made your heart light by the little laughable things that have occurred during our long journey—I am richly rewarded. I have not written with a view of even provoking criticism. My whole aim has been to tell you our travel's history in the first language that came up as I went along, and to try to make you see everything as I did myself.

Here the roads fork: you are to go one way and I am to go the other. May you have a better route and better entertainment for the rest of your journey, than I have been able to give you. Take to the right: there, that's it. Good bye!—God bless you!

A Dragoon Campaign
to the Rocky Mountains in 1845

CHAPTER I

OPERATIONS OF THE ARMY IN 1845—*Assembling of the Oregon Emigrants—Objects of the Dragoon Campaign—The labor of preparing a body of troops for the field—Objections to large baggage trains—Advantages of small ones—Subsistence stores—Luxuries and necessaries—Epicures—All things in readiness for a start—Officers and Guests of the Expedition—Western steamboats.*

H
E WHO imagines an Army Life to be one of idleness or filled with monotony, knows nothing at all of the Military Profession, and has only to select either of the fourteen Regiments in the service of the United States, and follow it through its fatiguing campaigns, or to witness its labors, in providing for the defence of our extended frontier, to satisfy himself conclusively of this fact. The operations of the whole army during the past year, particularly, have been of the most arduous character. While the Squadrons of the Second Regiment of Dragoons have been kept continually in the saddle in their active duties, under burning sun, upon the plains of Texas, the Regiments of Artillery and Infantry have, in the most trying season of the year, been hurried from the North, and concentrated upon the banks of the Rio Grande, or have been strewn—wherever their presence has been the most indispensable—from the forests of Maine along the Atlantic coast and the Lakes, to each extremity of the Mississippi. All these movements have been at the expense of incessant toil, but have been performed with the celerity and cheerfulness which has always distinguished the different arms of our Service, wherever the various requirements of the Government have rendered their presence necessary. The

operations of the First Regiment of Dragoons in the Spring, Summer, and Autumn of 1845, were likewise extremely laborious, and covered over an immense extent of country. While three divisions of it were kept continually employed in the Indian Nations situated upon the Arkansas and Washita Rivers, which pour their waters through the Mississippi into the Gulf of Mexico—two others were sent on a protracted campaign to the Red River of the North, which discharges itself into Hudson's Bay—while the five remaining divisions crossed the Rocky Mountains to the head of the Rio Colorado of the West, whose waters seek the Pacific Ocean through the Gulf of California. Thus, in May, for instance, they were all, as it were, within hailing distance of each other; but by the 30th of June they had spread out in their fanlike marches, until they had separated for thousands of miles, and were encamped on rivers that assist in draining the Eastern, Southern, and Western slopes of North America; while by September again, they had all returned to the various points from which they had severally radiated.

As it will be impossible for these rough notes to follow out all those movements, they will be confined exclusively to the one that extends to the Rocky Mountains; the others having been spoken of to show the reader that although he may elect for the present to accompany *this*, there were similar ones in the Artillery, Infantry, and Second Dragoons, equally as deserving of his attention. Having thus broken the ice, and—to use a nautical phrase—worked over the ground both at *Plain* and *Traverse Sailing*, the promised Sketches will be chalked off as fast as possible.[33]

During the winter of 1844 and 45, a greater number of families, whose intention it was to move to Oregon, had collected together at different towns along the Western frontier of Missouri, both from the several counties in that State, and from Tennessee, Illinois, Wisconsin and Iowa, than had been known to assemble for such an enterprise at any previous season.[34] Their object was to commence their movement in the Spring as soon as the grass upon the prairies had become high enough for the subsistence of their cattle; and the intervening time was occupied in organizing themselves into companies of from fifty to three hundred souls each, the better to insure their safety, and without loss of time, to overcome the natural obstacles of their journey by harmony of action and amity of purpose.

Five divisions of the First Regiment of United States Dragoons, under the command of Col. Kearny, were directed to proceed to the Great South Pass of the Rocky Mountains, partly to protect the emigrants thus far upon their route, and likewise to ascertain the military resources of the country;—its definite geography—the strength, manners and customs, and mode of warfare, of the different tribes of Indians that lay in their way;—together with their disposition towards the whites—their method of subsistence, &c. &c. And finally, to return upon the Trace that was opened between the United States and New Mexico in 1825, that by their presence they might secure the safe passage of the rich Caravans that would then be on their way from Missouri to the ports of Santa Fe and Chihuahua. Such at least are understood to have been the instructions given to Col. Kearny, either direct, or implied, by vesting him with discretionary powers for the fulfilment of every necessary duty that might come under his cognizance, while pursuing such routes at just such times.

The four divisions of the Regiment stationed at Fort Leavenworth, and that stationed at Fort Scott, which had been directed to proceed to the former post to form a part of the Expedition—were prepared for a four months' campaign early in May. By the 12th, Col. Kearny had arrived from St. Louis, where he had for a long time been stationed, as Chief of the 3d Military Department;—and the 18th of the same month was selected as the day when the troops should commence their long march.

Those of our fellow citizens who, from their peculiar vocations and remote localities, have but few opportunities for acquiring even a superficial knowledge of what is called "the regular service"—but who are perfectly aware of the various movements that are made from time to time of the several parts of the Army, and understand exactly their objects and the final results, would be astonished could they witness the labor it requires to put in a state of readiness a body of men for action and efficient operation in the fields, even in a settled country, where the different wants, as they may arise, can be easily provided for; but if the same number are to perform similar duties in an uninhabited wilderness—like the great prairies, for instance—when hardly a thing can by a possibility be obtained, except water and fuel—their astonishment would be proportionably increased at beholding the thousand little preparations in detail, which *have* to be made before those men can be fitted for the numberless emergencies in which they may be suddenly called upon promptly and effectively to act. This is the case with every species of troops, but more especially with Dragoons; for it requires far more attention to see that the horses are in complete condition—that their equipments are so strong and in such good repair as not to be liable to become useless,—that they are so adjusted upon each animal as not to impede his action and power, or be in danger of injuring him from continued wear—than the men do who are to ride them;—and yet they need just as much as they would were they to move on foot.

To the rapidity of a march across a prairie country, where, generally, there are no roads—no causeways on the morasses, or bridges over the many rivers and streams that have to be passed—a large train of baggage wagons forms a greater impediment than can well be imagined; and, although it is reasonable to suppose that a more cumbrous one is needed than in an inhabited country, where, as before stated, many articles might be procured from time to time, or where these obstructions to the celerity of their transportation are provided for, still a smaller one has actually to be taken along for these very reasons. Besides its inconvenience in retarding the progress of the troops, it is one of the most expensive items in the whole service—and hence it is that commanding officers have a double object in cutting it down to the smallest number possible. In such cases, therefore, it requires quite as much experience and forethought on his part to know what to dispense with, as to take into consideration just what will be indispensable. Col. Kearny carried this doctrine out to the letter, and consequently caused us to dispense with almost everything but flour, coffee, sugar, and salt. It is true we had eighteen barrels of pork and bacon for the whole campaign—which, in addition to the other stores, would have to be hauled a little ways—and thirty head of cattle carried their own beef along to provide for emergencies; but the balance of our edibles in the meat line, both for officers and men, was saving the Government a vast deal of money on this score—by transporting itself over the prairies in the shape of buffaloes, deer, and antelopes; but like Mrs. Glass's rabbit, would have to be caught and killed before it could well be either cooked or eaten. We had an abundance of ammunition—and a plenty of hospital stores for those who might be sick;— besides axes for making bridges—spades for cutting down the banks of rivers—scythes for the mowing of grass to lay on soft ground—and ropes to pull wagons and mules out of the mire, &c. &c. &c.—for all these things would help us to overcome distance; but if an enemy had by chance captured the whole of our baggage with a hope either of rich booty or fat living, unless he could have found both in the above enumerated articles, he would have been most egregiously disappointed; that would have been some comfort to have sustained us under the mortification of a defeat. It is true that, together with the foregoing subsistence stores, a little soap and vinegar was added as sort of luxuries, but they were to be issued sparingly, and then only on great and important occasions. The reader can, therefore, easily account for the reason of our having, perhaps, the smallest train of wagons that ever accompanied the same number of troops on a similar expedition—and for the speed with which we travelled.

After the first ten days the officers were allowed to purchase from the Commissary the same proportions of subsistence that was issued to the men for a given time, and no more—but this restriction was perfectly satisfactory—all understood its importance; and knowing exactly what they had to encounter in the way of hardships, were determined, in doing a soldier's duty, to stick to the soldier's fare. However, one or two of the older officers, although preaching up this very thing—practiced, in an under-handed way, quite a different one; for they smuggled along a little pepper (!) in out of the way corners of their 8 by 10 mess chests—and attempted to justify themselves, when it was discovered, by saying, in a tone and manner only slightly embarrassed, "that they thought it would go well on fish!" And two or three of the others went so far as to stow away one or two of those little apoplectic jars of pickles and an emaciated bottle or two of capers; but these things were so utterly contraband, that they had the shrewdness to keep them well out of sight, during the day, at least. However, these gentlemen were acknowledged epicures, and to that fact may be attributed this extravagance.

So, reader, consider that a busy six days have elapsed in attending to these and hundreds of other absolutely necessary requirements, but that *now* everything has been thought of and prepared;—the troops inspected and found to be in perfect order;—the wagons all packed and hauled out in line, ready to start, and everything accomplished but to say good bye to those we are to leave behind.

The following[35] are the divisions that form the Expedition, viz.:

Col. S. W. Kearny, *Commanding*
Capt. H. S. Turner, *Assistant Adjutant General*
Dr. S. G. I. De Camp, *Surgeon U.S.A.*
Capt. W. M. D. McKissack, *Quartermaster*
Lieut. J. Henry Carleton, *Commissary*
Lieut. W. B. Franklin, *U.S. Topographical Engineers*

LINE

Capt. P. S. G. Cooke, *1st Dragoons*
Capt. B. D. Moore, *1st Dragoons*
Capt. J. H. K. Burgwin, *1st Dragoons*
Capt. William Eustis, *1st Dragoons*
Lieut. P. Kearny, *1st Dragoons*
Lieut. A. J. Smith, *1st Dragoons*
Lieut. R. S. Ewell, *1st Dragoons*
Lieut. John Love, *1st Dragoons*
Lieut. Henry Stanton, *1st Dragoons*
Lieut. T. C. Hammond, *1st Dragoons*

Capt. Alexander Macomb (late 2d Dragoons), goes with us as a guest, as does Henry Loring, Esq., of Boston, and Mr. Simpson, of St. Louis. Mr. Fitzpatrick,[36] who has for many years been familiar with the country in the neighborhood of the Rocky Mountains—and who accompanied Capt. Fremont in his exploring tour to Upper California, is to be our guide throughout the campaign.

CHAPTER II

G OOD-BYE–C OMMENCE THE MARCH–*Natchez–Scenery of to-day's march–Utilitarianism–Pen frisky–Soil and Minerals–Kicka-poos–Get on high horse about* "*Lo! the poor Indian*" – *The Past–Indian Mounds–Description of Camp*–"*Rocky*" – *His pack–Its contents–Our Sportsmen and* "*Sport*" – *Cockney hunters–Horse loose in Camp.*

SUNDAY, MAY 18, 1845

L AST night the heavens were covered with dark and massive clouds, and now and then, a heavy shower of rain came pattering down, and threatening a disagreeable day for the beginning of the campaign; but at reveillé, patches of blue sky, with bright stars in them, gave birth to a more favorable expectation. The sun soon after came up with his big, jolly countenance. At the same time a cool and invigorating wind from the northwest began to shake down the drops which had lazily been hanging on the dark green foliage like countless diamonds; and its merry faculty of setting the leaves to dancing, and the boughs overhead to swinging and balancing to their partners, seemed also to impart a correspond-ing cheerfulness to the body of stalwart men who were drawn up in line on the green turf beneath, and who were soon to wheel off and commence the long march which was to take them so many miles from the magnificent scenes then surrounding them, and from the dear friends with whom they had just exchanged a hurried, yet earnest farewell!

The order was at length given, and the rumbling of the earth, as three hundred armed horsemen moved over it, told, in a deep-toned and eloquent language, the touching truth, that they had already begun to leave those scenes and those friends far behind.

In a short time, the troops of the leading division reached the summit of the belt of hills that surround Fort Leavenworth like a zone of jewels, and as they passed over it, each one involuntarily cast

"A longing, lingering look behind,"

as if to bid an affectionate adieu to the beloved post, also. There it lay reposing in its May-beauty, with stately trees about it, holding aloft a canopy of boughs to shield it from a too ardent gaze of the sun.

The scenery around Fort Leavenworth is lovely beyond expression, particularly at this season of the year.

As we came along we saw beautiful hills on every hand as far as the eye could reach. Some of them were covered with groves of oak, hickory, and walnut, springing up out of a green turf like the trees of an orchard; and some were covered with fresh grass, and the blue and white flowers of spring, which seemed to furnish the breeze that cooled our temples, by loading it with perfume for kissing them, as it frolicked past.

The land over which we have travelled westward to-day, is based upon fossiliferous limestone. Its decomposition, mixed with vegetable and animal mould, has formed a covering of soil which is so rich that even for gardens, it can be tilled for years without requiring a particle of manure. Sandstone, coal, iron, and lead, have been discovered in it, and, no doubt, exist in sufficient quantities to be sought hereafter with profit. The Kickapoo tribe who ceded it to the United States, and timidly shrunk back to give place to this handful of their brethren. That great tide of the human race, which is sweeping over this continent, forced them to leave their hunting grounds east of the Mississippi. Hardly had they reached their present asylum, before its waves were again heard by them, tearing down forests and hoarsely murmuring through rivers in its resistless course. And now, it is once more lashing the shores of their blooming country with its advancing surges, and seems remorselessly waiting only for a renewed impetus to overwhelm their peaceful homes, and drive them still farther Westward; and finally, to blot out their very name from the pages of the world. To know that such will be their inevitable fate, we have only to turn to the records of the Past

On Pilot Knob, a picturesque landmark only five miles from Fort Leavenworth, are three tumuli composed of loose stones, which from the lapse of time have grown grey and moss covered, and which have almost settled down to a level with the surrounding soil. Within a rifle-shot, also, of where we crossed the same range of hills, of which Pilot Knob is only an advanced bastion, there are eight others clustered together in the form of a cross, as if those who erected them, ignorantly typified in building their tombs, the emblem of a coming religion they had never known while living. Not one month since one of these mounds was opened by three gentlemen from the garrison, with a view of removing a doubt as to their being natural or artificial—and far below, the pieces of human bones, which had not yet become resolved into their elements, answered that doubt by mutely upbraiding them in a visible language for their unkind desecration of a grave!

On other eminences there are more of them. Nature piled up those magnificent hills as monuments to her children.

By four o'clock we reached Independence River, and our first encampment is formed on the same ground where our second night was spent when commencing the Pawnee Campaign last year.[37] It is a sweet little spot, protected on two sides by deep woods, and on the other two by terraced hills, which seem to have been thrown up by a race of giants as intrenchments; (I liked to have gone off on the giants;) and are fashioned with crests—exterior slopes—berms— scarps—and (without any ditch—giants didn't use ditches) a glacis. At the foot of the latter, on a perfectly level plain (they belonged to the grenadiers, the giants did—and used to come down here for drills and evening parade), our tents are pitched.

The first night out of a garrison—although men may have been in the field half their lives—is always one of restlessness and excitement. There are so many things to attract one's attention. First—the beautiful appearance of the white tents standing in long rows over

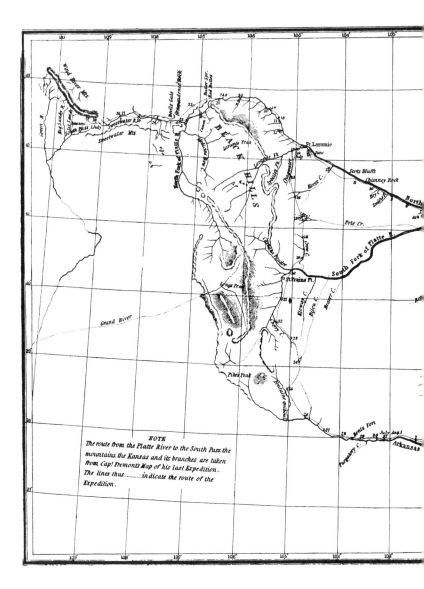

NOTE
The route from the Platte River to the South Pass, the mountains, the Kansas and its branches are taken from Cap.t Fremont's Map of his last Expedition. The lines thus..........indicate the route of the Expedition.

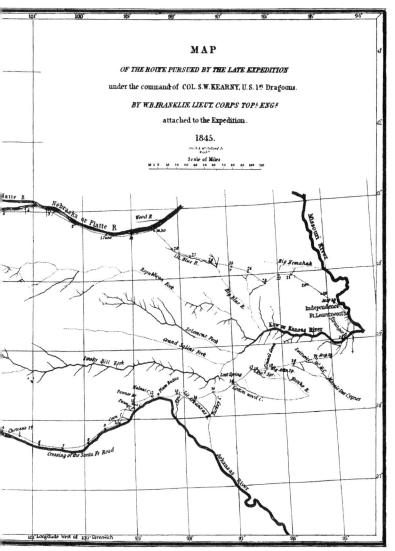

MAP

OF THE ROUTE PURSUED BY THE LATE EXPEDITION

under the command of COL. S.W. KEARNY, U.S. 1st Dragoons.

BY W.B. FRANKLIN, LIEUT. CORPS TOP! ENG!

attached to the Expedition.

1845.

Smith & M? Clelland S?
Wash?

Scale of Miles

From *Senate Executive Documents*, 1st Sess., 29th Cong., I, Document 1.

the green grass; and the blue smoke curling gently upward from the many fires. Then the athletic figures of the soldiers as they move about hither and thither, intent upon their various duties; or the groups of them who stand and sit in picturesque attitudes, and are quietly talking over the affairs of the day and the probable ones of the morrow. Then the neighing of the horses, as they call out to one another as much as to say—"Look here!"—when they kick up—roll over—or, with their head and tail erect, and their nostrils distended, trot loftily around in a circle, of which their lariette is the radius and the iron picket-pin the centre; of, pausing a moment in a majestic attitude, with eyes that beam fire, they give a snort like a locomotive, and then trot on again until they are tired. And then the long-eared and comically, grave-looking donkeys, who, with widely distended jaws and spasmodically heaving bellies, fret the air with horrible sounds that seem to include the whole gamut of discordant notes, from the lower wheezings of a crosscut saw to the screaming treble of an ungreased wheel-barrow. And when they have completed their "linked harshness, long drawn out," and donkey-echoes are hoarsely repeating it in the distant woods—they look around as if they thought it a fine joke, and seem to say, "Hear that!" There are innumerable donkeys everywhere who make nearly as sensible a noise, who wonder that they are not appreciated or applauded. And then the cattle—they attract one's attention, too, as some of them are industriously grazing on the side of yonder hill, while others are lying down, and are quietly ruminating. And the sheep—sheep? —yes, sheep: we brought along some thirty of them—partly as an experiment to see how they would travel—and partly to go with those capers which have been spoken of. Poor creatures, they are tired enough; and though we have been here two hours, they have laid there in the grass panting and too fatigued to eat. It is thought by some quite impossible for them to keep up with the command for a long time. But to go on. All these sights, and all these sounds, together with thousands of others—though seen and heard fifty times before—still, they are novel now, and consequently, keep one's thoughts flying so rapidly here and there, that rest or sleep is quite out of the question.

There are several excellent sportsmen along this year who will no doubt have abundant opportunities to kill all kinds of game, to their hearts' content. When Lieutenant Graham, of the 4th Infantry, was out to the Rocky Mountains, with him who was then Sir William Drummond Stewart, but who has since been promoted to something higher—he rode a fine sorrel mustang which he called after those mountains, and which, on his return, he gave to one of his brother officers at Fort Leavenworth. That horse is along with us, and flourishes under his old title dwindled down to plain Rocky, for short. His time is mostly employed on this campaign in the light duty of carrying a small pack filled with all sorts of sporting apparatus. On the top of the pack is fastened a plain, jointed, fishing rod of decidedly a democratic turn, and which smacks strongly of a Connecticut manufacture; while down the sides dangles divers pairs of boots suspended by the ears, and various bundles of wearing apparel—a canteen or two—and coils of lariettes enough for a division of cavalry. But the main magazine of the load is the interior. It is said that there are stowed sundry brown paper parcels containing Dupont's powder, and quantity of plethoric bags filled with different sized shot, ranging from single buck and O's, down to common mustard seed; besides dozens of boxes of percussion caps done up in long rolls, together with a gross or two of different sized fishing lines, and a pound of tobacco—a dozen or so of pipes, of the T. D. brand—some lucifer matches, and an extra hunting knife or two— to provide for losses and breakage. That pack belongs in part to our hunter of last year;—and that is him sitting there at the mouth of his tent, and busily engaged in unscrewing the locks from his double-barrelled gun, and oiling them up for immediate service, by touching them here and there with a feather which he occasionally dips into a wicker bottle held in the hands of his black boy John. The tall gentleman with broad brimmed hat—finely fitting shooting-jacket—dark smalls and gaiters, who had already been out in the grounds to try his hand, forgetting that so near an Indian settlement game is apt to be scarce, and who—having been consequently unsuccessful—is now standing nearby leaning upon his gun and nodding frequent exactly so's, at the various periods of the essay our hunter is giving him as he continues his labor,—setting forth, as it does, the secrets of his former good fortune, and concluded by—"Now, if you do so and so, (alluding to the already explained modus operandi,) you will be equally as lucky"—As another of our sportsmen; and if he follows the instructions he has just received, will no doubt realize to the fullest extent their concluding promise. He lacks a dog, it is true; but Sport there—that liver-colored pointer lying upon the grass is him—has the rare talent of being able to keep at least six hunters in full blast, if game is plenty, at one and the same time. He is as famous for his faculty of scenting birds, if not absolutely pointing them, as his master is for bringing them down after they are flushed;—and if possible, a trifle more so. Sport has his faults it is true—and if the precise fact must be stated—is really more fond of sky-larking than he is of grousing; but of his ability as a dog—looking at him in a mere abstract light—there never, I believe, has been the smallest particle of a question. His master has frequent cause of gratification from the daily proofs he gives of both his speed and endurance; for he has innumerable opportunities almost every hour of seeing them tried to the utmost in Sport's exciting race after rabbits. And although the rabbit always beats, still it is no fault of the dog's, for as his master often says— "He tried hard enough to catch him, dear knows."

We have other sportsmen besides. Our guide has a beautiful rifle that throws about a two ounce ball, which was made expressly for killing tigers in India, and presented to him by its former owner, Sir William Drummond Stewart. But with the exception of carrying, suspended in front, a powder flask and russet leather ball pouch, above which a small belt is buckled to keep them from swinging, he has made no preparations for its use yet awhile. He knows too much of the country for that. He is not like, is Mr. Fitzpatrick,— those Cockney gentlemen, who, hearing that the United States swarmed with game, particularly bears,—came over to this country for a summer's shooting, and before the ship had hauled in to the wharf at New York, jumped into a boat—guns in hand, and loaded down with ammunition—and after having been rowed ashore— went carefully on tip-toe up Broadway—each holding his piece in both hands, with a thumb on the hammer ready to cock it at a moment's warning—and without speaking above their breath, looking eerily around the corners, expecting every minute to see "My hyes, vot a big un!" Not he. When the proper time arrives he'll have it ready enough, you may be certain.

Several other of the gentlemen intend, by and by, to enter very largely into the business, also; and have amongst them a ricketty old rifle or two, to say nothing of a decrepit shot gun that hangs suspended by two strings from the interior of the bows of the staff wagon.

So with one other fishing pole of domestic fabric, with not so many pretensions to elegrance as the jointed one already spoken of —and both of which are even now doing heavy duty at the river by exerting themselves in a remarkable degree in their endeavours at long intervals to throw out a three inch perch—you can see that we are well provided to furnish you with some exceedingly rare specimens of sport, both in the piscatorial, as well as in the hunting line.

But here it is too dark to put farther jottings down in my old note-book. The night air is cool—the dew heavy—and white mists settle in the valleys, or hang in graceful festoons around the distant groves. While high above—sailing in cloudless majesty—the bright moon goes on in her silent course; imparting as it were, to the attendant stars and all nature below, only a whispered light, that it may not disturb the solemn repose of a world.

Just as one's mind gets really interested on such subjects, the sound of iron hoofs is heard careering over the plain, and the watchful sentinel on yonder hill, sings out with the voice of a Stentor— "Company 'A'—horse loose!"—which is repeated by airy echoes, until away off on the distant prairie and through the still woods, most of Company A's horses seem to have gone—and with them the reflections. Company A's men turn out, and after five minutes hard run through the wet grass to catch the loose horse, have the satisfaction to ascertain that he belongs to Company K. However, they picket him and grumble along to their tents. And as it's getting late, we'll go to ours. Good night!

THOROUGHFARE FROM MISSOURI TO OREGON–*Route of the Expedition–Morning Exercises before the march–Order of march–Allurements of life on the Prairies–Arrival of Mr. Loring–Last adieus of the First Infantry to the Expedition–Clough Creek–First appearance of Game–A thunder storm.*

SUNDAY, MAY 18

THE main thoroughfare from the Western frontier to the Territory of Oregon starts from Independence, Mo. It then proceeds up the country south of the Kansas River until near the Kansas Villages, when it turns to the right, and after passing that river pursues nearly a northwest course until it strikes Little Blue River. This it crosses near the junction of one of its eastern tributaries, and then circles around to the left for nearly sixty miles before it gets its proper westerly direction. Such a crooked trace necessarily compels the emigrants who go upon it to expand much labor without overcoming but little of the direct distance they wish to travel.

The flourishing little town of Weston,[38] only five miles from Fort Leavenworth, is fifty miles farther up the Missouri than Independence, and is believed by many to be a much better point from whence to commence the journey. Several important reasons are given why such a belief is entertained, and among them the following appear to be worthy the consideration of those the most interested in the matter:—

First—because the former is situated in the extreme western bend of the river, and consequently makes the distance shorter to be travelled in an unsettled country; and is but a little south of an east line running from where the trace should fall into the valley of the Nebraska: and in the second place, because the crossing of the Kanzas is entirely avoided as are all the difficulties and dangers such an operation presents, to say nothing of the waste of much valuable time in the ferrying over of a large company, and which cannot well be spared at the most important season of the year. Likewise, it is said that several other exceedingly bad streams, which obstruct the trace from Independence, would not be met with at all in going from Weston. And finally, because such a route would leave those notoriously adroit and impudent thieves, the Kanzas Indians, so far to the left that the danger of having property and stock stolen by them, would, in a great measure be escaped.

There is another branch of the Oregon Road that leaves St. Joseph, Mo. But from the great bend it is obliged to make to the south, in order to avoid the difficult affluents of the Nemaha, and to arrive at the present intersection of the Independence trace—which is below the crossing of the Blue River—it subjects those who go upon it to a great deal of unnecessary travel. It would be a saving of much time and distance were they to rendezvous at Weston—only twenty miles off—and start from there likewise. Heretofore no direct road has been marked out from Fort Leavenworth westward to the most suitable point, where it should fall in to the one already made from Independence; but this year the commanding officer intends to take the column through the very route recommended. And certainly wherever we can go with our heavy wagons, the emigrants could follow with theirs.

Monday, May 19

The faintest possible cob-web of light had been woven over the eastern sky, and the chances were very doubtful whether a day or a night would be caught in it, when our ten stout buglers decided the point by arousing us all from our slumbers with their reveille. To wake up—dress—put on our trappings—seize our arms and be in line on foot—each division in front of its own tents, did not admit of a great deal of leisure time most certainly; for from the first blast of the bugles until the orderly sergeants commenced calling the roll, was invariably inside of two minutes. Immediately afterwards came stable call, when the animals were taken out to fresh spots of grass, then breakfast; then everything was packed and loaded into the wagons; then guard mounting; then to horse, when at last, by half past six o'clock, the signal of advance unwound the long string of the column from the compact ball of the encampment, and we were fairly under way again. It is but a short time since, in the account of the Pawnee Campaign, all the modus operandi of encamping at night and starting in the morning was given. It being the same on this expedition, except in one or two unimportant details, it is unnecessary to repeat it again.

We are now just leaving the hilly country and issuing out upon the undulating. In front, and on our right and left, there are numerous groves fringing the various water courses—while in the rear the vast valley of the Missouri is spread out like a dark ocean of foliage. The appearance of the cavalcade, as it passes over the successive levels of the bright green prairie—or winds through the intervening hollows—or makes an extended circle to avoid some projecting headland of timber, is exceedingly picturesque and beautiful. Sometimes the route lays over a straight ridge that runs perpendicular to the direction of the march for miles, and then it is that a person in looking upon it from either hand can see the command in profile at a glance; each individual of it brought out in strong relief by a "background" of blue sky alone. Such view of it are equally fine. First the guide is seen by himself, some quarter of a mile ahead of all: then the commanding officer, followed by his orderly and the chief bugler: then the staff officers: then a division, mounted on black horses, marching by twos: then another on greys—another on bays—another on sorrels, and a fifth on blacks again, with an interval of one hundred paces between each division to avoid one another's dust: then the howitzers, followed by a party of dragoons to serve them under charge of the sergeant major: then the train of wagons, with a detail to assist in getting them over bad places, under the immediate command of the quartermaster-sergeant, who receives his directions from the quartermaster: then the drove of cattle and sheep, followed by their guard of nine men under the command of a corporal—and lastly, the main guard, under an officer to bring up the extreme rear. Each day the divisions alternate in taking the lead—as do the several wagons. Such is the usual order of march—though occasionally, where the ground admits of it, the command moves in two columns abreast.[39]

So far the reader has had a general view of our appearance, both in camp and en route, and he must consider it as they say in the almanacks—calculated for any given meridian on the whole campaign, after making a liberal allowance for the variations required for time, place, and circumstances; all of which will be chronicled in due season.

And here we are once more upon the prairies, and surrounded by nature in all her purity and her bloom. No plough has ever furrowed these fields, nor has the axe sullied the loveliness of these groves. As they have always been, do we behold them now—clothed in the surpassing beauty with which they were decorated by the hand of the Creator. Who wonders that such scenes as these win men from the hackneyed gaities of the crowded city and the rife and affected blandishments of society?

In garrison the same scenes to look upon, and the daily round of duties, after a while become tedious. But talk to him of a campaign —picture to him the broad plains and the magnificent mountains— the luxuriant groves and the beautiful rivers—and he will fire up in a moment, and his heart will pant with impatience to mount up and be away again. What though his fatigues and privations are to be increased tenfold—that does not dampen his ardour—not a bit of it he loves fatigue because his rest is sweet after it; he loves privations, partly to show he can endure them, and because they teach him how to enjoy that part of his life which has less of them. Talk to him of the long days' marches under a burning sun or in a cold storm; of the hunger and of the thirst he is to experience—but faster than you can enumerate them his mind will call back such scenes as these that are delighting us—and will picture the quiet encampment —the romantic bivouac—the staunch and cheerful comrades—the big camp-fire—the roasted buffalo ribs—the broiled venison—the pint cup of hot coffee—the sociable pipe—the enchanting story—the joke—the song—all these things, and a thousand others which will put down at once all your preachings of hardships, with an eloquence, that to his heart is perfectly irresistible. And now, as we move on, the mind of each man is sketching for itself some picture that is pleasing. All are cheerful and full of hope. The monotony of the garrison has given place to the excitement of the march, and each one is in the full enjoyment of that indescribable sensation of freedom which is so fascinating both to the sailor upon the ocean and the soldier in the field;—and which can never be felt amidst the bustle and the smoke, the noise and confinement of the city.

To-day our course has laid something north of west, and we have followed a greater part of the line of last year's expedition—leaving it only to cut off the great bends it was then obliged to make from the grounds being unusually wet that season; and to-night we are encamped on "Clough Creek," named for the soldier who so suddenly died on that campaign, and whose grave is on a little eminence just opposite to us.[40]

Mr. Loring of Boston, who left that city for the purpose of accompanying us, did not arrive at Fort Leavenworth until the evening of the 18th. We had then gone. Supposing he would get there soon after that time, a carriage had been engaged to bring him on until he overtook us, while the horses and the other necessary articles he might require, we brought along to save him any delay or trouble before starting. However, when he got there he did not even wait for the carriage, but took a horse and a guide, which Major Wharton kindly furnished him, and immediately left upon our trace. He came up with us to-night, pretty well tired out from the fatigues of his long ride. There are a few more passengers whose names are registered, whom we are yet to take aboard still farther along.

The gallant officers of the 1st Infantry, stationed at Fort Leavenworth, sent us by Mr. Loring a still later edition of their blessing and kind wishes for our success, and with it wherewithal to drink their healths—God bless them!—and sundry goodies and nicknackerie besides. In one sense, like the jolly old monks of old—and they looked upon such things in a pious and sensible light, did the monks —they speeded their departing brethren with a benedicite, a bottle of wine and a scrip. The first to encourage—the second to cheer, and the third to sustain. So having been comforted by the blessing and eaten the scrip, we will finish both the comparison and bottle by another—God bless them! merely remarking at the same time that when next we shall have an opportunity to gladden the cockles of our hearts with such good wine as that is a problem more difficult of solution than any in Newton's Principia and infinitely more dry. It is said that in the navy many of our ships have conducted their cruises throughout entirely upon cold water, and this may be set down as a military campaign carrying out that principle, for, with the exception of the Hospital stores, it would be hard to gather enough liquor together to drown and preserve even a decent specimen of a marmot.

On the morning of the 20th, by building a bridge across a small branch of "Clough Creek," we were enabled to cut off all of three miles, which we were obliged to travel last year in order to avoid it. At nine o'clock we struck the old trace again, and at four in the afternoon encamped on the head waters of Stranger river, a tributary of the Kanzas. Our course to-day was W.N.W., and lay over the ridge that divides the water falling into Wolf river and those running into the Stranger. The soil has been of an excellent quality the whole distance, but there was hardly any wood nearer than five or six miles on either hand. The upper branches of the Great Nemaha, those of the Stranger, and some eastern tributaries of Little Blue River, interlock so much with one another as to make it impracticable to follow the sinuosities of their "divide;" but by crossing the upper branches of each of those streams, although one or two bridges are required to be built, and here and there a rough place to go over, still it is cheaper in point of both time and labor to keep the straight course than to endeavour to avoid the streams by pursuing the tortuous one of the divide.

The 21st we marched N.W. all day. We kept until four o'clock on the waters of the Stranger—two considerable branches of which we crossed without much difficulty. At that time we passed over and encamped upon a small creek that runs into the Nemaha. On the divide in question, the Oregon trace from St. Joseph runs, and at the point where we intersected it, it bore due south; evidently making an immense detour to avoid the branches of the Nemaha that here cut up the country in every direction like the sticks of a fan. Our course is nearly the chord of the arc it describes, but that trace keeps clear of the streams, while ours passes them with but little trouble.

This day there were several deer seen, and our sportsmen made quite an expenditure of powder and shot by sharp practice at a grouse or so. None, however, were injured—the proper gauge for the charge not having yet been ascertained. As soon as it can be definitely known, it is believed that the closeness of the firing will be sensibly improved.

The 22nd we made a long march through the broken land drained by the Nemaha, and crossed the main river on a smooth limestone ford, several miles higher up than we did on the Pawnee Campaign. We fell into the trace made at that time from the left at 11 o'clock A.M. and followed it for eight miles, when we came to a very miry creek running to our right, which we were obliged to bridge. The old trail crosses the same creek two miles higher up by bearing away to the south and describing a half circle. We fell into it again from the right about two o'clock P.M. and kept it then till we arrived at the "sulphur spring," where we encamped. Our general course to-day was W.N.W., and we have cleared the net which was spread before us this morning with much less difficulty than we anticipated. Why these dry details have been spoken of at all, has been to show that the route from Weston across this way is practicable, as the very worst part of it has already been gone over by our column:—and, also, on account of the obstructions the country here offers to the progress of commands from Fort Leavenworth to the Pawnee Villages or to the head of Grand Island on the Nebraska.

The soil has grown poorer each mile of the last two days' journey —especially on the uplands where it is more or less mixed with coarse gravel and pebbles. The intervales along the smaller streams are quite narrow, and support only a slight growth of timber; but along the main Nemaha there is an excellent soil and some pretty extensive groves, and all the way from its source down, there might be a fine range of farms. Besides, limestone and sandstone make their appearance frequently enough for all necessary purposes for which they might be required, and no doubt but coal could likewise be found here in great abundance.

Just at dark we were visited by a tremendous thunder storm, and the lightning seemed to strike the earth on every side of us. It continued to rain heavily all night, but at daybreak on the 23rd a thick fog set in, which, with a cold southeast wind, made all the cloaks we could muster in great demand. During the day a regular storm came on, which completely drenched us from head to foot. Our course was W.S.W., and lay between two eastern tributaries of the Little Blue, and after nine o'clock in the morning we did not cross a single water-course for the whole day. The country passed over was very flat, with only a slight inclination towards the west, and the soil thin and clayey. Nearly all the time we were out of sight of land—or in other words, there was not a tree to be seen as far as the eye could reach. It was as disagreeable a day's journey as one could well imagine. Under foot it was so muddy and slippery the animals could hardly keep their feet—while the leaden sky overhead poured down a perfect flood of water, and besides, presented every appearance of having just set in for a six weeks' rain. Everybody was wet and trembling with cold and there was nothing to attract one's attention but a monotonous ocean of thin and consumptive grass extending in every direction to the horizon. On every countenance there was the same cheerful expression around the mouth—but it gradually faded off into a moody frown by the time it got to the fore-head. Even our sportsmen became taciturn and dejected. Early in the forenoon they attempted to get up an excitement at an unfortunate curlew that was too low spirited to fly; but finding that their guns hung fire, they only snapped a dozen or so of caps at him and let him run. And after making a few bets as to whether one of the horses that belonged to a citizen teamster, and which had given out—would ever live to reach camp or not—they wrapped their cloaks snugly about them and rode silently along to await the issue. The horse died.

At evening we encamped in a point at the junction of the two streams between which we had been marching nearly all day, and but a mile or two from the Little Blue. For the whole night the rain came down in torrents—but by daybreak next morning it ceased, and by eight o'clock every vestige of the storm had left the heavens.

It took two hours to complete a bridge across the stream on our right, when we were again on the march. In a short time we reached Little Blue—but it was some time before we could find a spot suitable for passing it, owing to the depth of the water and the steepness of the banks. At length a ford was discovered, where, after considerable labor with spades in grading down a road, and in forming a matting of willows on the first shore to keep the animals from miring into the quicksands as they descended into the water, we commenced the crossing. In one hour the whole command was over. Nothing had to swim but the sheep, and by driving the cattle in first, they took to the water without any hesitation.

Little Blue River is about sixty yards wide and has an average depth of three feet. Its banks and bed are composed of quicksands and alluvium—and it runs with a very rapid current. It is bordered by a heavy growth of timber consisting of cotton-wood, sycamore and elm, in its immediate vicinity, while back—as the land begins to rise from its bottoms—it changes to hickory and oak. From being often overflowed, the intervales upon each side are heavy and wet, and as soon as they are left, a series of those peculiar eminences commence which are graded by successive slopes and terraces, with frequent out croppings of limestone—similar to those which are met with near the Missouri. Their summits mark the general level of the surrounding country, and back from them there is only a poor barren soil filled with gravel, which offers only an apology for vegetation in sending forth a short, thin, and sickly crop of grass.

We had proceeded westward only about five miles farther when, with the help of our glasses, we discovered a long train of wagons on a distant ridge, which we knew must belong to a company of emigrants on the trace from Independence. At one o'clock we came into that road which, without a single branching out to the right or left, extends from the Missouri River to the Pacific Ocean, a distance of over two thousand miles. From this point to Fort Leavenworth across the country it is one hundred and twenty miles, and we have been six days and a half in marching it—having moved at a moderate pace on account of the animals not yet getting fairly accustomed to their change from grain to nothing but grass. But to show the difference in the length of the road, one of the emigrants of this company informed us that they had already been out from Independence nearly three weeks.

A COMPANY OF EMIGRANTS—*They thought we were Indians—How they should be regarded—Description of them and of their march—The poor Irishman's home—Mail for Leavenworth—Sportsman's consolation for loss of his horse—Wonderful intelligence of his mule—Grouse shooting—Peeps—Nubbins—Pass another Company—The Country—The Sandy—Its Valley—Five more companies—An Oregon Belle—Capt. M.— The Oregon Guide—His stump speech—Marriage upon the Prairies— A wedding night.*

WHEN we discovered the long train of wagons it was so near the edge of the horizon it was difficult to determine what it was by the naked eye, but when the spy-glasses had been got out, and some one exclaimed "It's a company of Emigrants!" we felt the same interest and excitement which a passenger, who had been long at sea, would experience as the cry "Sail ho!" would greet his ears from the look-out aloft. The direction of the emigrants was north-west, while that of our column was nearly west, and we gradually approached each other, until finally we struck the big trace just ahead of them. When they first observed us they felt a much deeper interest than ours was at seeing them— for our wagons not yet having come in sight, they supposed us to be a large band of Pawnees; but as soon as we had come near enough for them to witness the compactness and regularity of the column, they knew at once we were dragoons, and three or four of the principal men of the party came galloping over to meet us. They expressed the utmost gratification when they were informed that it was the purpose of Colonel Kearney to take his command so far upon the route as the Great South Pass, as at that point of their journey they would have escaped all danger of attack from the Indians.

The progress of a company of emigrants across what the geographies denominate as "The Great American Desert," is one of exceeding interest; and although the original idea of that progress presents to the mind only a large number of ox-wagons, with rustic drivers—yet, underneath it are matters that afford ground for far more serious consideration than one would at first thought imagine. It is not the mere performance of a long journey by these families, with their flocks and herds, and their little all of worldly wealth, that calls for particular notice; though that alone, when looked upon in connection with the loneliness, the dangers and the privations which attend it, is a matter worthy of peculiar attention: it is their destiny when that journey shall have been completed, and the influence that destiny may hereafter exert—not only on the country they have left behind, but on the world at large—that makes the simple passing along of these people—humble though they may be —a subject inviting the most profound reflections. They are journeying to the fulfilment of that destiny, and in that light, above all others, should they be regarded.

The company which we first saw, consisted, as we were informed, of seventy men capable of bearing arms, besides a proportionate number of women and children. They had fifty large and well made wagons, each covered with white canvass, and drawn by three or four yokes of oxen. Wherever the country would admit of it the trace was formed by two parallel roads, five or six rods apart, and in such places the wagons moved in two columns opposite each other, there being twenty-five in each column. The men were well armed—each one having a rifle, and many in addition to it, had a brace of pistols and a large knife, which they wore in their belts. Generally, they were clad in coarse homespun cloth, with broad brimmed glazed hats. Some had buckskin hunting frocks, but the most of them wore loose blouses made of Kentucky jane. These were secured around their waists by the broad leathern belts—and outside of all hung their powder horns and ball pouches. Every man seemed to be in fine health—full of energy and spirit, and so browned by exposure to the weather, as to make him appear like anything but an individual who would shrink from hardship or danger. The fact of their moving to such a distance, and by such a route, is in itself a sufficient proof of their enterprise and courage, though they are abundantly able to show a still stronger one to whoever may have any curiosity of testing the point by molesting them while on their way, or even after they may arrive at their destination.

It was really a beautiful sight to see this company while on the march. The white topped wagons—the long line of cattle—the horsemen upon each flank, with their long rifles—the drivers with their big whips—and all moving so regularly forward, that when viewed from a distance, it seemed as if they were united and propelled by the same power. A quarter of a mile in the rear came the loose stock, driven by some ten or fifteen mounted men, and consisting of horses, mules, oxen, cows, young cattle and calves. The continued rumble of so many heavy wagons—the tramp of so many hoofs, together with the lowing of the cows—the bleating of the calves—the occasional neighing of the horses and braying of the mules, as they saw the animals of our long column sweep past them; the tinkling of innumerable bells—the loud voices of the drivers— the sharp and frequent cracking of their long whips; and in addition, now and then rising above all might be heard the measure of some familiar hymn, or the burden of some old song; and the boys and girls laughing and shouting as they frolicked along between the two columns—and mothers singing to their little children in the wagons, or calling their wondering attention to us and telling them "those are the soldiers who are going with us"—all these sights and all these sounds, though common and homely, have a peculiar attraction anywhere, but seen and heard here, and considered in connection with the purposes which have drawn them away from the bounds of civilization, are doubly interesting.

As we marched a great deal faster than the emigrants, we had only time to take a hurried glance at this company. This sketch may give the reader a faint idea of how they appear to the mere traveller, who has had but a few moments in which to give them a passing notice. One mile further along we went over a fine and well timbered stream, which ran S.E. into the Little Blue.

After marching a few miles farther we encamped upon the bank of another well wooded stream, which also runs into the Little Blue. Several of our wagons belong to citizens, and to save expense they are to be turned back as soon as their loading of flour can be issued. As two of them are to start for Fort Leavenworth to-morrow, all the gentlemen are busily engaged in writing back to their friends. These teams are the "slow line" of our mail route to the States, but as a horse belonging to one of our sportsmen considerately took it into his head to start home on "express" this morning, it does not so much matter, as he will be received there if one might judge from the speed with which he set out, long before the information which they will convey. From this unfortunate elopement of his proud and high mettled charger, his owner has been razed down to one of the lowest, longest-eared and "kickingest" donkeys that ever a man bestrode—and when compared with the action, the grace, the power and beauty of the runaway horse, personifies to a shade the most opposite extreme from the sublime. His rider, however, looks upon his loss with real philosophy.

Sunday, May 25

We had not proceeded more than six miles this morning before we passed another large company of emigrants, with an immense drove of stock. Before noon we marched over a high and barren prairie, which was the divide between the Little Blue and Main Blue. The soil is so poor through this part of the country, that except in the immediate vicinity of the water courses, there is but very little grass. At twelve o'clock we crossed quite a large stream running South, and which was well fringed with timber. The balance of the day's march was over an elevated table-land, nearly destitute of vegetation, and here and there intersected by deep ravines, which were washed out by rains in wet seasons, but which are entirely without water in dry weather. They are generally very deep, and their sides are so steep from the continual sliding down of sand, gravel and clay, that it is impossible to pass them with wagons, or even horses, except at unfrequent intervals, where their sides are less precipitous and partly covered by turf. This is the character of the uplands through this whole section of country. In order to avoid the ravines the trace is frequently very tortuous in its direction. When we came to the next stream the grass had been so completely eaten off in its neighborhood by the cattle of the companies that had gone on, that we were obliged to turn back a mile, where, in a large hollow, we were fortunate enough to find sufficient for the night. The only clump of timber within five or six miles was upon the stream we had just left, and from thence the wood for cooking our meals had to be brought. The water for our coffee, and that required for our animals, we found in some holes nearer by. So far the horses, mules, cattle and sheep have hardly "fallen off" at all. With but one or two exceptions the days have been quite cool, and they have travelled with much ease.

MONDAY, MAY 26

Our general direction for the whole of to-day's march was but little north of west. At four miles from our last encampment we crossed another affluent of Blue River, called "Sandy." Its course, so far as we could see, was nearly south. The scenery, as we descended from the high plains to its valley, was very beautiful. The level prairie above slopes down to it upon each side by a series of small hills and steps, which being covered by grass, and here and there groves of oak sprinkled sparsely upon them, gave the whole landscape much the appearance of a highly cultivated country, as one sees it in some of the old towns of New England. The oaks were very nearly the size and shape of apple trees, and sometimes acres would be covered with them, in such a manner as to give a perfect resemblance, when viewed from a distance, of an orchard; and but for the absence of houses and fences, it was difficult to realize that the whole valley had not been improved by the farmer. The stream that meanders through it has a slight border of cotton-woods, elms and willows. Its water is very clear, and runs over a smooth bed of sand. The soil of this valley cannot be considered good, as it is so light and filled with gravel that if it were torn to pieces by the plough and exposed to the sun, it would be incapable of holding moisture, or dressing sufficient to sustain a crop. But protected by its present covering of thin turf, it is able to furnish enough grass to make it do very well for a stock range. About two miles west of the Sandy, and encamped upon a little branch that runs into it, we passed upon our right another company of emigrants, having some sixty wagons and a large drove of animals. On account of the difficulty they have of finding sufficient grass where two or three companies arrive at a stream on the same night, some of them are obliged to lay by until the others have gone on so far as to keep out of their way. Where there are such immense herds of cattle and but little feed they are compelled to let them go a great ways from camp to find enough to eat; and besides the danger of losing them entirely, a great deal of time is wasted every morning in getting them together, ready to move on. If it were not for these serious inconveniences, four or five companies might be united for mutual protection. We then began to ascend a high and nearly barren prairie, with a small stream upon each hand, until mid-day, when we were completely out of sight of every vestige of either wood or water, and nothing but a wide plain stretching out on every hand, like an ocean. Sometimes we would come to the dry beds of some wet-weather brooks, but they were too small to break the uniform level that surrounded us. A large cloud of dust just on the edge of the horizon ahead indicated that still another company was near us, and on the march in that direction, although as yet no other signs of it were visible. Soon, however, the white canvass wagon-tops began to loom up through the mirage—then the horsemen, and then the dark mass of moving cattle. It was but little wonder that this company raised a dust, for reckoning in the cattle they worked, and those they drove, they told us as we passed them that they had fifteen hundred head. It was with much difficulty that we could keep our little herd from being swallowed up in their big one. And the only way we could get our cattle by was to turn out

to the right long before we got up with those belonging to the
emigrants, and then hurry them along with a rush. Every now and
then some of ours would break through the guard and gallop as
hard as it could for the large flock, when three or four dragoons
would start after, at a dead run—after they had got by it a series
of dodging took place on both sides, until the ox would find the
horsemen were getting the best of it, when he would turn and scam-
per back as fast as he could, and bellowing at every leap. It was
the same way with the cattle of the emigrants; as soon as they saw
ours a general lowing commenced, and sometimes whole rafts of
them would attempt to come over, when a still more active scene of
running and dodging took place before they could be got to return. This company was from Tennessee, and seemed to be composed of good substantial farmers, with their families. Many of the
young ladies belonging to it were very pretty, and their travelling
dresses were made with some pretensions to taste and fashion as well
as comfort. A Miss Williams seemed to be the belle of them all—
and if a beautiful figure, and a handsome face, whereon ripe lips,
red cheeks and large black eyes were set off by the most roguish
kind of an expression, are calculated to make an impression upon
the young beaux of the valley of Wallamette, there will certainly be
a sensation when she gets there.

However, many created one even before then, and several mar-
riages have taken place first and last on the route—one quite
recently, and in a party we have already passed. A wild harum-scarum
sort of a man, by the name of Captain M., having been out to
Oregon a year or two ago, and returned again to Independence,
endeavored to hire himself as a guide to one of the companies that
was just organized. The men to whom he offered his services told
him they had heard there was a plain road all the way, and they could
not see why it was necessary to have any one to point it out to
them, especially when so many other companies would be going
along at the same time. Upon that Capt. M. got up on a barrel, and
gave his reasons why a guide was absolutely necessary, and that,
too, in a set speech. "Feller beans! you don't know what yer under-
takin' you don't by the eternal Moses! Jest you tell me whar you

think you'll bring up if you pretend to start without nerry guide. If you have any idee of bringin' up short of—you'll find yerself mistaken, by—! Now, I've bin to Oregon, an' I reckon as how I know the way. I offer to take on with you out of pure love for my fellermen—not that I care a—for the dollar a day. No query. You think thar's a trail—well, so there is, and feller beans, that thar trail leads through a howlin' wilderness, and in that thar wilderness thar's injuns, by—! I've been thar an' I know 'em. Ask anybody. An' them injuns will not only take the har of yer own sculps, but off'er yer wives an' yer innercint prattlers, by the eternal Moses! No query. *I've* seen 'em—ask anybody. I tell you I've been thar, and I know the whole story, from a to izzard. An' why moutent I? can you reckon? No, by—you jest can't. Bekase thar's a road is nothin'. Who has ever hearn of erry crowd, I don't care a—how small it was, that didn't have a guide on the big perarys. Why, even *one* man couldn't travel alone without one—not to save his life. No query. I've been thar, I tell you, and I *know*. Ask anybody. Jest you go on, and when them injuns come upon you jest you think what I tell you. But injuns isn't half. You git on the big deesert an' yer'll want water, an' so will yer wives an' your helpless orphins, an' so will yer beasts; an' grass, too, by the eternal Moses! Well, yer'll jest naturally not find any 'less you have a guide! An' you'll famish even when you've passed by *fifty* bilin' springs that *I* know."

Notwithstanding Capt. M.'s profanity and his broad assertions, the company employed him, sure enough. He had not a thing in the world—so we were informed—but the horse he rode, his soiled buckskin hunting dress, and a long rifle and bowie knife, yet, for all that, he won the heart of a young lady who had made up her mind to seek her fortune on the other side of the mountains. And although her friends advised her not to have him, (her father and mother were both dead,) marry him she would, in spite of all they could say to prevent it. The night the company arrived at the Little Blue was the one set apart for the ceremony, and it was performed with due observances by a quondam justice of the peace, from some State on the Mississippi. The company unanimously voted the happy couple a nuptial wagon, and after the evening was spent in enjoying the good things that could be raised by the joint exertions of all the families, the bride was conducted to her new home. Soon after the bridegroom followed, and in a few minutes the lights in all the wagons were extinguished, and a profound silence reigned throughout the little encampment, broken only by the heavy tread of the sentinels on duty, and the noice made by the feeding of hundreds of cattle. However, about twenty of the stout, hearty young fellows, who were along, were determined to have some more fun before the night was out, and after everything was quiet they got a long rope, and tying it to the end of the tongue of the extemporaneous car of Hymen, at a given signal they started with it at full speed through the line of sentinels and out upon the wild prairie. This way and that—over rough ground and smooth, did they go, as if Beelzebub himself was after them.

"H-11 upon *trucks*!" roared the bridegroom, "what upon earth is to pay now. Indians, by the *eternal* Moses! Whar in *thunder* is my rifle."

The bride shrieked and the captain hallo'd, but it was no use; on they went like lightning, scaring the cattle into a perfect stampede, and giving the sentinels as much as they could attend to to keep them from running off. After a moment's reflection the captain understood the whole matter, and pacifying the bride by telling her "it was only the boys, after all," he ran to the bow of the wagon and attempted to leap out; but he might as well have jumped from a locomotive, for just then the wagon was going down an inclined plain like jehu. "Fellers! now by—! it's time to stop. Fun is fun, you know. I tell you, by the eternal Moses, to whoo!—WHOO!! Jeems *Rice*! aint yer never going to stop! If you hadn't stole my gun I'd pepper you—d—d if I wouldn't—WHOO-O!" Just then they let go the rope, and separating, returned to camp in different directions. The Captain came in, but every soul was snoring like the seven sleepers. He got the sentinels to go and help him haul back his bride, and after giving one a dollar to keep an eye on the boys, he again retired to spend his first

"Nicht wi' a wife."

That is the way the thing is done upon the prairies.

CHAPTER V

ARRIVAL AT THE VALLEY OF THE BLUE—*Awful storm—Captain M—the Oregon Pilot—Description of the Valley from the ground—Hunting—Lieut. Franklin and Mr. Simpson overtake us.*

MONDAY, MAY 26

IT WAS late in the afternoon, and we had long since passed the company of emigrants spoken of in the last chapter. The dim outline of their white-topped wagons—the dark masses of their immense herd of cattle—and the high cloud of dust that shot up from them like a dense pillar of smoke—were all indistinctly visible upon the level waste far away to the rear. For hours not a tree or hardly a spire of grass had refreshed our eyes—nor had we, during that time, seen a drop of water with which to slake our thirst. Nothing, in short, had broken the dreary monotony that surrounded us, but the tramp-tramp-tramp- of our long column as it kept steadily on its course—or the clang of hundreds of sabres as they swung heavily to and fro against the iron stirrups. But all at once we came as it were, to the edge of the barren prairie over which we had been travelling so long, when a scene of indescribable loveliness burst full upon our gladdened sight, as if called into being in a moment by a wand of enchantment. It was the Valley of the Blue!—covered with verdure and strewn with flowers.

We descended into this valley by a circuitous road and encamped close upon the margin of the river. Near night-fall—just as evening was beginning to stretch its sombre and lengthened shadows over the land—the company of emigrants, which we had passed, came into view on the distant verge of the prairie, and began to wind

189

slowly down the declivity by the same trace on which we had marched. Their poor cattle—tired with their long day's travel, and faint for the want of food and water—expressed their joy as they caught sight of the crystal stream and fertile fields below; and lowing and bellowing as they hurried downwards past the cumbrous and tardy wagons—they frantically galloped across the plain and dashed by hundreds into the river,—from whence, after their thirst was quenched, they one by one emerged and scattered in every direction to feed on the rich repast that nature had so bountifully spread out before them.

The emigrants encamped upon the bank of the Blue nearly a mile above us—and by the time their wagons had been placed in a compact circle—their tents pitched and fires lighted in the interior of it—and the chain of hardy and vigilant sentinels had been thrown around the whole, every vestige of day had left the heavens and darkness the most profound had fallen over the earth. During the evening until tattoo, we could at times hear the loud voices of the men here and there hallooing to their cattle as they gathered them up nearer to their encampment; and, as the lazy breeze of night floated slowly down the valley, there came borne upon it, now and then, the fitful cadence of some old and familiar tune, sung by women and children: now rising to distinctness as the winds freshened, and now sinking to a murmur as it died away; yet all mellowed by distance to a plaintive sweetness. But after that time all was still; except, where from some far off hill the unearthly and prolonged yell of a hungry wolf went echoing away into the gloom and silence; or when answering back to it from some remote grove, the dismal whoop of the owl came booming upon the ear through the darkness.

Such, as nearly as these rough notes have power to describe it, was the appearance of this Fairy Land of the West before the sun went down, and before our command and the travellers for Oregon had reared within it their two busy little cities;—and in such a manner did the deep night slowly and solemnly envelope it. We had all expected—as we spread our blankets upon the grass floor of our tents, and rolled ourselves up in them to forget our fatigues in a refreshing sleep—that nothing could possibly occur to break our rest until reveille. But in this we were most sadly disappointed. It seemed as if the storm-gods had determined to punish us for coming so far from the haunts of life and bringing with us the harsh clang of arms—the braying of trumpets—the trampling of iron hoofs to disturb the repose and desecrate the beauty of this sanctuary of nature—wherein she had exerted to the utmost her matchless cunning to shadow forth her own sweet ideal of heaven, and then, with jealous affection, had hid it in the bosom of a desert,—and, therefore, sent upon us one of their most terrible tempests.

We were aroused from our slumbers by the roar of the distant wind and the startling peals of thunder which every minute broke with awful crash immediately above us, and then rumbled through the valley around, or rolling over the hills, muttered and wailed across the vast desert beyond. Like a war and struggle of hissing and fiery serpents—bright streams of lightning darted down to earth, or shot from cloud to cloud in a zig-zag and contorted course, and illuminated with their lurid and tremulous glare every object of the surrounding scene. Many of our horses broke loose and ran screaming hither and thither through the encampment; and the cattle of the emigrants scattered in frightened droves over the plain. Everything seemed to be in confusion and uproar where but a few hours since all was so quiet and calm; and mingled with the howling of the storm there could be heard the loud voices of the dragoons as they called to each other to assist in securing their alarmed animals, and the clatter of countless hatchets driving picket pins more firmly into the ground, or fastening down the flapping walls of the reeling tents. Nearer and nearer came the tempest, and at length burst upon us in all its fury. The cold rain poured down, not in drops, but in gusts and streams, and so hard as almost to take one's breath and completely to drench us through in a moment. The ground becoming soft from the moisture, would not hold the pins, and many of our tents, unable to sustain the weight of both the wind and water, vanished in a twinkling from between us and the sky—and then the flood came upon us direct from the open windows of heaven. There was no avoiding it by running, for there was no place to creep into that it did not pelt through; and the only alternative left, was to cover our faces with our wet and heavy blankets and lay quiet; at the same time running the risk of being trampled to death at any minute by the horses. It could not possibly have rained so hard at the time of the flood.

TUESDAY, MAY 27

When reveille aroused us from our beds every trace of the storm had vanished, and the whole heavens were as clear as a bell. A mild wind blew gently from the westward, and the surrounding groves were vocal with the songs of birds. The sun soon came up, and, as if smothering a laugh in a vain endeavor to appear not only dignified, but astonished at the doleful figures we cut, he seemed to say—"Hail Col-*um*-bia! why how damp you look!"—just as if *he* did not know all the time what had been the matter.

The command was given until nine o'clock to get everything dry and in order again. When that hour arrived we took up our line of march and continued it along the left bank of the river towards its source. The emigrants had suffered as much from the storm as we had. Their tents had all blown down; but fortunately the women and children had been lodged in the wagons and none but the men got a drenching. As we passed along by them, Capt. M. of their party—a gentleman whom the reader may possibly recollect—accosted us in his modest and peculiarly elegant manner.

"Hail—*low*, feller sodgers! by the eternal Moses *didn't* it blow; an' *no* query? and Jeemes *River*! *didn't* it rain? Why con-*trive* such durned weather, I say. It does beat all natur' sure enough. I allow may be some o' yer might have got wet. Eh? Well, 'mong us, feller sodgers!— 'cept the women and plunder, yer couldn't find a dry har, by the eternal Moses. No query? Ask anybody. Come, 'light; and we'll jine yer in a jiffy. No? Well, then, just tell 'em all at the Pass that, by—! we're *coming*—the whole of Greenbriar, and peert at that. So good bye to yer!"

All of which we promised most faithfully to perform; and again left them far behind us. The Blue is upwards of three hundred miles in length, and receives through its tributaries the most of the water that flows southward from the elevated table that lies between the

Lower Nebraska and Kanzas Rivers. When swollen with heavy rains it is quite turbid from being filled with a brown detritus, caused by the falling in of its banks, which are of dark alluvium. But usually it is very clear and runs with a uniform and rapid current. Its general course for the first third of its length is considerably north of east. It then runs east to the point where we first struck it, when it turns to the southeast, and keeps that direction to its confluence with the Kanzas. As has been already remarked, it is bordered by a fine growth of trees, consisting principally of cotton-wood, sycamore, oak, and hickory. This timber is not continuous, however, but divided into groves by frequent tongues of grass land stretching in from the prairie on each side.

Late in the afternoon, after having made a long march, we came to where the river formed a bend nearly into the bluffs. These we were obliged to ascend; and, after describing a wide detour upon the uplands to avoid a deep and impassable ravine, we again returned to the valley and pitched our tents just under the hills upon the second embankment, which at this place was some twenty-five or thirty feet high and stretched along in a straight line for five or six hundred yards like the curtain of a fort, and terminating at each end in a natural bastion. Back from the edge of this there was a level parterre just large enough for our square. All of our animals were picketted in the fine grass upon the plain below, while the sentinels were posted along the eminences some fifty feet above us: the guard tents perched on a still more elevated promontory, which required no effort of imagination to make it resemble an ancient watch-tower. Our old campaigners all agreed that they never had seen a spot so beautiful, or so admirably adapted by nature for the purposes for which it was then occupied. In almost every respect it was our realized ideal of just what a cavalry encampment ought to be.

We have passed two varieties of the cactus to-day. One—the common—just in bloom, and another resembled in form the pineapple, with a single dark purple blossom upon its top. The whole valley has been painted with flowers of every hue from pearly white to deep carnation. Some of which were very delicate and fragrant.

We also saw considerable game. Spanish curlews (*sickle-bills*), upland plover, grouse, and ducks were scared up at almost every rod; and antelopes were seen from time to time, but not near enough to be taken. Our hunters rode at some distance from us upon the flanks of the columns, and enjoyed fine sport in keeping up a sort of running fire at the birds; some of which it is thought were seriously wounded; especially a few killdees; for they would only fly a short distance at a time—and then hobble along over the ground as if every leg and wing had been broken. However, whenever the sportsmen dismounted to pick them up, they seemed suddenly to recover strength enough to fly away, and that, too, with wonderful alacrity.

The two fishing rods were very successfully employed this evening. The homemade one, by the way, was by far the most in luck, and landed a basket full of cats, kittens, sun-fish, perch, and hickory shad, in a very short time. Some elegant "casts" were made with the other, but the fish did not seem to appreciate them, and either kept at a wary distance or went to bite at the hook depending from the one of less pretensions. After dark its owner thought he felt one most glorious nibble. "Ah! them's um!" said he, and giving a vigorous jerk he had the misfortune to lose both the fish and his line, which snapped in two within a foot of his rod. However, he recovered the latter the next morning—the fish having had the honesty to disengage the hook from his jaws and fix it firmly into the top of a willow which bent over into the water, and was kept in continual agitation by the force of the current.

WEDNESDAY, MAY 28

To-day we continued our course up the valley for the most of the time, though to cut off the distance, made by its occasional bends to the southward, we now and then went over a point of high prairie; but always descended again to the bottom lands whenever they swept northward sufficiently to allow us to keep our direction while marching upon them. The timber along the river has fallen off considerably as we have advanced, and the soil become less fertile. The uplands have, also, changed somewhat in their general character; their surface, in place of being level, is bent into long undulations, and is composed of sand, with only a slight admixture of gravel. We have seen in the distance several affluents well skirted by wood which have fallen into the Blue from the south, but have crossed only one stream that ran into it from the north, and that was very small and bordered by a few willows, with here and there a stunted and diminutive cottonwood. The vegetation, even in the valley, has become thin and short in proportion as the soil has grown more sandy and sterile; and to-night our encampment extends for nearly a mile along the bank of the river. The various divisions are detached from each other at uncertain intervals and their animals are picketed wherever a sufficient quantity of grass can be found to furnish them with only a scanty supply for the night. The elevated table-lands make no further pretensions to a dress of green—but everywhere present to the eye a brown and desolate expanse, with not herbage enough to be considered even an apology for a garment wherewithal to cover their nakedness. It is true, that here and there can be seen a thin clump of withered and shrivelled grass, or meagre and sickly artemisia, or it may be a few yellow and dwarfish cacti.

Lieut. Franklin of the Topographical Engineers had been directed by Colonel Abert, the chief of his corps, to joint Col. Kearney and go out with the Expedition. With a view of doing so he started from the East by the way of the Lakes. From the violent storms he encountered on those waters he was detained so long upon the route that he did not arrive at Fort Leavenworth until some days after we had left. He there procured his horses, and being furnished with an escort of dragoons, and a pack animal on which to convey his instruments, he immediately started upon our trace. He was accompanied by Mr. Simpson, of St. Louis, who had also been detained, but who was likewise to go with us as a guest of his brother-in-law, one of the officers of the regiment. They arrived at our encampment to-night; having ridden two hundred and seventeen miles in five days and a half. They brought us the latest and only news from the "States" which we shall probably receive for many a long day.

CHAPTER VI

THURSDAY, MAY 29

SOON after we started this morning we ascended to the elevated prairie, diagonally from the Valley, which now bore too much to the southward any longer to be followed. After marching about five miles we came to a small stream—affluent to the Blue. It had a narrow margin on which we found some tolerable grass. Here the column was halted and the horses permitted to graze until the wagons came up; and here, also, was encamped another small company of Emigrants. We had proceeded but a few miles beyond this stream—our course changing around to the northwest to avoid some deep and impassable gorges making back into the uplands from the south—when we discovered a party of Indians just upon the horizon and moving across the plain in a northeasterly direction. The day being very hot and there being hardly a breath of wind, a mirage rose from the dry and sterile prairie which produced a crinkling motion of the air near the surface of the ground, similar in appearance to that arising from a heated stove. The line of sight being tremulously refracted by it, every far off object had neither definite place or certain proportion; nor after it was once seen did it remain steadily visible; but rose into view or disappeared again, as one sometimes sees the "loom" of a distant coast from ship-board, as the vessel rises and falls with the long swell of the sea. Whenever upon the plains the air is affected in this manner, every remote depression of the general surface of the ground—however slight it may be—seems covered with a sheet of water;—and where repeated undulations occur these spectre-like as frequently appear;— the intervening elevations rising out of them like islands. Under such circumstances the whole country presents the most singular aspect; and any one who had never witnessed this phenomenon, if he were suddenly placed upon a given point, could never believe that what he saw surrounding him was not real land and water—a regular and positive Polynesia in miniature—and not an illusion which the first shower or high wind might dissipate in a moment, and leave in its stead nothing but an arid and uneven waste. On these occasions the column when viewed from a distance seemed now to be travelling over terra firma, and now wading through glassy firths; the lines

> "Tramp, tramp, along the land,
> Splash, splash, along the sea"—

precisely describing its appearance. And it was also the same with the Indians, who were now visible. Some of them were armed with long lances—some with fusees—but the most with bows—and had quivers upon their backs filled with arrows. Their horses and mules were loaded down with packs of dried buffalo meat and skins, which gave them an outline similar to that of camels; and as their owner lead or drove them forward—the whole party resembled a scattered caravan of Arabs. Those that were nearest to us seemed of natural figure and size—but those miles away had the most fantastic shapes. The men being giants excessively attenuate, and the animals about three feet long and ten feet high.

We intersected their trace—which was formed of eight deeply trodden paths running parallel with each other, and which from all appearances had been travelled upon for ages—just at the point where the head of their party had arrived when our column came up. They proved to be a large band of Pawnees returning to their villages upon the Nebraska from a successful hunt in the buffalo country. They informed us that in the direction from whence they had come—the southwest—the buffalo were only three days off— and that there the country was covered with them on every hand. This of course was gratifying intelligence as it gave us evidence of our vicinity to our anticipated and locomotive depots of subsistence stores. After a short halt near their trace, we again moved on, but changing our course to the south of west—and we soon saw them in the distance growing taller and thinner, as the mirage increased between us—until at last their shadowy forms flitted up and down— disappeared—then came into view again—then trembled upon the sight for a moment, and then finally vanished by being engulfed in a visionary sea.

After marching until three o'clock over this parched and sandy prairie which was here and there bent into gradual and shallow hollows where a sparse and blighted crop of grass enabled them to urge only a feeble claim to a suit of green—and where we found in holes and old buffalo wallows, now and then, a little tepid water filled with insects, by which our cattle could make out to quench their thirst—we came to a very respectable little pond—comparatively speaking—when a halt for an hour was ordered that the animals might refresh themselves upon the passable vegetation that surrounded it. From this place for the rest of the day our course hauled around to W. 15 N. We now began to ascend an inclined plain, and far off in the distance its upper edge ended by a long range of blue hills which from their conical and regular shape we knew at once to be what the prairie travellers call "the coast of Nebraska." From away to the southwest where in confused masses they were lost to our sight, and passing along diagonally in front of us to where they again disappeared in the northeast, they were pictured in strong relief against the bright sky like the huge and dark waves of a mighty ocean, could they be viewed in profile. These hills, or bluffs, mark the southern boundary of the far-famed Valley of the Nebraska; and before sun-set we had arrived at their summit, and looked down upon it as upon an immense. lake, level apparently as water, but covered with a variegated carpet of grass and flowers. The broad river lay along upon it like an Arabesque embroidery of silver,—embracing the line of dark foliage which covers Grand Island—and with its many channels, winding in and out among the wood-covered knolls that here and there seemed to sleep upon its bosom. While away beyond, the horizon was bounded by the faint undulations of the opposite "coast."

The hills that form the Coast of the Nebraska are composed almost entirely of sand, and from their appearance one might easily fancy that they are but the drifts piled up in ages gone past, by the force of the wind as it swept down the valley, long before it was covered by its present thin matting of turf and when it was only a broad and barren desert. They are clad by a slight crop of grass growing in little isolated tufts, which affords a scanty sustenance for the elk and antelopes that feed upon their sides—watch out from their summits, or hide in their intervening hollows. Several of the latter of these animals we have seen this afternoon, both upon our right hand and upon our left. After having approached us sufficiently near to satisfy their curiosity as to what we were, they galloped away over the hills with the fleetness of the wind, and were soon out of sight.

We descended to the level below through a sort of gorge—the wheels of our wagons cutting deeply into the sand the whole way—and after marching between three and four miles, we came to the bank of the river and encamped; the men *wading* across to a small Island for the night's supply of feed—there being no timber upon the main land. The point where we struck the Nebraska is in Latitude 40° 44′, and Longitude 99° 5′;—the bed of the river being 2000 feet above the level of the sea. It is also 247 miles from Fort Leavenworth—reckoning the distance from day to day by our rate of travel.

Previous to our coming over the bluffs, and about four miles back from them, we passed a company of Emigrants whose cattle were so exhausted by their long day's toil and the excessive heat, that they were obliged to halt and spend the night where they were—with not a stick of wood wherewith to build a fire, or drop of water to drink, and hardly a spire of grass about them, although their herd numbered some five or six hundred animals: and besides, there is encamped about half a mile above us, yet another company, and having a still larger drove of stock. The men of it came down to visit the commanding officer, and through him kindly offered us as much fresh milk as we might want. We gladly availed ourselves of their generous hospitality, and soon had all our coffee pots—tin cups and canteens, brimming with that sweet luxury.

As the sun went down its yellow rays lay like a flood over the land, and bathed each object in a glorious light. And while the western sides of the distant hills gleamed as if covered with gold, those toward the east were already mantled in the dark shadows of evening. It was a quiet and beautiful scene—that valley—and our two encampments seemed to add a charming diversity to its loveliness. Here the tents of the Dragoons stood in one long line upon the bank of the river. In rear of them were dozens of men bringing large bundles of wood over the water; while in front hundreds of horses were feeding upon the plain; and armed sentinels were marching to and fro outside of all. Yonder was the little circular village of the Emigrants, nestled, as it were, close up to the side of an oasis of timber. Long columns of blue smoke were curling up lazily from it —and clustered around were the numerous herds: some of the cattle industriously grazing—some lying down, and some playing; while here and there might be seen a hardy horseman with his long rifle: sometimes riding this way and that, and keeping vigilant guard— and sometimes pausing to enjoy the prospect around, or perhaps to muse upon the serious and uncertain one ahead. Such in brief was the rough outline of the picture that surrounded us—its stillness only disturbed by the tinkling of bells and the lowing of cows; and although we have seen others more sublime, and, from their stern features, better calculated to stamp a deeper impression upon the memory, still, this possessed an indescribable attraction which we can never wholly forget.

We remained encamped for the whole of May 30th, in order that our horses, mules, and cattle, might recover somewhat from their fatigue. Besides the grass where we were was much better than any we had yet seen since we left the Nemaha. An ox being killed we got a taste of fresh meat—the first we had eaten on the campaign. One or two turtles were caught during the day, and a catfish or so;

and when the dinner hour came—what with the milk the Emigrants gave us—and a taste, or such a matter, of butter—to say nothing of some French Portable Soup—a little old Cheshire cheese—a few olives, and a bottle or two of claret, with a pipe to top off with—we fared right well; indeed, one might say sumptuously, when everything had been taken into consideration.

Some of the officers amused themselves with hunting for elk and antelopes out among the bluffs; and the old gun from the staff-wagon was called into active service for the first time. The gentleman who carried it tolled up a fine buck antelope—(one that was very fat about the kidneys, and of broad saddle and deep brisket withal—) within thirty yards; and after drawing a charming bead upon him, the cap alone exploded. The animal thereupon ran away, and he did not see him again any more. The company that was obliged to stop out upon the high lands last night, came into the valley to-day, and, also, encamped a mile or two above us; and we are now so many that we just make these old solitudes ring again with all sorts of bustle and animation. In fact, it is quite lively anywhere around. Judging from the way they go on, by the time the leading company reaches the valley of the Columbia, there will be a broad stream of the real Anglo-Saxon stock stretching from the Atlantic to the Pacific, and having a steady three-knot current. A regular Life-River, as Carlyle would say: and onwards-flowing, and tending to resolutions not yet defined, though not lacking definitionality wholly, though in part somewhat. The future is the only Sphinx: yet not a Sphinxiad in this case completely; for the reasoning Essence of the Man-soul—I like that phrase: there's marrow and fatness in it—the Man-soul—the Intellect without death, forces the Present to prophet the One To Come.

On the 31st. we again took up our line of march. Our route lay along the wide bottom-lands on the south side of the river. The grass as we proceeded seemed to grow poorer and poorer; and in the evening although we encamped on the best spot we could find, there really was not enough forage on a mile square, could it all have been collected together, to have furnished even one squadron. The river at this point is all of two thousand yards in width—and we are now just above the head of Grand Island. To-night, there being no wood within a distance of a mile and a half, our men have to bring what they need to cook their suppers with, that far, and upon their backs at that. After a hard day's journey such labor is no child's play, the reader may be sure. However, as the commanding officer firmly, yet encouragingly remarked last year, at the time when his column got caught in the trap of the Nemaha—"*Nil desperandum!*" We had harder times then than we have had yet.

Sunday, June 1

This morning the mirage again enveloped the country on every side. In looking up the river it was almost impossible to determine where the water left off and the sky began. And the distant bluffs in that direction appeared exactly like islands far out at sea; while the real islands in the river—having here and there a few trees upon them—resembled ships and boats lying at anchor near the mouth of some great roadstead. About noon we saw a company, having some fifty wagons and seven or eight hundred head of loose stock, away off upon the side of the bluffs on our left, and some two or three miles in advance of us. The men, women, and children of it appeared for a time to be gathered in a cluster upon a beautiful little eminence above where the wagons were halted. Soon, however, all but two or three men slowly descended, and then separated for their several vehicles. In a few minutes the whole train was again in motion, and winding around to the right, fell into the trace just as our column had passed along. We were wondering what such a singular departure from the known and perfectly plain road could mean, and two of the gentlemen went up to one of the emigrants who was slowly riding by himself, with a view to ascertaining the cause. He was the leader of the company; a large and stern featured man of forty. They asked him what had been the reason of his taking his party to the bluffs, and what those few men were still remaining there for.

"Strangers," said he, and his voice trembled as he spoke and big tears came into his eyes, and, one by one, rolled down his sun-browned cheeks—"the cause were a funeral, and them men thar are covering up the body of my own pretty boy.[41] Last night he left me for a better world than this—did the poor little fellow—but 'twas hard to give him up and to leave him thar in such a lonesome place."

The gentlemen both expressed much sorrow at his loss and endeavored to console him all in their power.

He was much affected and said in reply—"I should have felt better if the poor little thing had died nearer home, so I could have buried it in a grave-yard whar other children lie; but then again, strangers, if a body thinks a minnit on this pint, I allow he'll say my dear child sleeps as near the angels here as thar—so it matters but little whar I laid him. He had suffered a good deal—my little boy had."

"And without doubt he is happy now," said one of the gentlemen.

"If he isn't, strangers—the gentle little thing, who didn't know how to sin, I allow us older people stand a mighty poor chance for heaven."

CHAPTER VII

VALLEY OF THE NEBRASKA, CONTINUED—*Exciting antelope hunt—Charming shot of our Fisherman—Consequent discussions—Buffalo sign—Prairie dogs—More Pawnees—Effects of drought—Gloomy prospect—No fuel but Bois de Vache—Manner of using it—Good fare and good appetites—Bad grass and no grass mixed—Valley grows narrower and Bluffs higher—Growth on Islands—Last mail, slow line, to Fort Leavenworth—Sedentary duties, and the beauties of letter writing.*

SUNDAY, JUNE 1

THE Valley of the Nebraska from where we first entered it to the middle of to-day's march has extended from the river back to the foot of the bluffs—an average breadth of, say, five miles—without any perceptible difference in its height—except here and there, where the wind had probably blown the sand into slight mounds and drifts before they were turfed over. But about noon to-day we came to where the bottom began to be characterized by two plains as is that of the Blue, only on a larger scale. The first is not over four feet above the ordinary surface of the water and runs back generally a half mile, when a step rises from ten to fifteen feet; and from its edge, the second one inclines gradually upward to the base of the hills. The first no doubt marks the former bed of the river, and the step, its bank;—but having scooped from the sand a deeper channel it has forsaken its old ground to return to it only when swelled up with occasional conceit of a freshet. The first level has a slight crop of grass—a great many wet and miry places where flags and coarse rushes grow—while the upper plain is hard, dry, and barren. The islands in the river correspond in height with the lower bottom.

For the whole afternoon we have been travelling along the upper elevation and close to the slope that divides it from the one below. A beautiful stream of clear water has run at its foot in a direction parallel with, and about a mile distant from the river. On this plain between the stream and the Nebraska there was some exciting sport for the whole afternoon. Two fine antelopes that had been sleeping in the grass, were aroused by the noise of our column which stretched along for nearly a mile between them and the bluffs, and which was immediately followed by two companies of emigrants extending upon the trace for quite another mile. Having such an obstacle on the one hand and the river upon the other, it seemed as if to escape from our sportsmen, and a large reenforcement of hunters from the companies, would be next to impossible. A volley from the rifles of the emigrants sent them coursing up the valley with the speed of the wind, and although they were some quarter of a mile off, a desultory fire was kept up at them from shot-guns, carbines, and pistols, until they got near the head of the column, where our sportsmen lay in ambush, industriously waving to and fro their handkerchiefs fixed upon the ends of their ramrods, to attract their attention. These flags had the desired effect; and the antelopes halted and stood at gaze long before they got near them. Then came a terrific discharge of double barrels—the buckshot raising a cloud of dust as they fell in a shower upon the ground all of one hundred yards from the shooters and about three hundred from the shoot*ees*, who thereupon would turn and run this one-sided gauntlet away to the rear again—the bullets screaming through the air and knocking up the sand all around them as they went,—when another waving of flags would bring them to a stand—and then another volley would set them off for the head of the column again. A large number of our dogs that belonged to the emigrants, and a few who followed us, fired up with excitement, and ran out and yelped with a great deal of ferocity; yet having too much sense to try their speed with creatures that seemed to fly over the ground as if they had the wings of Mercury tied to their feet. This rare fun was kept up until nearly

night, when the immediate supply of ammunition which our sportsmen carried, began to run low—and the barrels of their pieces to
wax hot and white about the nipples from such an extensive explosion of caps. The flags began to droop also, for when they were not
waving at the antelopes—without being taken from the ramrods they
were in constant requisition from the profuse perspiration of their
excited owners,—and for a while there was quite a cessation of
hostilities and the poor animals slackened up their speed to an unpretending trot. By this time the command had crossed the stream
and turned in toward the river and began to encamp. This movement
made an opening through which the antelopes saw they could gain
the bluffs, and off they started. A black trundle-tail, followed by six
or eight yellow, spotted, and bow-legged tykes, getting out of all
patience—now started after them at full speed. But as soon as the
firing commenced again, and the bullets and buckshot to whiz
about their ears, the tykes one by one, gave up the chase. Not so
with Trundle. He was made of sterner stuff and kept on, as much as
to say "shoot and be damned to you, for here goes hit or miss!"
And go he did, like a quarter-horse. The antelopes kept an easy and
graceful canter, while he was down to a dead run all the time, and
losing ground at that. However, he did not seem to mind it, and
believing he could make up in bottom what he lacked in heels, he
pulled foot like a hero, the bullets falling a great deal more plenty
around him than about the chase. At length they came up near our
encampment,—when one of our fishermen, who was arranging his
tackle for a cast, dropped everything, and seizing a carbine, drew a
beautiful bead, and brought the biggest antelope down in a moment. "It's out of my line," said he, "and nothing but the absolute
danger of the animals getting away could have induced me to interfere in the matter." Trundle followed the other off over the bluffs
and out of sight. About an hour or so afterwards he came trotting
leisurely back; and having acquitted himself so handsomely our
fisherman sent his master—(one of the emigrants)—two quarters of
the buck. He generously divided the other two amongst his comrades, and gathering up his gear quietly started off to the enjoyment
of his favorite amusement. By the time our hunters came up with

their guns upon their shoulders and the little flags still in their hands —and enquired if we had seen anything of two badly wounded antelopes hobbling along that way with a black cur after them—he was perfectly absorbed from all sublunary thoughts in the intense excitement afforded him by the sport of throwing out, right and left, lethargic cats,—volatile hickory-shad,—and frisky shiners.

So ended the day's hunt. It occupied so much time and occasioned such an extravagant expenditure of ammunition, that it was no more than justice to all concerned to give a full history of such a spirit-stirring incident. Throughout the balance of the week the subject was talked over by our sportsmen with evident relish. The manner in which each shot was made,—the quantity of powder used for different distances,—the effect of the flags,—the peculiarities of the animals, and the pertinacity with which Trundle followed them, together with the danger *he* ran, &c. &c.—were all satisfactorily discussed and definitely settled. This being the first game we had taken except the turtle and fish, we all began to feel encouraged to a remarkable degree, particularly when we were credibly informed by the Captain of one of these companies, that he yesterday saw from the top of the bluffs a herd of five hundred buffaloes upon the bottom on the opposite side of the Nebraska. The grass of to-night's encampment is unusually fine and our animals are enjoying it most wonderfully;—their appetites having been sharpened by their meager fare yesterday and their long day's journey on an empty stomach. To-day we passed the first Dog-Town we have seen. The appearance, gregarious habits, and remarkable intelligence, of the little animal commonly called the Prairie Dog but which naturalists recognize as a species of the Marmot (Arctomys Ludoviciana)— have been so often described as to render a farther notice of them in these notes unnecessary. Mr. Fitzpatrick, who has spent the last twenty years upon the plains and in the mountains—and whose good sense and close observation entitle his opinions on any matter connected with them—to the highest credit—informed us that no animal with which he is acquainted—not even the beaver—bears any approach in point of shrewdness and sagacity to the Prairie Dog. They display these qualities in the selection of sites for their towns—

the manner in which they protect their burrows from water—the spiral windings of the interior galleries which makes the digging of them out next to an impossibility—the fine police which is everywhere discernible—their councils—sentinels, &c. &c. And yet they suffer rattlesnakes and owls to enjoy their municipal immunities scot free;—but whether these unpleasant associates remunerate the inhabitants for such privileges by acting in the joint capacity of public executioners, and animated sarcophagi for the victims, is a matter that has not yet been fully determined.

MONDAY, JUNE 2

By half six o'clock this morning we were on the march again. We soon came to where the deeply trodden trails of buffaloes descended from the bluffs—which by the way have been growing more high and precipitous as we have advanced—and crossed the valley from the south to the river. Besides, we passed several carcases of these animals that had been recently killed, as portions of the flesh and the hide were still clinging to the bones. At noon we thought we discovered a herd of them standing in the water on the opposite side of the river, and about a mile distant; but upon getting out our glasses we ascertained that it was but the shadows of the embankment—and the excitement that had begun to kindle at the thought of boiling hump ribs for supper as speedily died away. To-day, also, we met another hunting party of Pawnees coming over the bluffs from the southwest. They were on their return to their villages from the neighborhood of the Republican Fork of the Kanzas—and all their animals were heavily laden with dried meat and skins. There can be no doubt that we should have found buffaloes in abundance at this point, if there had not still other companies of emigrants passed along a-head of us. As we go on, the ground is hourly becoming more sterile, and the grass thinner. And what there is, seems so closely cropped, that for the whole day we have not gone by a single spot that would afford even a tolerable supply for the night. At the most favorable seasons, the crop of vegetation through this whole upper country, must from necessity, be very meagre, as the

soil is too dry, and sandy, to afford sustenance sufficient for a fruit-
ful growth; but this year the unprecedented drought has so parched
up the prairies, as literally to render them a desert, except immediately along the river. With such a long march still before us, as
we are obliged to perform—and our whole dependence for its successful accomplishment being upon what food we may find by which
to forage our animals, the prospect a-head is certainly discouraging.
The emigrants suffer still more than we do. During the night their
large herds of cattle wander off from camp for a great distance, in
their endeavors to find grass—and the whole of the cool of the
morning has to be spent in getting them together before a move can
be made. Many of them are never found again—and besides, many
are obliged to be left behind from having their hoofs so worn out
by constant travel over the hard and unyielding earth, that it is impossible for them to keep up. After making an unusually long day's
march, we encamped to-night upon what in an ordinary season,
might have been a small brook, but which is now so dried up, that
only here and there, a little stagnant water can be found standing in
puddles and filled with animalcules. This answered very well for our
horses and cattle, while for ourselves, we have to dig holes in the
black mud and sand, into which a sufficient quantity filters to supply our wants for the night. It is so impregnated with the dock-smell
of the mud, as to be extremely nauseous—but we can do no better.
This spot is nearly half way from the river to the bluffs, and the
reason why the Colonel selected it is because a few acres of old grass
grows about it, while down on the shore there is none of any kind.
Not a stick of wood can be seen within miles of us, and for the first
time our fires are built and suppers cooked with *bois de vache*, or
"buffalo chips," as the soldiers call this species of fuel. We find it in
great quantities all over the plain—and a dozen men with horse-
blankets soon collect a sufficient quantity for the use of a company
for the night. The men dig holes in the earth a foot deep—about the
same in width, and four or five feet long, with another little hole
entering it near the bottom to let in a draught. A little dry grass is
then placed in it and set on fire, when the pit is filled full of chips
that soon get to burning with a slight flame, and uniform heat like

peat. Camp kettles filled with water for coffee, or with meat for boiling, are then set on top—while tin plates with thin cakes upon them are placed around, and in a short time "supper is ready." There is nothing unpleasant in having fires made, or a meal cooked with such a material;—and the odour arising from it while burning, is far from being disagreeable. The old hunters say that buffalo ribs and marrow bones, should never be roasted before a fire made of anything else but *bois de vache*—no more than should Porter or Mountain Dew, be drunk out of any other kind of a vessel than a pewter one. The reader, surrounded by all the comforts and elegancies of life, will naturally conclude if such is the fare of campaigners upon the prairies—*i.e.* bread, meat, and coffee, prepared in this manner—for his part he had rather stay at home. It is true, a good dinner made up of a dozen fine dishes ranging from tom a la cod, in the fish line, —calf a la head, in the meat,—with pastry varying from pies a la mince down to tarts a la cranberry—to say nothing of dessert, and a bottle or such matter, of old wine, and a few regalia cigars just to take the bad taste out of one's mouth—is not difficult to set down to, though often troublesome to get up from. But then one soon gets used to all that sort of thing, and tired of it, in the bargain. While out upon the prairie, if a man rides from sun-rise to sun-set, without a mouthful to lay his jaws to for the whole time, at night plain bread and pork, with a good hearty drink of strong coffee, and a quiet and unpretending pipe of tobacco—are a kind of living he is not very likely to get sick of so long as his active exercise and long periods of abstinence continue. And as for relish—he need not trouble himself on that score;—he will enjoy his meal by the time he gets it—that he may set down as certain.

Tuesday, June 3

To-day we did not march over twenty miles as the grass grew scarcer and scarcer as we proceeded;[42] and about two o'clock in the afternoon we turned down to the right—and finding a small intervale upon the lower level where by frequently changing the animals from place to place, they could manage by industry to pick up a sufficient quantity to keep themselves from absolutely famishing, provided they had the whole afternoon and night to do it in—we encamped. This spot was like a little field of a hundred or two acres—and was surrounded on every hand by a thicket of willows and small cotton-woods. For miles the whole bottom has been cut up by an immense herd of buffaloes that must have swarmed over it quite recently, as their "sign" was still fresh. There is hardly a shrub or bush that is not covered by large mats of their hair, as they have scratched against every knot and dry limb that might in any manner assist in robbing them of their uncomfortable winter coats. And the herbage in every direction is cropped off close to the ground. The poor creatures must have fared hard, also—for we discovered along the bank of the river and amongst the willows, where they had even rooted in the earth for wild potatoes (the *arachis*) with which to appease their hunger.

For the whole of to-day's march the valley upon the south side of the river has grown much narrower, and at this point the bluffs are not over a mile and a half off. Opposite to where we are to-night they are nearly twice as high as they were when we first crossed them; the summits of the highest being estimated to be between three and four hundred feet above the surface of the water. They are piled up in the most fantastic forms, with narrow and deep gorges here and there splitting them asunder, or furrowing their sides. These gorges are filled with a scrubby growth of red cedar, whose long lines of almost black foliage present a singular contrast to the grey and arid surface of the grotesque pinnacles to whose ungenerous bosoms they seem to cling to like so many famished leeches. Some of the islands that we passed to-day have been very well wooded. The timber upon them consisted principally of cotton-wood, interspersed here and there with a few dwarfish and gnarled hackberrys, and now and then a stunted ash. We also noted a few sumachs growing along the shore whenever the bank of the river was rendered high from points of the second table that shot in close to the water.

We are now very near the Forks of the Nebraska. As the Colonel contemplates sending back to Fort Leavenworth the two remaining citizen-teams, and thirteen dragoons, whose horses have become too much reduced to proceed any farther, the officers are nearly all employed to-night in writing home. The teams are to commence their return march in the morning, and this is the last mail that will probably return from us to the settlements for many a long day.

The facilities for writing letters that a campaigner upon the prairies usually possess, do not lay claim to any undeserved and therefore arrogant pretensions to being peculiarly adapted for the convenience of executing the mechanical part of them in a style which, for neatness and beauty, would ever be considered as remarkable. Far from it. But looked upon so far as their capabilities may extend for doing all manner of duties which shall serve to make the epistles permanent and strong, then it is that their legitimate character and office are understood as they should be. It is quite amusing to see the gentlemen engaged to-night in what the General Regulations of the Army denominate as "Sedentary Duties." They are nearly all sitting upon the ground in front of their respective tents, and each one has a little bottle of ink propped up beside him to keep it from upsetting, a steel-pen in his hand, and upon his knees a roll of wrinkled and dogeared paper which, every time he makes a dive for a new supply of ideas, rattles and rolls over in the wind and duplicates the old ones in all sorts of inverse order on various parts of the page. It is equally as interesting—after he has speared a fresh lot—to see the way in which he glues them to the sheet. He scorns dressing them in anything like straight lines. But just sticks them down from left to right up hill, down hill, serpentine, and zig-zag; and as he dots the *I's* and crosses the *T's*, his head keeping exact time with his pen, and in all the skirts of the *y's* and bonnets of the *h's*, moving up and down *pari passu*, he may be regarded as just naturally putting in what might well be termed the intellectual licks in an exceedingly earnest and creditable manner. As for big blots, they get to be a perfect drug, and punching the pen through the paper and spattering the ink right and left, is such an ordinary occurrence that it is not minded at all, notwithstanding the *tout en semble* of the page when completed is so extremely ornamented from these fortuitous causes. Then the pen has to go through the final exercises of punctuation that are called for by a second reading; now cutting a quirl and quiddity on notes of interrogation—or making a punch and thrust on those of admiration; then giving a single parry *in quarte* on a comma—a stoccado and parry on a semicolon—two rapid stoccadoes on a colon, and finally making a grand lunge on a period. After this, dashes begin to be cut, and an extra flourish or two under the signature finishes off the inside of the affair. Then comes the folding—the pocket invariably getting too large for its contents; and then the sealing with a wafer moistened in the mouth; and to complete all—the superscription. At last, as the letter is held out at arm's length, in order the better to regard its proportions and appearance, the ink bottle capsizes, and its contents seeking the lower level where the writer sits, apprise him of the accident, by soaking up through his clothes, when a fierce "Curse the luck!" announces for the time being a cessation of his literary labors.

FORKS OF THE NEBRASKA—*A buffalo chase—Killed—Feasting—Accident—Some of the peculiarities of the buffalo—Sport of a donkey—High bluffs give out on south side of the river—Another buffalo chase—An exciting and dangerous encounter with a bull—A hope that the compositor will not hereafter habitually set up "was" for "were," "has" for "have," "manifest" for "manifold," or "Natchez" for "watches," and other words in proportion.*

WEDNESDAY, JUNE 4

OUR trace to-day has been near the foot of the bluffs, and generally about two miles from the river.[43] As we have advanced, the growth of timber upon the islands has become less and less. The bluffs, also, have diminished in height. This forenoon we observed upon their sides a stratum of white calcareous stone, it being the first of any kind that we had seen since we entered the Valley. About noon we passed the junction of the North and South Forks of the Nebraska. Some fifteen miles above where the two rivers unite, the wide bottom on the north side appears to terminate.—There, the elevated prairie runs in to the very edge of the water; and, from the force of the current continually wearing away the earth below, and the consequent sliding down of that from above, a sheer precipice all of an hundred and fifty feet in height and something over a mile in length has been formed. It marks the exact point where the North Fork enters the big valley, and is, according to our reckoning, three hundred and forty-six miles from Fort Leavenworth. The land that lies between the two rivers for two or three days journey above that place, is very high and broken into abrupt hills, some of which descend directly to the water of the North Fork; we shall therefore be obliged to proceed for some distance up the South Fork, (although it takes us considerably out of our course,) before we shall be able to cross over and follow the valley of the former river which marks almost our direct route to the South Pass.

About four o'clock this afternoon, as the head of the column ascended to the summit of a range of sand hills that ran off into the bottom like a little spur from the highlands upon our left, a small herd of buffaloes was discovered. A party of men was immediately detached to kill some of them. Several of the gentlemen volunteered their services for this exciting duty, and in a few minutes a very spirited and lively chase commenced. It was not long before the hunters came up with the buffaloes and began to fire upon them. At that, the herd divided, and each animal started off for the distant bluffs on his own responsibility. This movement separated the party in pursuit, and consequently every individual of it had his particular portion of the fun all to himself. It was a regular up and down hill business all the time, and every now and then, both hunters and buffaloes were entirely out of sight from us. Then again, we could at times see a big black bull with his pursuer hard after him, ascending a ridge a mile or so off. An animated chase would then take place along its crest. Then perhaps, the smoke of a carbine would be visible, but from the distance no report could be heard; and then the bull would go out of sight, and then the hunters, as they successively dropped over into the next valley beyond.—Then again we could see another away in a different direction—and coursing it along on a level plain between two hills, with a horseman just abreast of him, and both going forward at a killing pace—just nip and tie, with a cloud of dust rising up behind them, and the bull puffing like a high pressure steamboat. Pistol-shot after pistol-shot could then be heard; every bullet seeming to retard the buffalo's headway as it crashed in amongst his engine and boilers; until at last, to use a nautical term—he would put his helm hard down—sullenly round to, at bay, and then crack on a full head of steam for a charge. In an instant the hunter might be seen to wear ship, and ranging up abeam, again give him a broadside just under his pilothouse. This would cut away his tiller ropes so badly as to make him steer wild. Another shot would make him collapse a flue and set the blood to running through the forward scuppers in torrents; until at last, when there was no longer a soul on board able to fight, down would come his flag. Then the hunter would dismount and throwing his grappling tackle over the bull's cat-heads, board him knife in hand. So they went on; all kinds of fights in all kinds of grounds. The store-ships rigged like pack-mules soon got under way and stood across from the column to where the hottest of the battle took place. Shortly afterwards the squadrons came to an anchor near a small run about two miles from the river. Here a very good supply of grass was found and a plenty of water, but there was not a stick of wood in sight in any direction. In an hour or so, the hunters began to drop in, having in tow the pack-mules loaded down with the rigging and spars of the enemy; nice tender-loins, fleeces, humpribs, and marrow bones. Eight line-of-battle buffaloes were reported to have been captured in this engagement, and a small tender—an antelope. And, strange as it may seem, our fishermen took the most of them. A plenty of *bois de rache* was soon collected—pits dug, and fires got a going; and it was not long before all kinds of broils, and roasts, and stews, loaded the air with a fragrant odour, which to a hungry man, was exceedingly pleasant, as it betokened such a great variety of most glorious feasting. Now, reader, we are just beginning to live.

Two more companies of emigrants are encamped within a mile of us. We have come through two or three deserted Dog-Towns to-day. When they have been abandoned long enough for the grass to hide their burrows, it is extremely dangerous riding through them at a rapid pace. One of the officer's horses accidently stepped into a hole as we came over the last town and fell. His rider was thrown and very severely injured.

THURSDAY, JUNE 5

If there are many travellers along the valley, the buffaloes are apt to stray out in the highlands during the day; but as there is no water

there, they are obliged to descend to the river every night, in quest
of it. If not disturbed, they stop and feed along the intervale until
after sunrise, when they return to the hills again. However, at any
time, on the least alarm, they will gallop away for the uplands as
fast as they can go. On account of the large quantity of hair that
hangs down over their eyes they cannot see but a little way. When
the wind is blowing from them towards the hunter, they can be
approached very closely. But if the wind blows in the contrary direction, their sense of smelling is so remarkably acute, they will scent
a man at an astonishing great distance, and immediately commence
running away. They have been known to become aware of the vicinity of hunters when several miles from them.

For instance, a body of men in passing over a plain where there
are many of these animals on every hand, will notice that all those
to the leeward, though almost out of sight, will become frightened
and move rapidly still farther off; while those upon the windward
side will feed along within, it may be, gun-shot of the trace, and be
apparently unconscious of danger.

This morning before reveille, there was a brisk wind from the
south, and a small herd came leisurely down from that direction
toward our encampment, evidently to get water from the creek we
were near. They approached within less than an hundred yards of
our park of wagons without noticing us at all. The officer of the
squad, fearing that the horses would become alarmed, pull up their
picket-pins and start off in a "stampede"—directed the signal to be
blown that the men might turn out and take care of them. The
buffaloes at that stopped where they were, and began to look around
as if to ascertain what it could be that made such an unusual noise.
Just then a large donkey that had broken loose from the wagons,
walked directly up to them. When he got within about twenty
yards he brayed out a blast both loud and long, and passably awful.
No sooner did they hear that, than off they started, with the donkey
after them as hard as he could go. If now and then they paused in
their fright to listen if their pursuer was still upon their track, the
horrible sound was again sent forth, when away they would go
again—their terror increasing their speed to the utmost. The donkey

seemed determined to have a little private chase on his own account, and consequently endeavored to run in as creditable a manner as possible. He therefore husbanded his wind for a long race, and only expended a little now and then in an economical bray, just to keep the buffaloes down to what might be called convenient though respectable time. So they went on for all of a mile and a half, before the two men who had mounted their horses and started in pursuit, could gallop in ahead of the mule and turn him back. He was very loth to abandon his sport, and endeavored to dodge by and commence it again two or three times; but finding at last it was impossible to do so, he trotted leisurely to camp with as good grace as he could command.

By twelve o'clock to-day, the bluffs upon the south side of the South Fork had entirely ceased. A small range of hills that ran across our trace to the river's bank, marks the point where they terminate. The summit of many of these hills were bare, and at the time we passed over them the wind was sweeping off the sand in clouds. For a few miles farther along we found the land quite broken. Our trace through it was very circuitous. At times we were at the top of some commanding eminence from whence we could obtain an extended view of the undulating country upon our left, and then again we were winding through some quiet valley— scooped out here and there like a great basin—and opening through the hills to the river, by long, green and picturesque vistas. It was down one of these dells that a herd of buffaloes had gone for water, probably the night before, and had been tardy in feeding along back to the inlands. When they got scent of the command, they were between it and the river, and immediately commenced galloping up towards it. They seemed undetermined at first whether to pass between the rear division and the train of wagons, or to turn off diagonally, and endeavor to get by the company the fartherest advanced. The latter course they at length adopted, and swept along close to the right of the column in beautiful style. Just as they were turning by the leading files about a dozen officers and men dashed in amongst them, and for ten or fifteen minutes a real jewel of a race took place all in plain sight. The rumbling of the ground—the dust

—the rushing throng of bulls with the horsemen just flying here and there amongst them—the frequent shot—the animated hurra—the huge black carcase now and then dropped far behind with pack-mule fellows gathering around it and flaying off the red meat—and the sudden silence as they all passed out of sight over a distant ridge—like the dark shadow of a cloud—seemed to press all sorts of excited feelings through the minds of those who looked on, which can be more easily imagined than described.

Every person who has ever seen a very old buffalo bull must have noticed that his formerly long shaggy mane, and the frightful elk-locks that once hung over his face and fringed his fore-legs, have dropped off and left only a spare crop of hair to cover his now meagre and attenuated frame. Several of these antiquated veterans may be observed in every herd of any considerable size. If the younger ones get alarmed and start off at speed, the aged have to bring up the rear in the best kind of trot, or walk, as the case may be, of which their several degrees of infirmities will admit. In the chase that has just been spoken of, there was one bull of this character. He was extremely venerable, and was soon left far behind. At first he struck quite a breeze in the way of a gallop, and kept it up until the herd had gone by the head of the column and was some way off upon the prairie. He then began to fail and slacken down his speed to a swinging trot; the rest of the band fast dropping him astern. Finally as he became more and more exhausted he pulled up to a moderate walk, and every now and then stopped to rest and breathe a little. There was one young gentleman engaged in the attack who never before had hunted the buffalo, consequently the sport to him was as novel as it was fascinating. He went on in the first place pell-mell with the crowd, but being unable to get his pistol off—and his horse becoming greatly distressed from the protracted rapidity to which it had been urged—he concluded to give up the chase. As he descended into the hollow on his way back, he unexpectedly saw the old bull standing perfectly still from sheer feebleness. He stopped, pricked a little fresh powder into the nipple of his pistol, put on an undoubted cap—and boldly advanced and shot the monster on the head. The buffalo then moved on and tried to get by. The hunter having heard how ferocious these animals become when wounded and at bay, imagined that this one was now in that state, and so turned cautiously out to avoid him; meanwhile keeping a wary eye upon all his motions and loading up his pistol again as fast as possible. Again the old fellow halted and then came another shot. Then the same manoeuvres were repeated; the bull again trying to go past, and the hunter circling round and dodging about, alike to prevent him from escaping and to keep out of his way, as the exigencies of the case from time to time seemed to require, but all the while loading and firing as fast as he could. Fortunately the seventh shot dropped the bull upon his haunches, and the eighth finished him effectually. Then came the process of prying open his toothless jaws and sawing off a half or such a matter of his tongue, with a small two-bladed knife. This trophy the hunter ostentatiously hung at his saddle-bow, and then in a perfect fever of exultation and pride, at his unexpected success in this fearful combat, he mounted up and came galloping back to the column.

"Well, what luck—what luck? What did you kill?"

"Oh, gracious, gracious! don't ask me. Oh I had such a battle! To kill a cow is nothing, but to see a bull etre au abois—regularly showing fight, is the sport. So I on with a new cap and dashed at him. Bang! struck him in the head. Mon Dieu! how he came at *me*. Il a le diable au corps, says I, getting out of his way and loading up. Bang! hit him in the rump. At me he came again. Never mind says I —ruse contre ruse. And so we had it. Six shots I made at him, still he showed game. Ma foi! says I, this is regularly ouvrage de longue haleine—terrible! bad! horrid! But nul bien sans pien, says I, and banged again. That time I knocked him down in rear. Gracious, gracious! but I was glad."

About three o'clock P.M., we found some very good grass on a little creek that ran into the South Fork—and encamped. An abundance of fine fish were caught during the evening. The wood has entirely disappeared from the islands. They are now clad only by a growth of small willows; none of which are over six or seven feet in height. To-day the mercury has been 90° in the shade. As the mail is just closing, au revoir!

CROSS THE SOUTH FORK OF THE NEBRASKA–*Description of the surrounding country–March across to the North Fork–Our sportsmen obliged to hold up–A slight quandary–Our descent through "Ash Hollow"–Wretched description of a picturesque place–Beautiful trees and sweet water–Fatigues of the emigrants–Grizzly "bars" and peeps–Tolerable scenery for a new country–Vultures–Swallows–Martins–Robbing Peter to pay Paul–Bullo solo–Perilous situation and wonderful escape of an officer–Eagles–Mackinac boats aground–"Suhaws" or Sioux within striking distance–A rare curlew–A successful day's hunt for one of our sportsmen–An approximation to his account thereof, with an ending out of keeping, and in decidedly bad taste.*

FRIDAY, JUNE 6

THIS morning we continued our march up the southern bank of the South Fork for ten miles farther, when we came to a point where it was practicable to cross to the opposite shore. As nearly as we could judge, the river at this place was all of a thousand yards in width. We found its bed composed entirely of quicksands closely packed, and rendered quite firm by the rapidity of the current, which has a velocity, say, three and a half miles an hour. The water is filled with detritus, which gives it a yellowish grey color—and is so opaque in consequence, that where it is only two or three inches deep, the bottom cannot be seen. The channels are numerous and quite narrow, and vary in depth from one to three feet. They are divided from each other by sand bars that rise nearly to the surface. The islands are small—many of them being but a few rods in length. They have a covering of coarse grass, interspersed with willows some four or five feet high, and of the thickness of a man's finger. With the exception of these diminutive bushes, nothing that looks like wood can be seen in any direction.

The appearance of our column, when crossing the river, was very beautiful. All the divisions were marching by twos—and that which was leading had not reached the northern shore, before the one in the rear had entered the water. The howitzers and provision train then followed without any difficulty. However, it was very hard pulling for the mules, as the wheels kept continually cutting into the sand and giving the wagons a rapidly jolting motion, such as they would have if passing over a cord roy road. The cattle went across very well—but the distance was so great, the poor sheep liked to have perished. Whenever they could get on a sand-bar they waded along pretty well, but the moment they struck a channel, away they would go down stream until they made the next bar, when they would trot up again and recover lost ground by the time they reached the succeeding deep place. And so on. But this alternate trotting, and wading, and swimming, was so fatiguing that when they got on shore they lied down for nearly an hour from sheer exhaustion.

As the main trace to Oregon is hereafter to cross the South Fork at *this* point, it may be amiss to state that by our computation it is three hundred and eighty-four miles from Fort Leavenworth.

We kept up the northern bank of the river for the rest of the day's march. On our right hand there has been for the whole afternoon a perpendicular wall of limestone all of an hundred feet in height, and extending along in a direction generally parallel with the South Fork, but varying in distance from the shore from a half a mile to two miles; as here and there long points projected into the valley like bastions, while between them deep bays were formed.

To-night our encampment extends for over a half a mile along a little second embankment some two hundred yards from the river. There is a low wet interval between us and the water which is covered by the best grass we have seen for some days, and our animals are picketted upon it. Our fuel is still *bois de vache.* We have seen several buffaloes upon the plain on the south side of the river during the afternoon, but as we have meat enough to last for a few days we did not disturb them. Many of our cattle are getting very lame and are daily falling off in flesh.

SATURDAY, JUNE 7

After proceeding up the river for six miles farther the high precipices upon our right became less and less, and finally changed into hills with an ascent gradual enough to permit us to gain the elevated prairie above. When we had done so we found ourselves some two hundred feet higher than the valley we had just left. A fine view was then obtained of a large extent of the country south of the river, and as far as we could see it was only slightly undulating, and quite low when compared with that upon the north side, which was very broken, high, and precipitous. Our direction was then W.N.W. across a very uneven and barren prairie. After having marched a few miles we found that the whole surface of the land about us was hollowed by immense sink holes or tunnels, into which the water collects during the storms, and afterwards gradually escapes through subterranean passages to the river. About noon we passed two more small companies of emigrants. They had halted for the purpose of refreshing their cattle in the large hollows just spoken of, where some very good grass was growing. During the afternoon we saw a great many buffaloes, antelopes and white wolves, both upon our right hand and upon our left—but as a cold raw wind was blowing in our faces for the most of the day, our sportsmen found it much more comfortable to ride quietly along with the column, than to freeze themselves and exhaust their horses by doubtful chases over such a broken country. Once in a while, however, they could hardly restrain their ardor; and as we occasionally passed along close by some big bull, they would dash fiercely towards him for a hundred or two yards, but by that time their temporary excitement would gradually have become subsided, when they would trot back and travel on with us again; but meanwhile slowly gathering a new supply of animation and energy, which the sight of the next bull was sure to call forth and expend, in a like manner.

After keeping our new course for seventeen miles our progress became suddenly arrested. We all at once came to the edge of the high prairie, and from thence down to the valley of the North Fork, a distance of three miles, nothing but a chaotic mass of rocks, hills, precipices, and chasms could be seen; and through which it seemed as if it were impossible ever to proceed. We here found another large company of emigrants. They were halted and had been searching for a pass for sometime, but without success. We then turned off to the left, and having kept along for more than a mile just at the head of the deep gorges by which this "*mauvaise terre*" first begins, we also came to a halt, and Mr. Fitzpatrick started off down one of them to see if he could not find a way by which we could descend to the river. In an hour or so he returned and reported that we were then at the head of the Ash Hollow—a celebrated defile with which he was well acquainted—and through which, with but little trouble, it was practicable to take the command. We were immediately put in motion again, and commenced following our guide through a perfect labyrinth of ravines; now around some high jutting point— now along some steep hill-side—and now close by the very verge of deep and rugged channels, that ages past, had been worn down into the solid rock by the attrition of water.

After proceeding in this way for a mile, and descending all the time,—we came to a steep declivity, down which we were obliged to lower each wagon separately with ropes. By the time this was accomplished the sun was nearly set.

Down where we were the deep shadows of evening had already obtained possession, and were fast forcing the retreating light of day up the surrounding precipices. Crag after crag had relinquished its dress of gold for one of grey, until at last only a few of the highest pinnacles made any pretensions to a robe of sunshine. We now found ourselves at the bottom of a gloomy defile but a few rods in breadth, and walled in by hills that rose almost perpendicularly hundreds of feet above us. It was so crooked and so abrupt in its turnings that as we proceeded along it was sometimes quite impossible to tell in what way we were ever to get out of it. And rarely was it the case that more than one squadron at a time could be seen from any given point. Through this defile there lay a wide, dry, and sandy bed of a wet-weather stream. Here and there, strewn along upon it, we passed a great many skeletons of buffaloes. Growing along its sides, also, were several clumps of wild-cherry and current bushes; and holding to the naked crags and barren hills far above, were some dwarfish and gnarled cedars that with their long, bare, contorted, and serpent-like roots, seemed to cling there with an "agony" more painful than that huge rock suffers, which Shelly gives so much life to in his tragedy of Beatrice Cenci. One more mile, and we came to a beautiful grove of ash, and soon after a cool stream of water gushed out from the sand—the first drop we had seen since morning. By this time it got to be nearly dark. The defile now began to increase in width as we advanced, and at last we came to a fine spot of grass large enough to supply half of the command for the night. The Colonel directed one squadron to encamp near it—and pushed on with the other three divisions to the bank of the North Fork, something like a mile further. We had been so many days without seeing any trees that the reader can hardly imagine how grateful to us was the sight of those which we here so unexpectedly found. And the limpid water that flowed over the sand seemed to taste sweeter than any we had ever drank before.

The company of emigrants we left upon the high prairie had followed on after us. But their delay was so great in letting their wagons down the steep descent, that it was ten o'clock at night before they reached our first encampment. They there halted—unyoked their cattle, and let them wander in search of grass in every direction. Long before this company came up, we could hear the echo of the wagons as they rumbled along in the tortuous and dismal passage, from whence we had just emerged—and the loud voices of the men as they urged forward their tired and almost famished cattle. And the reflection that women and children were there in such a gloomy place, and that they had been without water and food for a long summer's day, was anything but pleasant to us.

We had a distinct view of a comet to-night. It was in the northwest, and set about half-past nine in the evening. It was perfectly visible to the naked eye, and its luminous projection was some 25° or 30° long.

Ash Hollow[44] has been the scene of many fights between the Pawnees and Sioux. In the winter time, several families of the latter tribe generally encamp in it. The men employ their time in killing buffaloes, and the women in dressing the skins into robes. We saw the remains of some of their temporary winter lodges which had been built of stick and straw—and also the scaffolds where they had hung their meat to dry. A new red blanket, cut by innumerable gashes, was found hanging up near this deserted village. Why it had been left there we could not tell; but afterwards ascertained that it is a custom with the Sioux whenever there comes up a heavy thunderstorm, to give as an offering the most valuable garment they may have, in order to appease the wrath of the Great Spirit, whom they suppose is angry with them. And we concluded that this must have been left there on such an occasion and for such a purpose.

Sunday, June 8

One of the emigrants sent the Colonel a fine large antelope this morning, and it was divided out to the different officer's-messes. In all the companies we have passed, frank and open hospitality has ever manifested itself. No one could visit the emigrants' camp at night without being offered the best entertainment their humble means could afford; and when they were on the march, even, they were always ready to share their drink of milk or bit of bread with their fellow travellers—the dragoons.

This morning the immense tracks of a grizzly bear were discovered in the sand of Ash Creek. They were fresh, and some hopes were entertained that the animal might be discovered before we started—but he had probably seen us and secreted himself in the neighboring ravines. There is a material difference between attacking a grizzly bear and shooting at peeps. The former is considered to be decidedly the most dangerous sport of the two, and requires entirely another order of talent to carry it on with success.

The traveller in coming down the North Fork would have no difficulty in finding Ash Hollow, as its entrance from the valley is over a half a mile wide—and has upon each side a high buttress of rock which resembles the ruins of some old fort. Between them is a grove, all in plain sight from the river—the only one that is seen for fifty or sixty miles, either above or below.

To-day, our course was nearly due west, and extended along the bottom, which upon the south side is in places quite narrow, as the lofty precipices here and there, are advanced into it nearly to the water. The soil has been very sandy and barren, though at times we came to low strips of intervale, where a tolerable crop of coarse grass and equisetum managed, by taking advantage of the increased moisture of such places, to attain a respectable height. Many of the bluffs which we have passed upon our left, have been worn by time into the most picturesque shapes: some of them shooting up like pyramids—some like old castles—and some standing by themselves like watch towers. Upon the north side of the river the country has been quite low, with a wide and level bottom stretching back some ways from the water, and then gradually rising in gentle swells as far as we could see. We made but a short march to-day, as our animals, when we started this morning, had not entirely recovered from the protracted fatigues of yesterday.

The character of the high bluffs along the North Fork of the Nebraska, is continually changing as one advances westward. Near the junction of the two rivers they are composed of limestone, more or less filled with marine fossils, with a slight admixture of sand. There they are of a dark grey color. Farther along the proportion of sand in them becomes greater, and they change in color to a dirty white. Such is their composition and complexion in the neighborhood of Ash Hollow. For fifty or sixty miles westward of there, they consist of alternate but irregular layers of calcareous sandstone—(which is sometimes nearly as white as chalk, and sometimes the color of ashes)—and of indurated clay, which is, also, of different hues—but the prevailing ones are bright yellow and reddish brown. These strata of clay—or rather of clay and carbonate of lime mixed together—are in many of the bluffs seventy or eighty feet in thickness—and as the action of frost and rains, and the air, is continually decomposing and wearing them away faster than it does the intervening layers of sandstone,—large shelves of the latter material here and there project from the sides of the precipices, and give them a very singular, yet beautiful appearance. In many places these bluffs are isolated—but many of them, although they stand out in the valley all by themselves, are as high as those that form the boundary of the elevated prairie. Some of these are shaped like large domes, and some shoot up like turrets with overhanging battlements. The upper stratum of nearly all of them is composed of sandstone of a much harder and more durable quality than any below; and as it presents greater resistance to the action of the weather, it projects out over the whole like a huge cornice. Large blocks of it break off from time to time, and drop to the plain beneath, where they lie scattered about like the capitals and other portions of old ruins.

There are many vultures in this country, and at times we see great numbers of them perched upon the highest crags and pinnacles. Sometimes they will stand for an hour or so with their long wings extended as if they were about to fly; then again they will scale off into the air and circle around at a giddy height, apparently without the least effort—as if they were floating rather than flying.

In the summer-time colonies and colonies of swallows come to build their nests under the jutting shelves of the bluffs. In some places we observed hundreds of their little mud edifices clustered together, and as we went past them the birds issued forth in clouds, and went skimming and twittering over the plain below, and darting this way and that all around us, and appearing to try all in their power to make matters as lively and cheerful as possible. A great many martins spend their summer here also. They occupy crevices and holes which they find high up in the sides of the precipices. Although they are not so volatile or garrulous as their little neighbors—or so numerous either—still they can sing a better song, and on the whole make themselves quite as agreeable.

There are two of three companies of emigrants still ahead of us, who came across and descended to this valley by a pass several miles above Ash Hollow, and in the afternoon we fell into their trace. As we were marching along to-day, a large buffalo bull happened unexpectedly to find himself between our column and the river. No sooner had he discovered his situation than he attempted to get by us with a view of escaping to the highlands through the narrow and difficult gorges that here and there led up to them through the bluffs. One of the officers, who was exceedingly well mounted, gave chase to him, and, when at a long distance, gave him a pistol shot as he ran, which dropped him dead upon the sand. A detail of men soon took from his huge carcase a sufficient quantity of the best and most tender portions to last the command a day—and having stowed it into the wagons—left the remainder for the vultures and wolves. We saw several others, both on this and on the other side of the river, but did not molest them.

MONDAY, JUNE 9

During the night immense numbers of buffaloes came down to the river for water, and were still feeding along the bottom on both sides of the river when the command commenced its march this morning. However, those that were nearest to us soon scented us, and as we proceeded each successive herd galloped away for the hills. There was one band that had four or five hundred in it, which had been attacked by a small party of men that had been detailed as hunters for the day, and sent on ahead of the column under the direction of an officer. No sooner had the men got amongst them than the buffaloes started three or four abreast up the side of a high bluff that had an inclination of forty-five degrees at least—and rose all of two hundred and fifty feet before its top sloped off to the level of the great plain beyond. It was astonishing how rapidly they ran up such a steep place. If a horse could have clambered after them at all he could not possibly have been urged out of a walk—but they went lumbering up that side-hill at full speed, and raising a cloud of dust which we could see long after the last one had gone out of sight over the edge above. But the hunters stopped as many of them as they required—and, having loaded their pack-mules with as much meat as they could carry, came on after the column. Lieut. Smith, who had charge of this party, liked to have lost his life. By some accident, a large bull, which he was in pursuit of, fell into a hollow, and almost at the same instant his horse stumbled in likewise, and threw his rider completely over his head, and on to the buffalo. Fortunately Mr. Smith was able to clear himself from the bull before he rose, and so escaped with but little injury. It was the greatest wonder that the furious creature had not turned at bay and gored him to death, for the horse had recovered his feet and galloped off, and there was not the least chance to avoid an attack of the bull, as it was an open plain all around. However, he made no manifestations of hostility, but ran off for the bluffs as fast as he could go.

The soil to-day, has grown more dry and sandy as we proceeded. The bluffs have gradually receded farther from the river upon the south side—while those upon the north have gradually increased in height and advanced in some places close to the water's edge. The bottom over which we have travelled has been quite uneven: sometimes rising into high and barren ridges, and sinking into low swales covered with a fine crop of equisetum and coarse grass. Upon our left, the hills have occasionally been darkened by a scattered growth of red-cedars, and a few cottonwoods have here and there ornamented the river's bank. In the branches of one of these trees, and nearly over the water, we saw a large nest of the bald-eagle. Some of the men climbed up to it and but one eaglet, which was full-fledged, and so nearly grown, that it was with some difficulty they could capture it. At last, however, they got it down, when one man took hold of one of its wings, and another of the other, and stretching them apart, they ran for the wagons with the eagle between them. But he punished them severely on the way, by turning up first to the one on his right and fixing the sharp claws of both feet into his leg, and then serving the one upon his left in the same manner. The old eagles came around and filled the air with shrieks at the loss of their off-spring; but they did not attempt a rescue. It is the intention of the officers to take this belligerent captive "to the states" if possible—and he has been provided with a perch upon one of the howitzers. If any one approaches him he shows his game blood at once, and immediately commences bristling up for a fight; but if he sees in his neighborhood a fine piece of meat or fish, he is very conciliating until he gets hold of it, but after that it is quite as well to keep out of his reach.

Early in the afternoon we found a few hundred acres of very fair grass upon a low intervale near the bank of the river, and have encamped upon it for the night. There are four Mackinac boats aground upon the sand bars immediately in front of us. Many of the men who have them in charge, waded ashore, and informed us that they started from Fort Platte, an hundred miles above here, several days ago. There was then a little freshet which they hoped might last them until they reached the Missouri River on their way to St. Louis; but when they had floated down this far, their boats ran aground, and before they could get them off again, the temporary rise of the water had passed by. Each boat, they informed us, is laden with one thousand buffalo-robes, which the owners will have to haul back to the Fort, transport by land to Independence, Mo., or guard where they are until the next rise of the water, which will not take place, probably, until another year.[45]

They told us that the country in our immediate vicinity is called "Prudhomme's Prairie;"—having been named for one of the hunters of the American Fur Company, who many years ago accidentally shot himself and died near here. They, also, gave us information of an hundred and fifty lodges of Sioux, whom they say, are encamped fifteen miles back from the river amongst the "Sand Butes"—a name by which the voyageurs denominate the surrounding hills.

This evening we were visited by quite a respectable shower of rain, the first that has fallen upon us for many days. It is what we have been earnestly hoping for, for a long while. The whole upper country is so parched up with the drought that we are continually fearful that the grass will entirely give out, and our progress, from that cause, be arrested. We are not, however, so solicitous about ourselves, as we are for the emigrants.

A curlew was shot by one of the gentlemen to-day, which belonged to a species different from any we had ever seen before. It was quite as large as the Spanish curlew, or sickle-bill, but had a brown head—white body—black wings, and blue legs. Capt. Eustis prepared it with a view of sending it to the National Institute. Although it has probably been described, it must be quite rare, and will therefore be interesting.

CHAPTER X

FIRST VIEW OF THE "CHIMNEY" – *Pass the advanced Companies– An emigrant captain a Martinet–Valley increases in width–Isolated towers–Description of the Chimney and the cities in its neighborhood– Remarkable clearness of atmosphere–Scott's Bluffs–Note in relation to them–The Dahcotahs–Their divisions into bands–Great for fighting– Regular Ishmaelites in that respect–Brule Village–Brule toilette–View of Indians crossing the river–Their alarm at our presence in their country–Antelope chase and magnificent horsemanship–The way the Dahcotahs travel–Passage of the gorge–Grizzly bar range–First view of the mountains–Human bones dropping down from tree tops–Arrive at Laramie River.*

TUESDAY, JUNE 10

W E ARE still continuing up the valley of the North Fork. Early in the forenoon we crossed a fine stream of clear water, affluent to the river from the south. It is called "Smith's Branch" by the mountain men. At ten o'clock we came in sight of the celebrated "Chimney Rock." It was upwards of thirty miles distant when we first saw it, and yet the mirage brought it so completely above the horizon, that its general outline and comparative height could be very well determined. For seven or eight miles after leaving "Smith's Branch" we found the ground so wet and soft, we were obliged to make a large detour towards the bluffs to avoid it. This low land was covered almost entirely by equisetum. At the termination of it, we passed two more companies of emigrants. They were the first that started this year, and are still the fore-most of all. They were at a halt when our guard came up, and the officer commanding it dismounted his men and let them rest until our little herd of cattle should be got through their large and widely scattered one. The emigrants with their usual kindness and hospital-ity, gave to each of the dragoons a fine draught of milk, and to those who were hungry, a generous slice of bread and of meat. Reader, this may appear unworthy of notice—a drink of milk and bit of bread;—but travel on the prairies and you will recollect even poorer fare than that. The "head man," or captain of these two com-panies, made not a few pretensions of having all manner of duties performed with a method; and where ever there was an opportunity for the introduction of military discipline, and military commands, he was sure to improve it. He was amongst other captains of emigrants, what in the army would be called, a martinet. Hardly a yoke of oxen could be permitted to drink without a command;—and if a wagon wished to halt, only to adjust a clevis and pin, it could be done with but an order. Cattle were expected to march with a cadenced step—and horses to keep their eyes to the front and resting upon the earth at fifteen paces distant; to say nothing of their passing their feet near the ground—toeing out, or taking the goose step, whenever they were obliged to make a diagonal movement in order to pass a mud puddle.

"*Attention. Prepare to mount. Mount. Form ranks. By twos—march. Guide—Left,*" said the officer, giving the necessary commands to put his guard in the saddle, and to have it move off in column. All ears were endeavoring to catch each word that was said and all eyes were attentively watching how it was done. The captain, particularly, came striding forward with a martial gait, and his brow bent into an imperious frown. He regarded the whole movement with a con-temptuous manner, and with his lips curled in a sort of "Phew!" expression. No sooner had the dragoons started, than he turned around to his party with an air, and sang out in a loud and fierce tone—"Blow the horn! (whereupon a tin trumpet was made to groan two or three doleful notes.) Start on, you cattle-drivers! Jeems Priestly! together, I saw. Hitch up, teamsters! Are you ready?"

"Ready."

"Forrerds!" When off they would all move simultaneously.

The "Sand Buttes" upon the north side of the river have become lower and less precipitous as we have advanced to-day, and the main chain of the bluffs upon the south side have receded back ten or twelve miles, and begin to be darkened in all the gorges by a faint shadow of cedars. By four o'clock in the afternoon we passed another very considerable stream, called "Laran's Creek." It was some fifty yards in width—but very shallow and muddy, and filled with quicksands. We crossed it without difficulty, and having marched a mile further, encamped upon the bank of the river. The grass at this place was very poor—and but enough barely to keep our animals from starving. About six miles to the southward of us, a large, natural structure, resembling the ruins of an old castle, rises abruptly from the plain. It is about three hundred feet in height, and some quarter of a mile in length, by two hundred yards in breadth. Its outline, and general proportions are such, that it is difficult to look upon it and not believe that art had something to do with its construction. The voyageurs have called it the "Court House"; but it looks infinitely more like the Capitol than it does any building bearing the name they have bestowed upon it. There is something remarkable in these isolated towers, &c. They are composed of precisely the same materials as the distant bluffs; their strata and general height correspond; yet why they have sustained themselves when the whole country round them has been dug out and carried off by ages, until this great valley has been formed, whereon they stand in all their loneliness, like huge monuments to what was, is a wonder. If they were composed of more enduring substances than that part which has been gnawed off by the tooth of time, and transported away, there would be a cause easily understood why they remain:—but such is not the case.

WEDNESDAY, JUNE 11

For the whole of to-day's march the valley has been very unequal in its width. Sometimes it has stretched off to the southward for twelve or fifteen miles from the river, and having each bay so formed surrounded by the sculptured walls which have heretofore been

described thereby giving it the appearance of the arena of a coliseum.
And then again, as long points of the bluffs have at irregular intervals advanced toward the water, it has diminished in breadth to
five or six miles. At the termination of one of these points, and at a
distance of, say four miles from the river, stands the "Chimney
Rock," one of the greatest curiosities—perhaps the greatest—in
the whole valley of the Mississippi. It is a much more beautiful
structure, and of far greater magnitude, than one would imagine it
to be, from Mr. Preuss' drawing of it, published in Capt. Fremont's
first Journal.[46] As before stated, it stands at the outer end of one of
the large ranges of bluffs that run off into the valley the same as high
and narrow promontories advance into the sea. In fact, it is itself,
only the extreme point of one of those promontories divided from
the rest by a gorge some four or five hundred yards in width. At first,
it rises from the level plain by a cone, say one thousand yards in circumference at the base, and shooting upwards some two hundred
feet. From its top a perpendicular shaft, that is about forty feet in
diameter, runs up for one hundred and twenty-five feet more. This
column, or shaft, is composed of chocolate colored marl, here and
there interlaid with strata of yellowish white sandstone. The cone is
nearly all white sandstone, and its several layers, as well as those of
the column, correspond precisely with those of the perpendicular
wall of the promontory from which, no doubt, they have become
separated. As the materials of which it is formed are decomposing
very fast, in a few years it will have worn entirely away. The shaft is
already rent from top to bottom, and one would suppose that the
first high wind would topple it down. The reader will have a better
idea of how perishable it is, when he is told that with the strength of
his hand he can crush to powder a piece of it as large as he can grasp.
Different travellers have varied a great deal in their estimate of its
proportions. The Rev. Mr. Parker, who visited it in 1835, says:—
"We were going up on the north side of the river, and being anxious
to have a nearer view, I concluded to take an assistant and pass over
to it. We found the river a mile wide, and then travelled three miles
over a level plain before we arrived at its base. The whole distance at
first did not appear to be over a mile. This beacon hill has a conical

formed base of a half mile in circumference, and one hundred and fifty feet high; and above this a perpendicular column twelve feet square and eighty feet high, (230 feet). Near the top were some handsome stalactites, at which my assistant shot and broke off some pieces, of which I have taken a small specimen."*

There are no stalactites upon it now. Washington Irving says of it—"The lower part is a conical mound rising out of the naked plain: from the summit shoots up a shaft about one hundred and twenty feet in height, from which it derives its name—the Chimney. The height of the whole, according to Capt. Bonneville, is an hundred and seventy-five yards."** (525 feet.) Capt. Bonneville visited it in 1832. This year, 1845, the top of it, above the plain, is somewhere between 325 feet, and 350 feet—as near as we could judge without positive measurement. Mr. Loring and myself ascended to the summit of the promontory in rear of it. The highest point at which we went, was so far above the Chimney that we could see the Dragoons near the bank of the river, four miles distant—the line of sight passing immediately over the top of the shaft. We found it very fatiguing to clamber up through the gorges to where we then stood, and judging, step by step, our ascent, we believed ourselves then to be four hundred feet above the plain below. The atmosphere in this upper country is so remarkably clear, that even at that distance we could see each object near the river as plainly as we can one that is a half mile off on the Missouri. And the gentlemen, who were with the column at the time, informed us that they could see us as well as they could in an ordinary atmosphere had we been only six hundred yards away. However, the perspective is not changed, and everything diminishes in apparent size; in proportion to its distance, the same as it does where the air is less transparent. Let a person look at a near object through a reversed spy-glass, and he will have precisely the same view of it, that in this mountain air he would obtain with the naked eye, were it at a great distance.

We found upon the summit of this promontory but little grass; but there were many beds of the common cactus, and large clumps

*Parker's Exploring Tour beyond the Rocky Mountains,—3d. edition: pp. 64–65
**Irving's Rocky Mountains—1st. vol., page 45

of the "Spanish Bayonet" (*Yucca Aloifolia*) in full bloom. As we descended we found in the deep ravines that are ploughed into its northern side, several mountain pines—the first we had seen. They were covered with immense cones that were very beautiful. There were a few red cedars growing amongst them also: and a small shrub, having something the appearance of a barberry bush, with the fruit growing in the same manner, but continually distilling a kind of balsam, which covered the berries in drops like a heavy dew.

The view from the elevation, where we then were, was most enchanting. No pen or pencil could ever do justice to its surpassing loveliness. East and west of us, two of those deep bays, which have been spoken of, stretched inland for miles. They were oval-shaped like the interior of a theatre, and opened out upon the valley and to the river, as through a proscenium on to a stage. These bays were surrounded by fortresses, towers, and castellated walls, which had pinnacles shooting upward from them like the pagodas of the East—or like the light and graceful minarets of the Saracens. Long facades of old Gothic ruins, propped by quaintly chiselled buttresses,—Hindoo temples, with domes like inverted pears,—and *all* other kinds of edifices that were ever seen, or could, by a possibility, be ·conceived of, there found a counterpart, with hardly an effort of the imagination on the part of the spectator.

With these exceptions everything was inanimate, and an oppressive and painful silence reigned over the scene, so profound, that one could hear the beating of his own heart. Sixteen miles further up the river—yet all in plain sight from this promontory—that immense and celebrated pile, called "Scott's Bluffs," advances across the plain nearly to the water's edge. If one could increase the size of the Alhambra of Grenada, or the Castle of Heidelberg, which Professor Longfellow has so poetically and so graphically described,—twenty fold in every way but in height,—he could form some idea of the magnitude and splendor of this *chef d'oeuvre* of Nature at Palace-Building. And it constitutes a Mausoleum which the mightiest of earth might covet. Queen Artemisia, with all the wealth of Caria at her command, and inspired by her deep love, and her tender recollection of the husband she had lost, did not erect one to his memory, which, for magnificence and wonderful beauty, could at all equal this. And yet this stands by the grave, and will bear down through all time, the name of an humble and obscure trapper: a poor sick man, who in agony crept for sixty long miles, unconsciously to win for himself such a monument, and then perished at its foot.*

About four o'clock in the afternoon, we encamped upon the bank of the river eight miles below Scott's Bluffs, and directly opposite a large village of Dahcotah Indians.** Their high and conical lodges, formed of painted hides—their numerous herd of horses grazing upon the vast plain round about—the crowds of men, women, and children, clustered together, here and there, along the shore, intently regarding our approach with alarm, and filled with wonder at the magic appearance of our little regular city of tents, so soon after we had come to a halt—all contributed to form a picture, which, taken in connection with the wild and peculiar beauty of the surrounding country, would have been of the highest interest to either a poet or a painter. And more especially, when the thought was entertained, that we were the first troops these Indians had ever seen; the first decided evidence of that power which had swept so many nations of their brethren away, and was now grasping onward toward them, sooner or later, inevitably to crush them to turn.

The Dahcotahs are said to be more numerous than any other nation of Indians within the jurisdiction of the United States. The territory they claim, is a broad belt of country stretching from the Mississippi River north of Iowa, to the Rocky Mountains. They are the Ishmaelites of the Prairies, for, with every tribe by which they are surrounded, they are now at war, and have been for time out of mind. To this, the small tribe of Cheyennes are too few to maintain an independent existence, and have therefore been annexed to their more powerful neighbors, and are fast becoming absorbed into the great nation by intermarriages.

The Dahcotahs are divided into many bands. Each band has its own chiefs, and its own customs, and laws. One does not owe any

*Irving's Rocky Mountains, Vol. 1, p. 46.
**Throat-Cutters. For no earthly reason called by the worse name "Sioux."

allegiance to another—nor is there any national control over them, for they have no central government. If our states were not united, and each managed its affairs to suit its own convenience, without reference to any other one—then, to that extent, would they resemble the divisions of this people.—Every band goes to war, or makes peace, when it pleases. But when, collectively, they are considered as belonging to the same great family, they are never at peace. For instance, the Warpeton Dahcotahs might be at war with a neighboring tribe—the Chippeways—and to gain a point, or, because for the time being, they were tired of fighting,—they might smoke the calumet—shake hands—and declare themselves friends. But at the same moment the Sisseton Dahcotahs might dig up the hatchet, and commence a bloody campaign on their own account. So with the Yancton and Santee Dahcotahs, &c., &c. Some one of them is sure to keep the frontier of their common country in a state of continued warfare. And they battle with their neighbors for the love of the thing, and not for any other particular reason. The chase is their labor—and war their pastime. Nothing is more common, when they have laid in a good stock of meat, than to get up a little frolic of a war-party, and making a foray into some enemy's country in the vicinity, way-lay, and shoot down a dozen, or such a matter of them; and slashing around their heads with their long keen knives—peel from thence the reeking skin—and then, highly elated at the fun, carry them home; and, after hanging them up on a pole in the centre of their village, invite everybody to that greatest of sprees—a Scalp Dance. So they go—But we'll tell of all that by and bye.

In the great valleys that lie between the parallel ranges of mountains west of the Dahcotahs, dwell their hereditary and mortal enemies, the Blackfeet, Crows, and Snakes. There is never any peace made with them, and, by the way, they are as implacable foes to one another for that matter, as they are to the Dahcotahs. If a party of either of them accidentally meets with a party of the other—somebody has either to run or be whipped.—There is never between them, so much as a solitary whiff toward reconciliation; and either side that would propose such a thing as a pipe, would be incontinently scorned at as most arrant cowards. Such has been the condition of the Dahcotahs with respect to the internal management of their political affairs, and their foreign relations, so long as the whites have known anything about them.

The village opposite to our encampment this evening belongs to the Brule band of Dahcotahs. Soon after we had halted, Mr. Fitzpatrick rode over to it. He found the Indians very much alarmed at our unexpected appearance in their country; and it was not until he had assured them of our amicable feelings towards them, and the friendly purpose with which we had come, that they could be induced to accompany him to our camp. At length, however, they decided to do so—and the chiefs, and some fifty or sixty of the principal warriors, decorated themselves and their horses in a manner befitting such a great occasion. They put on their best garments —donned all the bright colors they could muster—and then retouched themselves, here and there, with their jewelry (those who were fortunate enough to possess any), consisting of feathers, hawk's bells, a few scalps, ear-bobs, wampum, necklaces of grizzly bear's claws, "medicine" bags, medals, &c., &c. After their elaborate toilette was completed, they mounted up—and dashing into the river, crossed over to where we were.

The North Fork at this place is about three quarters of a mile in width—and the horses they rode were sometimes nearly swimming, while at others they would be passing a bar where the water was not over a foot in depth. After they had got fairly started from the opposite shore, the scene they presented was exceedingly picturesque. Every now and then, a horse got into the quicksands, and came very near precipitating his rider over his head; and at times, while a dozen or so might be wading upon a bar, fifteen or twenty would be floundering along through some channel, where the water would come up so high each rider was obliged to curl up his legs to keep them from getting wet. A score of large wolf-dogs swam along on each flank, and a few colts, whose mothers were doing duty in the cavalcade, followed in the rear, as best they might.

As has just been stated, some of the Indians were in grand costume, and glittered with brilliant ornaments,—while others again, though they had taken equal pains in arraying themselves, in proportion to their means, could hardly boast of what is called the full dress of a Georgia gentleman.* They therefore presented with each other, a pleasing contrast; and as the rich yellow rays of an evening sun fell over them as they came swimming, wading, and spattering, towards us, the effect was extremely beautiful.

It was some time after they had arrived in our camp before they felt sure they were not in danger; and although they apparently paid profound attention to what the commanding officer said the them, still they would look furtively about, as if they distrusted us, and were on the watch for evidences of our treachery. Some of the warriors—who, to a sculptor, might have stood as models for statues of Achilles or Hector—who probably had never felt the emotion of fear during their lives—and would have met torture and death in their most terrible forms, without a sign of trepidation, had they combated with Indians—absolutely trembled like aspen leaves all the time they remained in camp. It was astonishing to see what a deep and powerful impression the appearance of the troops made upon them. The commanding officer took them through the camp, and showed them everything which would serve to render that impression, if possible, still more forcible.

The howitzers—the long sabres—the carbines, that could be loaded and fired so rapidly—the pistols—the powerful horses, from which they saw there could be no escape—the stalwart and athletic men, who were to ride those horses, and use those weapons—*all* these things, served to convince them, beyond a doubt, that although their great father had an open hand to give, he also had a strong arm to punish.

While these Brules were in camp, a young antelope sprang out of the grass near where they were. A dozen of the young men gave it chase on horseback, and a more exciting race it was never our fortune to witness. Back toward the bluffs there was a perfectly level plain about four miles wide. Across this the antelope took its way. From being not over six weeks old it was just a fair match for their horses in point of speed. Some times it would run in a straight line

*A dickey and a pair of spurs.

for a half mile, with the Indians all abreast, and going over the ground at a killing pace—with their long hair floating in the wind, and the fringes of their robes and feathers flying like streamers. Then it would double to the right or left, and their horses would all turn toward the new course simultaneously, and so suddenly, that their riders might have touched the ground, so great was their inclination. Every now and then, an arrow was launched at the little fawn, but fortunately none struck him. After the chase had continued in this zig-zag manner to the farthest edge of the plain, the poor little creature fell down perfectly exhausted, when one of the Indians dismounted; then caught and brought it back to camp. The most wonderful part of this chase was the astonishing skill the Dahcotahs displayed in the management of their horses. The whole race—turning and all included—was conducted by them without so much as once touching their hand to the reins. The horses were guided entirely by the legs and feet of their riders, who used both hands in managing their bows and arrows, the same as if they had been at a halt. We thought we had seen some beautiful horsemanship in our day—but it had all been riding an old hack to mill, with three bushels and a half of corn, compared with this.

The commanding officer had a friendly and informal talk with the Brules to-day. It is two day's march from here to Fort Laramie; at that place he has appointed to meet the Ogollallah Dahcotahs, to whom he sent a messenger this morning to call them to a council. In order that both bands may be together at that time, he invited the Brules to proceed thither, also. To this they acceded—and about sun-set returned to their village to make the necessary preparations. When the Dahcotahs go any distance, they take up, not only their bed and walk, but their houses, provisions, and all their worldly gear. Then, they just naturally potter along, and, to save expense, sleep at home every night.

Thursday, June 12

By six o'clock this morning, the beautiful village on the opposite bank of the North Fork had vanished—and there was no indication of the spot where it stood, except a few faint columns of smoke ascending from the smouldering pits of *bois de vache*. However, we could see it, about a mile up the river, and wending its way to the westward. It had been folded up—the village had—and been placed upon horses, mules, asses, and dogs, in this way: Each animal had a rude packsaddle, into which the thirty foot lodge poles were thrust like fills: the large ends trailing on the ground far behind. On top of these poles were lashed indiscriminately, folded up lodges—packs of meat—buffalo robes—traps—babies—and brass-kettles. The squaws and larger children trotted along on each side: only jumping on and riding a little ways now and then—when the prairies were particularly fine. The "chiefs and warriors of the Brules," rode on ahead—on the flanks—or in the rear, as best suited their convenience. So they got at a dignified distance from the women and young ones, it mattered but little on which side of the cavalcade they rode. Like all other Indians, the Dahcotahs make their women perform all the labor and drudgery—whether on the march or when encamped.

The ground between Scott's Bluffs and the river, being too wet to be travelled over with wagons,[47] we were forced to make a large detour to the left, to pass through a gorge in rear of them. This was a hard day's work, it being thirty miles around—that is, we were obliged to travel fifteen miles south-west to the gorge, and then fifteen miles north-west before we could find grass enough for a night.

The weather being extremely hot, and there being not a single drop of water to be obtained before we got to the gorge, we suffered a great deal from thirst, as did our poor animals. Our whole distance there lay up one of those beautiful bays before spoken of; and every rod we advanced, the bluffs seemed to assume some new and interesting shape—or, open to the view some pretty vista running away in perspective to a mere point. Arrived near the gorge, we found a little stream of tepid water that oozed from the marl, at the bottom of a ravine some forty feet in depth—and then, after running a half mile, lost itself in the hot sand, where the ravine debauched to the prairies. Here we found a little grove, consisting of stunted pines, scraggy cedars, diminutive hackberrys (*celti crassifolia*) with here and there a small ash, and wild cherry tree, with an undergrowth of wild currant bushes, and an over-growth of grape-vines, matted and snarled up, and running over the whole like a net. Such ravines are famous for grizzly bears when the cherries are ripe! And, by the way, speaking of bears, here's a bit of an extract from the Rev. Mr. Parker's Tour, about them. It speaks a great deal for their strength: —"Lieut. Steen, of the Dragoons, a man of undoubted veracity, told me he saw several buffaloes passing near some bushes, where a grizzly bear lay concealed, and the bear with one stroke tore three ribs from a buffalo, and laid it dead!" They are quite powerful—and at close quarters, say a hug, they are said to be very severe, indeed—especially if they have both "underholds."

When we arrived at the gorge, which the reader must understand was half-way up the bluffs, we caught our first view of the mountains. "James' Peak,"* the highest of that spur of the Rocky Mountains, called the "Black Hills," was distinctly visible, though upwards of eighty miles distant. "Hurra!" said we to ourselves, "there they are, sure enough!" The fact is, we had counted so much on this campaign—so much on seeing "whar the U-nited States war piled up a heap more mountainously than anywhar's else—and whar thar war higher pinnykills, an' colder snow, an' grizzlier bars, an' savager Injuns than England dared to have, by the eternal Moses!" as Capt. M. would say—that our delight when we first caught sight of them was unbounded.

After changing our course, we marched all the afternoon down an inclined plain, and encamped on a very beautiful stream called "Horse Creek."[48] Here we found but little grass, but a fine supply of equisetums, which was the best substitute for it we could have.

FRIDAY, JUNE 13

Last night, about eleven o'clock, we were visited by a perfect tornado of a blow from the north, which prostrated many of our tents. The mercury must have fallen all of 30° in a half an hour after

*Named for Dr. James.

it first struck us. To-day, our route was laid along the river bottom, which has grown very narrow, and has begun to support a few groves of cotton-wood and willow. The bluffs upon each bank have decreased very much in height—the river diminished in breadth—its water become clearer than below, and its current more rapid. To-night we have encamped on a little stream whose waters are as clear as crystal. Near us there are the remains of an old trading post, that used to be occupied by Mr. Peter Sarpy, who received us so hospitably last year, when we were on campaign at Council Bluffs, where he now resides. Nothing worthy of note met our attention during the whole day.

The reader knows that the Dahcotahs place bodies of their deceased friends upon scaffolds, and in the forks of trees, having previously wrapped them carefully in buffalo robes; so it is not worth while to describe how they do it, just at the bottom of a sheet. Many of the cotton-woods about our present encampment have borne aloft upon their branches this death-fruit. The fire having caught two of them and burned off their limbs, the charred and crackled bones have dropped down, and now lay in confused masses upon the ground below. I speak of this because one of the trees stands right in front of my tent, and while I sit here writing I can almost touch the bones with my feet.

SATURDAY, JUNE 14

After marching eight miles this morning we struck Laramie River, near its mouth, and just opposite a trading post called "Fort Platte"—which belongs to some merchants of St. Louis. The traders at this Fort informed us that we could find grass enough for the command four miles further up the North Fork, but upon going there we could not discover sufficient even for one division. So we were obliged to march through the hills until we again came to the valley of the Laramie, but two miles higher up than before. Here we found some very good grass, and have again encamped.

CHAPTER XI

INDIANS ARRIVING–*Dragoons detached to stay at Laramie–Scarcity of Buffalo–Large wolves–Council with the Dahcotahs–The exaggerated idea that the Indians had of our force–Arrival of the leading companies of the emigrants–Their discouraging prospects–Their cheerfulness in adversity–Their perseverance and piety.*

TO-DAY we shall rest: and it is only the second time we have done so since we left Fort Leavenworth. The Ogollallahs whom the Commanding officer had previously sent for, and, also, the Brules, whom we saw below Scott's Bluffs, are hourly arriving and encamping near Fort Platte, two miles and a half below us. To-morrow is the day on which the Council is to be held with them.

As stated in the last chapter, Fort Platte, and Fort John,[49] are situated immediately upon the Great Trace for Oregon, and are in the very heart of the Indian country. The emigrants usually stop in their neighborhood two or three days to rest their cattle and to make whatever repairs their wagons and other equipment may require. They regard this point as marking the first third of their journey; and here they may be said to leave the plains, and begin, first, to strike the ripple of the mountains.[50]

As many of their companies will, from time to time, as they arrive, be congregated here, Col. Kearny has detached from the command three officers and one hundred men, to remain in this neighborhood until his return from the Pass. As this detachment will have no heavy marches to perform, the weakest horses have been selected from each division to remain.

Since we left Scott's Bluffs, we have not seen a single buffalo; nor is it expected that the expedition will meet with any until it shall have marched an hundred miles or so, further up the river. The mouth of the Laramie River, where these two Forts are, is the great centre to which all the bands of Indians round about, come to trade away their buffalo robes and other peltry; and from which the hunters are sent out into the lands to procure a sufficient supply of meat for the numerous employes of the two rival establishments. Therefore, it is seldom that the buffaloes ever approach nearer than two or three day's journey of it, from any direction. So, now it is, we are obliged to depend entirely upon our little herd of cattle for subsistence. Our sheep are so completely worn down from travel, they are not fit to be killed for food;—and last night the wolves absolutely came inside of the chain of sentinels, and seizing three of them, carried them off bodily, to the top of some neighboring bluffs, and there devoured them. The wolves here are very different from any in Missouri or Arkansas: being nearly white, and three times the weight and strength of the Prairie wolf. The fact of their power to carry off a whole sheep speaks sufficiently for their strength.

Monday, June 16

Early in the morning, our tents were struck, and we moved a mile farther down the Laramie to a new spot of grass, and there encamped again. Col. Kearny, accompanied by about two-thirds of his officers, a guard, and a party with the howitzers, then proceeded to the Dahcotah encampment near Fort Platte, to meet the Indians in council. Arriving there, it was found that twelve hundred of them had already collected together. Of this number seven-eighths were Brules—but few of the Ogollallahs who had been sent for, having yet arrived. The day was an extremely disagreeable one. There was a raw wind blowing from the northeast, and every now and then the leaden clouds that flew past upon it, let down a drizzling shower of cold rain, accompanied at times with heavy flakes of snow, although it was the middle of June.

The Indians constructed a screen of buffalo robes, stretched upon lodge-poles, to break the weather from the officers. Beneath this they had formed seats for them to sit upon, and also spread skins on which they might place their feet. This screen was but the arc of a large circle—the rest of which was described by the chiefs and braves seated cross-legged upon the ground, from one end of it around to the other. Near the screen the Indians, in an excess of patriotism, had hoisted three American flags—and besides, they had complimented the troops and the occasion, by having decorated themselves in the most brilliant costume their limited means would afford. Outside of all, and making but few pretensions to elegance of attire, were gathered, promiscuously, the lower orders, and the women and children.

The officers having become seated, the Colonel shook hands with the principal chiefs, and then addressed them all, in substance, as follows:—"Sioux: I am glad to meet you. Through your Chiefs I have shaken hands with all of you. Your great father has learned much of his red children, and has sent me with a handful of braves to visit you. I am going to the waters which flow towards the setting sun. I shall return to this place, and then shall march to the Arkansas, and from there, home. I am opening a road for your white brethren. They are now following after me, and are journeying to the other side of the great mountains. They take with them their women, their children, and their cattle. They all go to bury their bones there, and never to return. You must not disturb them in their persons, or molest their property; neither must you on any account obstruct the road which I have now opened for them. Should you do so, your great father would be angry with you, and cause you to be punished.

"Your great father has warriors as numerous as the sands upon the shore of your river. As we have come to you without difficulty, so could they. But, although he is the enemy of all bad Indians, he is the friend of those who are good.

"I am sorry to hear that some of your war parties have killed white men; but we will bury the past: we cannot call to life those who have suffered. In future you must not trouble your white brethren, even though you meet them in an enemy's country. To the Indians with whom you are at war, and whom I may meet, I shall say the same.

"You have many enemies about you;—but fire-water is the greatest of them all. I learn that some bad white men bring it here from New Mexico, and sell it to you. Open your ears now, and listen to me. It is contrary to the wishes of your great father that it should be brought here; and I advise you, whenever you find it in your country—no matter in whose possession—to spill it all upon the ground. The earth may drink it without injury, but you cannot.

"I wish you to remember, particularly, what I have said to you—that all of you who have heard me, may tell those who are not present.

"Your great father is the friend of his red children, and will continue to be so, as long as they behave themselves properly. He did not direct me to come among you to bring you presents, but he has sent you a few things that you may remember what I have said."

This speech was interpreted to the Indians sentence by sentence, as it was delivered—by M. Bissonet, one of the factors at Fort Platte. It seemed to make a deep impression upon them. After it was concluded, the principal Chief of the Brules arose, and made a brief reply. He said:—"My father: what you have told my people is right, and it pleases me. I know now if they are good to their white brethren, they will be well treated in return; and will find that such presents as those they are about to receive, will often come. Now I have found a father: my people will no longer think of dying—but will live. They will long remember the words you have this day spoken to them; and as you have said, so, always shall they do."

One of the Ogollallah Braves succeeded the Chief by the following remarks:—

"My father; different bands of Dahcotahs are in the country, round about us. I am from one of them that dwells beyond the river. I am not a Chief, but have come here with some of my band to hear what you have just said to us. You have made me remember old times, my father. They were when Governor Clarke used to talk to *Blackbone*, my own father. And long afterwards, he went to see Governor Clark: but did not return to his people again—for he died there. Now since we have heard you, we know you are our friend; and the whole land has become smoother, and the clouds higher.

We shall tell our people to spread what you have said to us all about the country—so that others may be glad—for this day we have learned that we shall live."

A large quantity of presents, consisting of red and green blankets—scarlet and blue cloth—looking-glasses—knives—beads—tobacco, &c. &c. &c., were distributed amongst them. While they were being divided around, several of the old men expressed their delight by incessant singing. What they sang was called the "Song of Thanks"—but it was quite as difficult of translation, as a continued repetition of "*Huzza*" would be, The Council was then broken up; but before leaving the ground, several hollow shots were fired from the howitzers. This was something entirely new to the Indians, and seemed to fill them with astonishment. There can be no doubt but the impressions they have received of our prowess, and from the fact that we can reach them upon horses from which they cannot escape—are so deep, they can never be wholly obliterated.

The traders at the Forts, who could converse perfectly well with the Indians, informed us, that previous to our having come, the Dahcotahs were of the opinion the emigrants were all the white people there were. But that, when they saw the Dragoons, they were so terrified they hardly knew which way to turn. They told the traders when they first discovered us—and while we were yet a long ways off upon the prairies—that our numbers were so great we blackened the land.

Such were their fears, no doubt they magnified our force at least tenfold. And in their account of our coming, transmitted from one to the other of the bands that did not see us—their alarm and wonder will, in all probability, exaggerate our power still more and more, as the intelligence spreads.

After the Council was over, the rest of the day was spent in getting everything ready for an early start to-morrow. By the commanding officer's calculations, the expedition is to be at the South Pass on the 30th. instant, and again at Laramie River by the 13th. of July. To go there and back is estimated, by the traders, to be seven hundred miles. Twenty-eight day's provisions are all that are to be taken along for that distance, be it more or less.

This evening the leading companies of the emigrants reached Laramie River. Their cattle are very much reduced, and many of them they have been obliged to leave upon the road, as their feet had become entirely worn out. The prospect, for even so good grass as they have heretofore been able to obtain, is most discouraging. From reports which have reached here from beyond the Pass, it is learned that, from there down to Fort Hall the land is literally parched up with drought. From here on to the Pass it is said to be but little better. But there is now no receding for the emigrants. They are obliged to push on. If it were not that the fine, yet scanty, grasses that here and there paint with green patches of the river bottom, are infinitely more nutritious than any herbage their cattle have heretofore been accustomed to—they could not march ten consecutive days without absolutely perishing. Many of the companies have been visited by sickness. They have one or two very good physicians, who are emigrating with them;—and sometimes their services are needed sixty or eighty miles in advance or in rear, as the case may be.

The measles having broken out amongst them, many of the grown people have been attacked, and are entirely prostrated by the disease. But notwithstanding all their hardships—their cheerless prospect, or their sickness—they are all in fine spirits, and full of hope for the best. As most of the companies have devout and religious people in them, never a night passes by that all are not gathered together as the hour for repose approaches, and an earnest and heartfelt prayer sent up to heaven for its blessing and protection.

CHAPTER XII

THE BLACK HILLS–*Their formation–Minerals–The North Fork–*
An Arrapahoe woman and two children arrive at camp–Account of
their escapes and sufferings–Serious accident to a Dragoon–Surgeon De
Camp and seven men left in the heart of the wilderness–Grizzly bear–
Meet a party of hunters–Description of country–Arrive at the Sweet-
water–"Independence Rock"–"Devil's Gate"–Isolated rocks–Sage
cocks–Cubs–Powder River and Wind River–Mountains in sight–The
Great South Pass–Waters of the Pacific–Sickness–Return to Laramie.

O N THE 17th. of June the Expedition left Laramie[51] for the
Great South Pass. For nearly the first half of its distance
thither, its route still lay up the North Fork of the Nebraska, though at times, through the hills, several miles from it.[52] On
leaving the Forts spoken of in the last chapter, which are situated at
the extreme western, and upper edge of the vast inclined plain that
slopes down from the base of the Rocky Mountains to the Missouri
and Mississippi Rivers—and which are said to be 4470 feet above the
level of the sea,—it struck immediately into the first and lower
ranges of the Black Hills. The whole formation of the country
changes entirely, the moment the great plain is left. The white calcareous sand-stone, and marl, give place to the red, and variegated,
secondary sand-stone, here and there forced up by underlaying strata
of silicious limestone—some of which is white as the purest Parian
marble—while some is nearly transparent—and some of the most
delicate flesh color. The main bulk of the Black Hills is composed of
the red sandstone. It is overlaid by a thick stratum of fossiliferous

limestone—and above that, where the hills are high, there is found still another stratum of coarse conglomerate. From the lower hills the conglomerate has decomposed, and been washed away;—on those that are still lower, the fossiliferous limestone has also gone, leaving nothing but the bare eminences of red sandstone—here and there covered with a thin soil, which supports a scrubby growth of Norway pine, and red cedar;—the dark foliage of which gives the name to the hills. In passing through the several ranges of the Black Hills croppings out of coal were frequently seen; besides many confirmed indications of iron. Those ranges are nearly parallel with each other, and have a general direction from south to east, to a little north of west. The valleys that lie between, in ordinary seasons, are tolerably well clad with grass, which affords subsistence to the herds of buffaloes that find their way through them in their migrations to and from the South. The North Fork of the Nebraska cuts through the different chains of hills from the west. In the different valleys it spreads out a beautiful and smooth river; its waters being nearly free of detritus and quite limpid. But at each range of hills it is narrowed to forty or fifty yards—and with much brawling and commotion, forces its way through the deep chasms—or canons—walled in by perpendicular precipices hundreds of feet in height—to the next valley below,—when again it forgets its turbulence, and regaining its former width, moves gently along to the next gorge. And so on, until it finally bursts through the last ten miles above Laramie—and issues out upon the plain.

On the evening of the 18th., just before the command encamped, an Indian woman with two children—the eldest a boy of eleven, and the youngest a girl of about seven years of age—came in toward the column from the bluffs. They were brought in to camp, and through the language of signs by which Mr. Fitzpatrick could converse with her, the woman informed the commanding officer of the melancholy cause of the wretched and pitiable condition of which she, and the little children, had become reduced.

The story was briefly this:—Early in the spring, as soon as the grass began to start, a small band of Gros Ventres, who had been living with the Arrapahoes upon the Arkansas for many years, left there for their own country upon the Missouri, near the mouths of L'Eau Qui Court and White Rivers. During the long time in which these Gros Ventres had been residing with the Arrapahoes, they had intermarried with them; and when they started to return, many of them had Arrapahoe wives who accompanied them,—and many Arrapahoe men joined them, who had married Gros Ventre women. In all, there were twenty-eight lodges of people;—and they travelled with their whole wealth of horses, mules, skins, dried meat, and dogs.

Previous to their setting out from Bent's Fort, upon the Arkansas, they had heard that a large party of Dahcotahs were about to make a foray into the Crow country, and they were persuaded to delay their departure until that party had got so high up the Nebraska, they would run no risk of falling in with it.

But the Gros Ventres were anxious to return, and they concluded to set out early, so that, by making a wider detour to the left through the mountains, and crossing the Nebraska near the mouth of Sweetwater, they would get by the rumored war party before it had advanced that far upon its route. Accordingly they all set out. After they had journeyed nearly to the North Fork of the Nebraska, and while they were encamped in a secluded valley upon one of its tributaries, the Dahcotahs, whom they had turned so far out of their course to avoid, suddenly surprised them, and charged directly into their village. Every man, except three, who were guarding the horses at some distance, was put to death upon the spot. The approach of the Dahcotahs had been so unexpected, and so rapid, the Gros Ventres had not time even to seize their arms, before they were pinned to the earth by the long lances of their opponents, or were brained by their tomahawks. The women and children were spared, but were taken into captivity. This woman and the two children, managed, a few days afterwards, to escape from the Dahcotahs, and ever since had been wandering through the hills, with nothing to eat except the few roots they could here and there find, and the flesh of a dog that had faithfully followed them in their flight, but which they were obliged to kill to save themselves from absolutely starving to death. They had no knives with which to deprive him of life, but the woman beat him upon the head with a stone until he died. They then cut the flesh from the bones with flints, and devoured it raw. What they saved they dried in the sun, and then carried it along with them from day to day. The evening they fell in with the expedition, nearly the last bit had been consumed. They were almost famished with hunger, and were so emaciated by their constant fatigue, and protracted fasting, as to be hardly more than mere skin and bones. The first thing they made signs for was food;—and as soon as it was set before them, the poor creatures devoured it with the most astonishing voracity. Words can hardly express the gratitude they manifested for the kindness and protection they thus unexpectedly met with. The woman belonged to the Arrapahoe tribe. The little girl was her daughter, and the boy her nephew. As her people live near the Arkansas River, the Colonel sent her and the children back to Laramie under the charge of two dragoons, there to remain until his return from the Pass, when they are to be taken to the South, and delivered to their own people.

On the evening of the 19th.,[53] a very sad accident happened to one of the privates of "G" troop, named Smith. He was a member of the guard, and upon taking his horse out to picket him, he left his loaded carbine resting in a small clump of artemisia. On his return, when the order was given for the guard to form, he seized his piece near the muzzle, and in drawing it hastily forth, some of the branches of the artemisia caught in the lock, and discharged it. The whole of the contents of the carbine entered his right arm above the wrist, and ranging upwards, broke through the bones at the elbow joint, which it shivered entirely into pieces, and then passed out in the rear. Surgeon DeCamp was upon the ground in a moment, and immediately amputated it. Smith bore his sufferings with much fortitude. He was a good soldier, and a great deal of sympathy was felt for his misfortune, and distress. On the following morning—as it was impossible for him to be taken along without endangering his life—Surgeon De Camp, with only seven men, stayed back with him; having instructions, if Smith should recover sufficiently to admit of it, to return to the camp on Laramie River. The expedition then went on, and left the Surgeon and his little party there in the very depths of the wilderness. Every member of the command felt that he had rather run all the risks of sickness and accident to himself, than to have the wounded man's life jeopardized still more, by depriving him of the skill and attention of the Surgeon, at such a critical moment.

On the evening of the 21st., a large grizzly bear started up immediately in front of the command. Captain Moore succeeded in striking it with a charge of buckshot, and chase was immediately given to it by several of the officers. After an exciting race, the bear gained a small thicket, and finally escaped—though not without making three or four fierce charges from its cover at the horsemen, and scattering them right and left. The buffalo range was again struck on the 22d., and the flesh of two fine cows was brought into camp by the hunters, after night-fall.

On the 23d a small company of trappers, under the direction of an old mountain man, named Roubidoux, was met. Their pack animals were laden with furs which had been taken during the winter's hunt,—and they were on their way to the States. They reported the grass above to be very scarce from the effects of the drought—which for the whole winter and Spring had been more severe than had ever been known before. By these trappers another opportunity was presented for sending letters home, which was improved to the utmost. All over this whole region of country the soil was found to be sandy, and covered by a species of shrub called *Fremontia*, and by artemisia, —except immediately along the borders of the water-courses. High up the mountains, the pines and cedars continued to grow. Some of the artemisia was found to have attained the height of eight or ten feet, and to have a diameter near the ground of from four to six inches. It is called by the trappers "wild sage." Its leaves are so exceedingly bitter, hardly any animal will taste them, unless compelled to by extreme hunger.

The North Fork of the Nebraska has its source west of Long's Peak, in Latitude 40 N.;—it then runs west 15 north, to the 42d parallel, when it describes a semicircle around the northern extremity of the Black Hills for two hundred miles, and then emerges from them by a south-easterly direction near the confluence of Laramie River. At its most northerly bend the command crossed it for the last time during its westerly march, near the Red Buttes—a high landmark, composed of bluffs of dark red, indurated clay, and which is a great central point for the Indians, when travelling from the east, west, north, or south. The route of the expedition then lay through the country in a south-westerly direction, and leaving the North Fork all of twenty miles to the left. After two days' travelling through a barren region, in which the red sandstone abounded, with many indications of coal and iron, it arrived at the Sweetwater River, a fine tributary of the Nebraska, affluent to it from the west. This it crossed from its northern bank to its southern—some twelve miles above its confluence with the North Fork, and on the evening of the same day the trappers were met.

In many of the valleys that were passed between the two rivers, large pieces of ground, from one to six acres in size, were covered with chrystalized epsom salts;—and for the first few days' march up the Sweetwater similar places were frequently passed.

On the 24th, the command passed Independence Rock.[54] It was the first piece of granite of any considerable size that had been met with. It is an immensely large rock—entirely bare, and extending over several acres. Its name was given to it by a party of fur-traders, who, many years ago, celebrated the sabbath of freedom at its base. All travellers who have since passed it, have taken much pains to inscribe their names in full upon it. And some friend of the late president, Mr. Van Buren, has painted his upon one of its sides, in large letters that can be seen at a great distance. All the way up the Sweet-water, the country, in a geological point of view, became more and more interesting. The river was bordered on each side by mountains of granite, here and there, intersected by immense dikes of trap. All along its shores, numberless pieces of petrified wood and bones were discovered; besides, beautiful specimens of agate, jasper, chalced-ony, serpentine, cornelian, &c. &c., were collected by both officers and men. Just above Independence Rock, the Sweetwater bursts through a narrow gorge, only thirty or forty feet wide, and with walls more than three hundred feet high. The command was obliged to pass around the point of mountain through which the river had thus forced its way,—but many of the officers went to visit so great a natural curiosity. It is called the "Devil's Gate." As one stands near the upper entrance of it, a loud, deep-toned roar is heard, as the river dashes through, but the sight is soon intercepted by its winding course, and the darkness caused by the narrowness and deepness of the canon.

The Sweetwater is not a timbered stream, yet has a good growth of grass along its banks; but back, at a short distance from the river, and stretching to each range of mountains by which its valley is bounded—and which are distant from each other some twenty miles—the whole country is exceedingly barren, and produces nothing but artemisia. The plains upon both sides of the river are frequently embossed by immense isolated rocks, many of them in the shape of a hemisphere, and from three to four hundred feet in height. These rocks, standing in the midst of a dreary landscape, have a very imposing and even sublime appearance.

Buffaloes were met with in great abundance along the whole valley of the Sweetwater;—and in the "Sage Plains," spreading out on either hand, large numbers of the mountain grouse were found, which feed entirely upon the leaves and buds of the artemisia. Such food renders their flesh so bitter and unpalatable, that they are hardly fit to be eaten. Several of them, however, were killed, and preserved as specimens. They are much larger than the grouse of the prairies, the moor-fowl, or the ptarmigan. They are very dark, and beautifully mottled, and have longer tails than the pheasant. A fine cock, killed by Captain Moore, and the only one seen within gunshot (they are called the "*sage* cock"), stood some twenty inches in height, and was as heavy as a half grown turkey.

On the evening of the 24th, the snowy peaks of the Powder River Mountains were discovered, stretching along the horizon at the North, like a long chain of white and fleecy clouds,—and on the evening of the 25th, the Wind River Mountains were distinctly visible in the West.

While two of the hunters were in pursuit of buffaloes when near the Pass, they accidentally came across two fine grizzly bear cubs, one of which they were obliged to kill—but the other they succeeded in bringing into camp alive. It was the commanding officer's intention to have had him taken to the States; but a few days afterwards, unfortunately, he died.

After the expedition had reached nearly to the source of the Sweetwater, it left that river, and crossing over a broad sandy plain, for the distance of six miles, all at once found itself upon the margin of a beautiful stream flowing toward the West! As nothing in the passage across from the Sweetwater had indicated any particular elevation of the plain which would attract the attention, or any point which was so much higher than another, as to mark the precise place where the waters flowing toward the two oceans were divided—no one could hardly believe that the crest of the Rocky Mountains had really been crossed.[55]

According to the calculations of Brevet Captain Fremont, this—the Great South Pass of the Mountains—is in 42° 27′ 34″ north latitude, and in 32° 37′ 59″ of longitude, west from Washington, or 109° 27′ 50″ west from Greenwich. It is 7000 feet above the level of the sea.[56]

The stream which was met on the western side of the Pass, was one of the upper branches of Green River—a tributary of the Colorado of the west—which flows to the Gulf of California, and the Pacific Ocean.

It being the 30th of June, the command was mustered, and an order was published by the commanding officer, announcing that the expedition had reached the extreme western limit contemplated in his instructions, and congratulating the officers and men upon the successful accomplishment of that much of their arduous campaign. These were the first United States troops ever mustered on the Pacific side of the continent, and the first time the Head Quarters of the 3d Military Department had ever been upon the extreme summit of the Rocky Mountains.

The next morning—July 1st.—the expedition began to retrace its steps toward Laramie.[57] During the day, Colonel Kearny, Lieut. Kearny, Capt. Macomb, and several of the men, were seized with a sudden illness, which prostrated them immediately. Its symptoms were very much like those of the disease so prevalent in the East in 1843, and known as the "Tyler Gripe." All except the Colonel recovered in a few days. The effects of his attack were so very severe, that it was nearly three weeks before he had entirely regained his strength. I find upon examining Captain Bonneville's Journal, that he and his party suffered from a similar attack, in this same neighborhood. It was no doubt owing to the great elevation to which they had arrived. His party "complained of cramps and cholics, sore lips and mouths, and violent headaches."—and so did those of the dragoons who were taken sick.

On the 13th of July—the exact day calculated upon—the whole command arrived safely at Laramie River again,[58] having met on the return route nearly all the companies of emigrants which it had previously passed.[59]

The Oregon Emigrants

THE emigration from the United States to Oregon has more than doubled every succeeding season since it was first commenced—over three years ago.[60] The general character of the people who are so fast flocking thither—both for industry and integrity—is considered by many as being far above that of the *earliest* settlers of any of the territories that have, from time to time, immediately bordered the frontier of the corporate States.

Oregon is so extremely remote:[61] is reached at the expense of so much time, money, danger, and toil: and offers, at least for the present, so few inducements to the idle, the dissipated, or the dishonest, that, so far, it may be said to have entirely escaped being filled up by them. The restless—the worthless—the dissolute—and the outlawed, have had such cheap and easy facilities rapidly to reach Arkansas and Texas, that for the last several years, those two sections of the country, unhappily, have been, more or less, charged with the drainage from the old States, of much of the dregs of their society. The wide prairies and the rugged mountains are, in themselves, such a formidable barrier to all but those who have a great degree of courage, energy, and perseverance—qualities which, coupled with honesty of purpose, would, in any place, secure to their possessors both independence, respect, and advancement—that one may safely say, up to this time, none others have passed them.[62]

Nearly all who have gone to the shores of the Pacific, with a view of making a permanent settlement there, have been born and nurtured in the interior counties of the States lying in the Valley of the

Mississippi, and are, therefore, as a class, practical agriculturalists. They may be regarded as a straight-forward, simple, and well-meaning people, and shrewd and thrifty withal; and as having a fair share of good common sense. It is true, in the aggregate they are somewhat deficient in even the primary branches of education, and have but a limited knowledge of the usages of society, and a still narrower, of what is denominated "the world"; but there are many amongst them of creditable attainments, and of talents which in any country would be regarded as respectable.

Although they are buoyed up with the hope of ultimately bettering their own and their children's condition, still, their departure, their journey, and the first few years of their residence in the country towards which they are turning their footsteps, are now, and will be, marked by much sorrow, and with many disheartening toils and privations. Some idea of the causes of their emigration, together with the distress they have first to experience, may be gathered from the statement made to us by one of the leaders of a large company that this year came out from the State of Illinois, and from the rude picture of a parting scene which he drew for us.

"In the country we have left behind, our farms were probably of greater fertility than any we shall be able to make in that to which we are removing. We could raise from them with a little labor, more plentiful crops, than from any we ever expect to see again. But there, for two or three months every year, we have been, more or less, prostrated with sickness, which in itself not only caused us much suffering, but deprived us of the power of taking a proper care of what we had already accomplished, and completely unfitted us for a satisfactory enjoyment of what should ultimately be left us as the fruits of our previous toil. We thought that, although in Oregon we should be compelled to work much harder, yet, in the pure air, and the mild and equal climate we there hope to find, we should be blest with additional health to enable us to do so without inconvenience, and, likewise, to bestow so much the more care upon our lands as should cause them to yield, in the end, quite as abundantly as those we have heretofore occupied.

"But aside from these considerations, many of us had large families of children growing up about us, which, remaining where we were, we should not be able to provide for as we would be glad to. We were anxious, when they arrived at maturity, to see them all settled upon farms of their own. There was, it is true, unoccupied land enough about us, which we might have purchased, had we not been too poor to do so; and, so long as the markets were dull, to which we could take the little surplus of our crops over and beyond our immediate wants, so long were we likely to remain in indigent circumstances; each year bringing us nearer to the time when our children were to step out upon the world with nothing to begin life with, but their hands. But by going to Oregon we were sure that the government would supply us, free of price, with sufficient ground both for ourselves and for them. Had it not been for our solicitude for their welfare, probably we should have continued where we were; but as God had blessed us with them, we felt it to be our duty to sacrifice our own feelings for their future benefit.

"However, in addition to these reasons, and we considered them powerful enough of themselves, there were others of less weight, but which had no little influence upon our decisions. We believed that even in our own lives, the vast country bordering the Columbia, and the neighboring shores of the Pacific, was destined to become one of immense political and commercial importance; and where, even with our limited means and humble capacities, we could open for ourselves a field for enterprise and aggrandisement, of far greater moment than any it would be possible to attain, with our straightened circumstances, on this side of the mountains. Actuated by the motives for hastening thither, which this view of our prospective success presented, and aside from those already mentioned, our minds were finally made up to take the step we have taken, and which we felt sure, for good or for evil, was to affect our own, and our children's welfare, for ever.

"We suffer many privations on our long journey, and so we shall after our arrival there; but we try to endure them with patience, and ever hope on for the best. Our greatest sorrow was passed when we bade an eternal farewell to our friends. The agony of such a separation we had not fully counted upon. But it has gone by. We shall see them no more in this world—but we pray to meet them in a better.

"Until we were about to start, we knew not how many friends we had; how many there were who loved us, and who wished us well. When the day had arrived for our departure, and all our company had assembled at the place appointed, our neighbors from far and near, gathered there to bid us good-bye. There were hundreds and hundreds of them. The aged, with their silver locks and tottering decrepitude, whom we had looked up to and reverenced from child-hood: those whom we had played with in infancy, and who had grown up beside us to manhood—ever kind and true, generous and charitable: those, also, full of youth, and grace, and beauty,—whose hearts were brimming with purity and freshness, not yet sullied by a contact with the world: and even the little ones, with their sweet, wondering eyes—their curls—their dimples, and their innocence: all were there—gathered about us in sadness! and we were never to see them again! Our minister, who for years and years had watched over, and prayed for us,—he was there, too; and with a voice trembling with grief, and with the big tears gushing from his eyes, and, one by one, dropping over his furrowed cheeks, he spake to us a few parting words. How deeply they are engraven upon our hearts! But I need not repeat them to you. The circumstances of so melancholy an oc-casion as that which called them forth, will readily suggest to you what they must have been. Then we all kneeled there upon the ground, with him in our midst. I can see him now—his white hair streaming in the wind—his tearful eyes turned toward heaven so beseechingly—his clasped hands palsied with emotion, and his aged form bended in fervent supplication for us. Oh! how earnest and heartfelt was his prayer in our behalf: that our common Father would be with us and protect us till our next meeting; when each, though widely separate, had completed his allotted task, and had been called home for his reward. Then came the last embrace—the last 'May God bless you!' when weeping like children, we turned away from that spot and those friends, for ever!"

His story was but that of almost every emigrant with whom we conversed. To reach a healthy country, and to be able to get grants of land for their children, were the two great incentives for removal with all.

This year, according to Col. Kearny's report, there have gone through the Great South Pass, 850 men, 475 women, and 1000 children. They have taken with them 7000 head of neat cattle, 400 horses and mules, and 460 wagons. It would be safe to say that all of one-third of this number intended to make their homes in California, and the remaining two-thirds in the most fertile parts of Oregon, without much reference to degrees of latitude.

If the same number of troops had passed over, to remain permanently, West of the Mountains, it would have been known throughout the world, and perhaps two great nations would have been plunged into a long and bloody war in consequence. But emigrants have gone there in a measure unnoticed, and yet they have carried with them those elements of greatness and power, which the elaboration of but a few years will so transform, that the world will not only hear of them, but will, one day, attach far more importance even to their passive and quiet residence in that country, than to the active operations of thrice their numbers of soldiery.

They have borne away with them the strongest and most enduring sentiments of patriotism, and are so deeply imbued with the love of liberty, and the principles of republicanism, that no distance, however great, nor foreign or local influences, however powerful, can ever estrange their hearts—wean their affections—chill their sympathies, or, by their own consent, politically sever the ties that bind them to their Home-land. And though a wide desert separates them from it:[63] one which but few of them will ever re-cross to visit once more the scenes that smiled upon them in their child-hood—yet they will remain knitted to us, by all the pride they must feel in remembering the glories of the American Past, and all the hope that must inspire them as they look forward to the power and magnificence of the American Future.

How often, as they were moving along with us, were we struck with the deep affection and reverence they invariably manifested when speaking of the country they were leaving behind. How touching a proof was it, that the government, under whose fostering care they had been reared, was based upon principles of justice, and of equal privileges, so simple, and so pure, that even the most humble, and the most unlearned, could appreciate and love them. It is true they were not emigrating to a foreign land—but they were, for the time being, at least, stepping out, as it were, from under the protecting wing of their own; and were going to where their own choice might change, or materially modify, whatever they had before experienced, which was not entirely consonant with their settled convictions of right.

The thousands who are annually leaving the Old World, and seeking an asylum in the New, remember with an enduring love their Home-Land, from which they have been unjustly driven, by extortion that power alone had legalized—and by an oppression which, in its unrighteous might, could stalk abroad and trample upon them at noon-day. For it was there they were first surrounded by a living chain, whose every link was a warm heart, taught by its own sufferings to sympathise with them. It was there their earliest associations had their hallowed centre; and there the web was first woven about their being, whose warp and whose woof were made up of those endearing hearth-influences and affections, for which no tythes can be exacted—which tyranny serves but to strengthen—and which time nor distance can ever wholly unravel. For these—but only for these—do they love the land of their birth. And what better proof can there be of the magnitude of the wrongs they suffered, than the simple fact, that rather than to endure them, they chose to relinquish all that was so dear of friends and home! Poor and ignorant as many of them are, still they could readily understand the evils from which they sacrificed so much to escape, and the inestimable blessings that were here spread out like a rich repast, for their own and their children's enjoyment.

CHAPTER XIV

THE DAH-CO-TAHS

AS HAS been stated in a former chapter, the Dahcotahs are by far the most numerous tribe of Indians within the jurisdiction of the United States. The antiquarian and historian, Mr. S. G. Drake, has estimated them at 33,000; that number is considered by many to exceed their population; but if the accounts of the traders who reside in their country could be relied upon, it falls short of it, all of one half. Their exact strength has never been ascertained, but it may be safe to put it down at 30,000.

Within the last twenty years their country has extended towards the West to the base of the Rocky Mountains. In olden times, they lived on each side of the Upper Mississippi, and St. Peter's Rivers—and upon the Missouri—but in course of years they have forced the Crows and Blackfeet into the valleys that lie between the eastern ranges of the mountains; and those tribes in turn, have driven the Shoshonies, or Snakes, still higher up.

The Dahcotahs, as a race, may be regarded as being far above mediocrity, when compared with any others that have been, or are, indigenous to the Great Plains,[64] with the exception, perhaps, of the Mandans, Crows, and Blackfeet. The former of these tribes is now nearly extinct; the two latter are considered by Mr. Fitzpatrick as being superior to the Dahcotahs, in point of general intelligence, sagacity, and courage; or to any others, even, from the Missouri to the Pacific; and he may be looked upon as the best authority, on this point, of any man in the country. The Dahcotah men are considerably above the medium height, and are extremely symmetrical of form, well knit, agile, and easy in their movements. The girls and young women of the tribe have the most elegant figures, and are, also, very graceful and lithe in their every attitude and motion; but after they get older, and have had the severe labor to perform which falls to their lot as mothers of families, they soon lose all their beauty and elasticity, and become excessively coarse and ugly.

The Dahcotahs are not copper-colored, like the Indians who used to reside in the North, and in the Eastern side of the Valley of the Mississippi, but are of that clear red complexion, which is so peculiar to the nomadic tribes of the Western Prairies. Nor are their features so broad and angular, their foreheads so receding, their eyes so deep set, their cheek bones so high, or their noses so aquiline, as those of the Algonquin and Chippewayan races. But on the contrary, they are quite regular, and are often very handsome. Looked upon merely in a physiological point of view, their conformation would cause them to be esteemed as possessing, by nature, the elements of superiority, both of mind and body, over those who used to reside in the States proper; but as they live entirely upon the products of the chase, which are acquired with but little effort; and as in war, they meet the most of their enemies upon the open plain, where no great talent is required to fight in the manner to which they are accustomed—their faculties and powers have never, from necessity, been sharpened and called forth to their fullest extent. If they were compelled to incessant labor in cultivating the ground, as well as in hunting and fishing, and to a state of continual watchfulness and preparation, to subsist themselves, and at the same time maintain their existence, they ought to be far higher in the scale, as a people, than the Indians of the North were.

They reside in villages of from three hundred to two thousand souls each. Their lodges are made of buffalo hides, dressed in a similar manner as the robes which are taken to market, only the hair is shaved off, and both sides are worked over alike. Each one is composed of from thirteen to twenty-five of these skins. After they have been cut so as to fit the one to the other, they are strongly sewed together, with tendons of the buffalo split into threads; the whole then resembles, when spread flat upon the ground, a huge cloak of just half a circle; the radius of which varying in proportion to the number of skins employed. Every lodge, according to its capacity, then requires from eighteen to twenty-eight poles, for a frame on which it may be stretched. These poles are generally of pine, or spruce, and are procured at great labor on the upper affluents of the Nebraska before they issue from the mountains; none of those trees of a suitable size, straightness, and length, being found in their country, at a lesser altitude. They are then with much care shaved down, until they are about three inches in diameter at the butt, and gradually tapered toward the top, which is not over an inch through. Usually, when first made, they are upwards of thirteen feet long, but in time they become shorter, by wearing away at the lower ends, which drag upon the ground when the tops are fastened on each side of the horses and mules that transport them from place to place as the village is removed.

It requires a great deal of skill and practice to pitch one of these lodges properly. While encamped near Laramie River, we had two of them sent up to us from the forts. The traders who forwarded them, knew we should not be able to put them up without being shown how, and therefore obligingly directed some women to come at the same time, and erect them for us. This is the way they did it:—They at first spread the cape, or "lodge-skin," folded double, upon the ground, the two edges being together; it was then a quarter circle. Three poles were then laid upon it, the two outer ones being along the sides, and crossing each other at right angles at the top or point, and the butts just even with the arc, or bottom. The butt of the other was similarly placed midway the lower edge of the cape, and crossed the two first ones at the point where they intersected each other. One end of a strong rope—made of raw hide, and some fifty feet in length—was then employed to fasten them firmly together at their junction. They were then raised up, and the lower ends were placed at the points of a triangle, the rest of the rope hanging down. The remaining poles were then put up in such a way that each one bound the other—the butts being upon the ground, and describing a circle. To place each of them properly was the great secret; for the strength of the lodge, and much of its resistance to the force of the wind, depended on their being so interlocked that each one would bear its proportion of the weight, and come out from top to bottom as nearly even with the others as possible. The long rope was from time to time wound around the several layers, where they united, until all were fastened; the last end of it, like a main-stay, was then taken to the wind-ward side as far as it would reach, and being pulled tight, was tied to a stake driven firmly into the ground. The frame was then completed. The point of the lodge-skin was then lashed to a last, and much stronger pole—for its weight was very great—and raised up and leaned against the side of the frame opposite to that in which the entrance would be required. It was then brought around, and the two edges being lapped over each other, were pinned together by long skewers of wood, a boy going aloft and putting them in one by one, and placing his feet as he ascended, upon those he at first inserted. A flap at the top was left so that it could be kept open by a sprit, in order that the smoke could there escape in case a fire were needed in the lodge. There was a portion unpinned near the bottom, and that was the only door. In bad weather, or at night, it could likewise be pinned up; and by removing the sprit, and lapping the flap over at the top—which could be done by a small rope attached to it and hanging down within reach—the whole was remarkably tight and secure. The lower edge was pinned to the ground all around, the bottoms of the poles being afterwards moved out from towards the centre—the skin was stretched to the degree required to render it without wrinkle, and firm. Even when it is all closed up, it is, in the day time, sufficiently light in the interior, as the skins, though tanned, are more or less transparent.

When a fire is needed, it is built upon the ground in the centre; and long wooden hooks attached to a rope depending from the top, support the copper and sheet iron kettles, in which the Indians boil their meat.

The inside of many of the lodges is divided in several places by thin partitions of skin, running upwards five or six feet, and diverging like radii as they approach the outer wall. They are like little rooms without ceiling, and open on the side towards the fire. It is in them the robes are spread down upon which they sit or sleep. Others again, are all in one undivided space. Sometimes only one family lives in a lodge, but generally two or three do so. Sixty or seventy people might sit down in some of the largest of them, without inconvenience. They are decidedly the most convenient, cleanly, and comfortable habitations of any that are built by either one of all the tribes of Indians in our country. In the summer time, by pulling the pegs from the ground, the skin can be raised so as to admit of a free circulation of air, while the top still remains spread out, and casting a grateful shade. In the winter, a very little fire indeed, keeps them astonishingly warm; besides, at that season of the year, still another thickness of skin is placed around the inside, and carried so high, that any draught of cold air passing upward between the two, enters the lodge above the heads of the inmates.

The lodges are renewed every year, generally in the warm season. At that time the women have more leisure to make them, as no robes are then dressed. The hair of the buffalo being shed off quite early in the Spring, the men only kill enough, from time to time, until the cold weather sets in again, to supply their families with food, and to obtain hides for the construction of lodges, for the making of ropes, lariettes, and for other necessary purposes.

A village of an hundred or so of these lodges presents a very beautiful appearance. Many of them are ornamented on the outer side by fanciful devices, executed with considerable taste, and in various colors. It is no rare thing to see human scalps dangling from the points of the highest poles; the long black hair from them floating in the wind—a gloomy death-banner! Usually, before the door of every lodge, there stands a little tripod of poles some six or eight feet in height. On this are suspended the arms and amulets of the warriors within.

The Dahcotahs have many short fusees amongst them, which they have procured from the American Fur Company, and a very few rifles. But with these weapons they are not expert. Their main dependence either in war or the chase, is upon their bows and arrows, their lances and their shields. Their bows are not over three feet long, but are very stout. They are made of ash, elk-horn, or bois d'arc,* and to add to their strength they are carefully covered with sinews the whole length. The arrows are about two feet in length, are armed with iron heads, lozenge shaped and very sharp, and are feathered with great accuracy for one third of the distance from notch to point. Twenty-four of these in a quiver made of thick elk hide, and which is worn diagonally across the back a la Diana's, are a complement either for a battle or a "surround." When not required for immediate service, the bow is always unstrung, and is carried in a stout cover of dressed leather. It is said by gentlemen whose word cannot be doubted, and who have accompanied the Dahcotahs on their hunts, that frequently are they known to shoot their arrows directly through the bodies of the largest bulls. There can be no reason to discredit such a statement, when the weight of the arrows, the keenness of its blade, and the velocity with which it is thrown, are taken into consideration,—but no ordinary pistol, carbine, musket, or rifle, with the best powder in the world, could by a possibility drive a bullet so far. These arrows are sent with quite as much accuracy as force, and it is wonderful how rapidly one is made to succeed another. The shields are round, and are usually some twenty inches in diameter. They are made of bull's hide, which, when dry, is hard as horn. The outside is dressed until it is as white and stainless as snow. An arrow cannot be thrown through a good one.

The lances are about seven feet long. Just where the blades unite with the shafts, are usually fastened large tassels of war-eagle feathers. These lances are not thrown like the javelin, but are used principally to thrust down their antagonists when on foot, and in the charge against horsemen.

A great many of the Dahcotahs have swords, which they also purchased from the traders. They know nothing about using them, but only wear them for grandeur. To throw away the scabbard and to

*This celebrated and beautiful wood, is indigenous to Texas, Louisiana, and to nearly every fertile section of country west of the Mississippi, and as far north as the Arkansas River. It is a species of the *Citrus*, and is called by many the "Osage Orange." But along the frontier, and among the Indians, it is only known as the "Bois d'arc"—a name given to it by the French traders, from the use to which it is placed.

carry nothing but the blade, is the first thing to be done when they have bought one.

All these arms are hung upon the tripods just spoken of, whenever the band is encamped. The amulets, or "medicine bags," are, also, hung there with them.

The Dahcotahs are quite wealthy in horses, mules, and asses. These animals are the only currency they have when dealing with each other. If a young Indian sees a pretty girl whom he wishes to marry, he speaks to her parents to that effect, and asks what is the lowest price, horses down, they will take for her. If he is rich, they may ask him, say, three horses, two mules, and a jackass, more or less. If he is very deeply in love he may close with those terms at once; but if not, he and the old people might probably higgle for weeks about even a donkey, and perhaps at last have the whole matter kicked on the head by the difference of a jackass. One of our officers, mounted upon a beautiful bay horse, rode into one of their villages, and in a few minutes he was surrounded by all the jockeys of the band. They understand horses, do the Dahcotahs, next to buffalo; and they straightway began to consider the various points of the one then before them. They brought several of their own to "swap,"—offering three or four, as an inducement for the owner of the bay to give him up. Finding they could not get him with horses, they next tried with their daughters. No less than five women led their prettiest forward—girls from sixteen to eighteen—and offered, in succession, to exchange them for the bay. Finding that the charms of their children had no weight in procuring him, they became very indignant, and would have nothing further to say to his owner.

The Chieftaincy of each band is not hereditary in any particular family. When a young man wishes to be a chief, he commences giving feasts, and in bestowing upon his various friends all the valuable horses he can raise. In this way he gradually buys up a large party. When once he has got a majority of the band on his side, his friends declare for him, and his predecessor gradually falls back to the level of the common people. So long as the new chief is generous and brave, so long he remains in power; but whenever a more generous, and a braver man, can in turn buy up his party, his dynasty begins to cease, and that of the new ruler to come into the ascendant. In all these political changes, the candidate, in lieu of stump speeches, presents his friends with good eating; all who are inclined still to hold out, and have not allowed dog soup and buffalo marrow to change their opinions on the leading principles at issue, are then assailed by that most powerful argument, a horse or two. They immediately see wherein they were previously at fault, and pledge their votes without further discussion.

As has been previously remarked, the chase is the labor of these Children of the Desert, and war their pastime. When they have made a successful hunt, and laid in a good store of dried meat for their families, the next thing to be thought of is the getting up of a war-party. It matters but little who, of all their surrounding neighbors, are to be attacked, so the expedition promises to be rich in its return of scalps and horses. We were told that the war-parties of the Dahcotahs were usually raised in the following manner:—

Some distinguished chief, who wished to be its leader, at first started through the village of the band to which he belonged, and chanting his war-song as he proceeded. Every few minutes he halted, and was heard to proclaim in a loud voice, that the enemies of the Dahcotahs believed them to be asleep, or cowards, and were staying at home to die in their lodges like women. That he wished to show them that the Throat-Cutters were always awake, and were MEN—born to die in battle. That they were not dogs, to skulk away because the wolves were on the plain—but bears who never waited to be struck. And for this purpose he was about to go amongst those enemies to give them an opportunity for taking his life if they were able to do so. Who, he asked, would follow, and share the dangers he desired to encounter? And the glories and the spoils that were only to be won by the brave of heart and the strong of arm? This appeal would generally bring around him a large number of warriors. Having thus publicly pledged themselves to accompany and obey him, they would fall in behind him, when he would again move on—his followers joining in the chorus of his war-song. Soon another halt would be made, and another invitation extended, and loudly seconded by all the recruits, when more would fall in, and then the march and song would be again renewed. So they would go on, until the chief believed his party was sufficiently strong to be successful against any enemies whom he expected to encounter. A final halt would then be ordered, when the party would be perfectly organized throughout.

As the going to war is the most important of all their acts, a great deal of ceremony is observed in the various preparations which have to be made.

It is probable there are no people so foolishly superstitious as the Indians of the Plains. They have implicit faith in the predictions of their sorcerers, and believe there is a deep meaning in all the unnatural and incongruous phantasies of their dreams. It often happens, therefore, that the warning of some old seer, or the tale of some one of their party, to the effect that his "medicine" (his good genius) whispered in his ear while he slept, that if they then proceeded they would all be defeated, or would meet with some terrible accident, in which all their lives would be lost—delays for a long while the departure of the expedition—and sometimes has the effect of entirely disbanding it. If, on the contrary, every body's "medicine" talked propitiously, which generally happened where the leader was popular, the party strong, and the enemy weak—they set out with the greatest confidence of success.

On the day they were to start, there was usually a council of the whole Band, when all the old and feeble men of the village would come forward and exhort them to be true to their tribe; to be wary in all their movements; but when once they had closed with their enemies, then to die rather than to retreat, for only those who fell in battle were sure of reaching the happy hunting grounds away by the setting sun. The council being over, the purification of the warriors next took place. The chiefs and his braves having divested themselves of all their clothing, entered some small lodges that had been made as tight as possible, and having poured water on large heaps of red hot stones that had previously been placed there, they remained enveloped in the vapor that arose from them, until they were reeking with perspiration, and had almost fainted away from the excessive heat. They then came forth and plunged at once into the river. When

they had again attired themselves in their battle-dresses, and decorated themselves with their war-paint, they seized their arms, and
without touching a hand in good bye, or speaking a farewell, forth
they sallied to the country of their enemies.

When these parties go to fight the Indians of the mountains—say
the Crows and Blackfeet—it is common for them to do so on foot.
The difficulty of following their trail is then increased, and the
chances for their being seen, diminished. Besides, if they should
happen to be defeated, they would lose all their horses; but if successful, they would not be encumbered, on their return, by any but
those they had won by the enterprise. In fighting with the tribes of
the broad, open plains, where there are no rocks, defiles, or trees, by
which they could hide themselves, when pursued by a mounted
enemy—they prefer being on horseback, as then they can attack or
retreat with a celerity equal to that of their antagonists. The Crows
and Blackfeet are all mounted—but many parts of their country are
impassable except for footmen,—and through these the Dahcotah
warriors generally approach them, keeping well out of sight during
the day, and watching their opportunity when they can pounce upon
them at dead of night, murder them while they sleep, and then bring
off all the horses and plunder they can load themselves down with.

Most all the Indians in the upper country go into battle with not
an inch of covering except their centre cloths. All the fine dresses
which they put on when they leave home are (something like the
uniforms of our army) only an incumbrance to an agile, free, and
full exercise of the form and limbs they encase—and are thrown off
the moment the hard fighting is to be commenced. The buffoonery
of tassels, feathers, gold lace and embroidery, would probably meet
with the same fate, before hand to hand and foot to foot struggles
would voluntarily be entered into by their wearers.

When in view of their own people, the Indians believe it to be
grand to prepare themselves to meet their foes in all their array of
wampum, porcupine quills and vermillion. So with troops;—the
sight is very fine, that of a large body of sensible men lashed up with
straps, and bedizened with velvet and gold, strutting around after
the boys who are rigged out with red jackets, and who, with two

sticks, pound on the sheepskin heads of the little kegs they have lashed to their knees; or of others, mounted upon horse-back, who, to look fierce, have huge whiskers and moustachios, and sundry cords and toggery, and horse-hair switches in their caps, and who, also, for Buncombe, scowl a martial scowl, and curvette, caracole, and pirouette, as they prance around red-coated and cheek-distended fellows, who toot dismal discords through their brass training horns. In the din, and dust, and horror of battle, the bare right arm, and the free play of the chest and limbs, would take the place of all the glitter, stiffness, pomp, and harlequinism of dress parades: of the milles-fleur, white kids, affected attitude, feigned voice, and sentimental smile of ladies' men and carpet-knights.

The Indians, also, understand more about the secrets of command than we have hitherto been willing to allow. Mr. Fitzpatrick, who upon one occasion, many years ago, was some weeks with a war-party of Crows, informed us that the perfect discipline and harmony that prevailed in it, he had never seen equalled. The chief commanded with ease and dignity, and without any bombast and uncalled-for airs. He did not assume an undue, and therefore ridiculous importance; but knowing that whatever he directed would be performed, he gave his orders in the most mild and courteous terms. In return he was obeyed with cheerfulness and alacrity. He ever pursued the same even and uniform course; and as he never commanded anything to be done that reason and common sense did not suggest as necessary, there was no murmuring or bickering ever heard among his braves, nor did any one take pleasure, upon all occasions, to detract from his unquestioned merits. All the warriors were devotedly attached to him, and were ever ready to peril life and limb to serve him. Such a chief deserves to be remembered.

There was one thing Mr. Fitzpatrick told us of him which may not be uninteresting. He said he was conversing with him one evening about the power of the United States, and their intercourse with the Indians, and during the conversation the Crow leader made the following remarks:—

"I admit, my brother, that your people, the pale-faces, are very numerous and very wise. All the world has heard of them. So has all the world heard of the tribes of my red brethren, who live next to them. But who knows there is such a people as the Crows? Hardly any one beyond these valleys in which we dwell. And why is this? I will tell you, my brother. Those tribes murder the pale-faces, and steal from them their property. What punishment do they receive for doing so? None. The Big Chief of the pale-faces sends long-knives to visit them—to have large councils with them, and after a great smoke, and a long talk, in which they are to be told not to do so any more, then to give them a great many presents, and then to go home again. Now, my brother, what follows? The warriors of that tribe laugh when the long-knives have gone; and almost before they have passed from the country, robbery and murder are again committed. Again, my brother, what follows? I will tell you. The next year brings more long-knives, bigger councils, greater feasting and smoking, and again a new supply of presents. So they go on, my brother, and in a little while become famous. How is it with my people, the Crows? We have not molested the pale-faces, and yet we have never been heard of; we have ever respected both their property and persons, yet no long-knives ever come to meet us in council, nor has your Big Chief sent us so much as a piece of tobacco. Now what should we do to distinguish ourselves? Have we not an example in those of our red brothers of whom I have spoken? Surely we have; and it follows if we kill all the pale-faces we can find, and appropriate their property to our own use, the Big Chief of your people will often hear of us, and send us a plenty of presents likewise. We have long believed this to be true, still it is our desire to live at peace and harmony with you. But because we do so, the names of our warriors are never heard."

When upon the plains, the Dahcotahs bury their dead in the ground. Over the grave they build a little cairn, and place around upon its summit a row of buffalo skulls. But when their friends die near the groves of timber, they sometimes wrap them in robes, and place them high up in the forks of the trees. At other times they erect a scaffold, some eight or ten feet high, and lay the body upon that. We went to visit one of their places of sepulture near the mouth of the Laramie. Upon one scaffold the remains of a chief were reposing.

They were wrapped in the finest skins that could be obtained, and lay upon soft pillows beautifully adorned with beads and the stained quills of the porcupine. As we stood there looking up at the dead, with the magnificent landscape around us, smiling in the soft light of a beautiful summer's morning;—with, away in the distance, the blue mountains resting upon the horizon like heavy masses of cloud;—with the sweet west wind sighing gently through the embroidered pall that covered the remains, we questioned if it was not in better taste, and more congenial with their rude faith, so to leave their friends to their last rest, than to bury them in the chill earth, where, in darkness, the horrible death-worm would in silence revel at his gloomy repast.

All the Indians whom we saw are said to believe in a Great Spirit. They also believe in an Evil Spirit. Besides, they each have a particular guardian, to whom they dedicate some amulet, which they ever carry about them, and which they call their "medicine." There are several animals which they also venerate as "medicines," and many birds. Among the former, the grizzly bear and the white wolf are the greatest medicines, and amongst the latter, the black, or war-eagle. Notwithstanding these creatures are considered sacred, still, at times, they kill them as quickly as they would a buffalo.

The Rev. Mr. Parker states that "*he* never, while going to Oregon, witnessed lightning and thunder pealing from the clouds gathering around the summits of the hills or mountains. The thunder spirits who fabricate storms and tempests appear to have closed their labors, and the Indian tribes no longer hang offerings on the trees to propitiate the invisible lords of the mountains." The reverend gentleman travelled directly through the country, and of course had not many opportunities of knowing that what he asserted, as well as what he assumed, were correct. We were informed by people who have lived in the mountains for twenty years, that the Indians *do* still offer sacrifices of their most valuable garments, to appease the wrath of the storm-gods. Two of these offerings we ourselves found hung upon trees. One (already spoken of) in Ash Hollow, and one on Laramie River. Both were expensive scarlet blankets, and had been gashed with knives and then offered up, as has been stated. And besides, nothing is more common than to witness lightning and thunder pealing from clouds gathering around the summits of hills. One of the most severe hail and rain storms, accompanied by the most vivid lightning and terrific thunder, which we witnessed on the whole campaign, gathered around Long's Peak, and came down upon us while encamped near its base. Although he did not see these things, there were others he describes which would go to show the Dahcotahs in an unnatural light, and which we did not witness, although a long while in their country. He says—

"I was agreeably surprised to see tall young chiefs, well dressed in their own mode, walking arm and arm with their ladies."(!) This is what I did not expect to see among those whom we term savages."

This statement, made to any one at all acquainted with the manners and customs of *any* Indians, must be as replete with the ludicrous and the absurd, as anything he could possibly have said. Everybody knows that the wife is absolutely the slave of her Indian husband. Does he want a new lodge? She has to make it. When travelling, does he wish to encamp? He merely points out the place, and the wigwam is there erected. His clothes are all made by his women. They catch and saddle his horses, cook his meals, fill his pipe, and do every other work that can possibly be required of them. When he returns from hunting, he merely throws down his heavy fleeces of meat, and his labor is done. . . .

All the Indians of the West are said to believe in a future existence. But amongst the different tribes, different conceptions as to what the next world will offer to them as subjects of enjoyment, are often met with. The Dahcotahs, we are told, believe that if they fall in battle, they will at once be transported by their particular spirit, or "medicine," directly to a magnificent country in the Far West, where there are thousands of unsuspecting and easily to be conquered Crows and Blackfeet, which they can scalp to their heart's content, for ever; besides hundreds of beautiful women to wait upon them, and to minister to their gratifications;—and game to be stricken down on every hand. There have been no efforts made to teach them Christianity, but many to teach them some of the worst sins of the whites.

Notes and Appendix

NOTES

NOTES AND COMMENTS ON THE
LOGBOOK OF 1844

CHAPTER I

1. The total American army of 8573 men was scattered at fifty-two posts in 1844. The ten companies of the First Dragoons of about 623 men were stationed at six different western posts. Besides Major Wharton's march Captain E. V. Sumner's dragoons and those of Captain James Allen made "wide circuits in the Indian country of the West." *Senate Documents*, 2nd sess., 28th Cong., I, Document 1, pp. 130–133.

2. Immediately after Joseph Smith's murder on June 27, 1844, "I made application to the United States for five hundred men of the regular army, to be stationed in Hancock county, which was subsequently refused."— Thomas Ford, *A History of Illinois* (Chicago, 1854), 351.

3. Brief, official sketches of these officers are in Francis B. Heitman, *Historical Register and Dictionary of the United States Army* (1789–1903), I.

4. Charles Deas, a painter of western scenes, was born in Philadelphia in 1819. In the spring of 1840 he left the East and visited Green Bay, Fort Winnebago, and Fort Crawford. Later he travelled to Fort Snelling and Fort Atkinson. At these places he found subjects in Indians, fur depots, half-breeds, and frontier costumes and manners. Later he established himself at St. Louis. The Wharton expedition gave him the opportunity to observe Indians in their natural state. Little is known of the location of his paintings. It is to be regretted that pictures of the Wharton expedition have not been located. This sketch is based on correspondence between Mr. John Merryweather, an artist member of The Caxton Club of Chicago, and Dr. Robert Taft of the Department of Chemistry at the University of Kansas. Dr. Taft lists the names of sixteen paintings of which eleven are dated. Acknowledgments are due Dr. Taft for the data on Deas assembled by him.

CHAPTER II

5. A branch of the Stranger River in Leavenworth County, Kansas.

Chapter III

6. Sometimes called Fox, Livingston and Company. This was organized about 1841 and, as a rival of the Missouri Outfit and the American Fur Company, resorted to desperate and illegal methods. It was bought out by the latter company in 1845.

7. "*Delirium tremens* on his part explained all," noted Major Clifton Wharton, the commanding officer. Major Wharton's *Journal* of this expedition (August 12–September 21, 1844, edited with footnotes and a map) is printed in the *Collections of the Kansas State Historical Society 1923–1925*, XVI, 272–305.

Chapter IV

8. This likely was the Jesse Applegate party in the spring of 1843. His *A Day with the Cow Column in 1843* was printed for The Caxton Club of Chicago in 1934. This reprinted account is edited with Introduction and Notes by Joseph Schafer, then Superintendent of the State Historical Society of Wisconsin.

Chapter V

9. Major Clifton Wharton wrote, "The course of this branch of the Nemahas—whether it is the *Great* or the *Little* Nemaha, we have no means of determining."

10. This post erected in 1824 was located on the left bank of the Neosho River near its junction with the Arkansas River in the present county of Muskogee, Oklahoma. The fort was abandoned in 1857. R. G. Thwaites, *Early Western Travels* (Cleveland, 1904–1907), XX, 105.

Chapter VII

11. "At 12 M. we commenced unloading the wagons, our India rubber boat or raft was inflated and launched, three pontoon wagon bodies were put in the waters for the purpose of carrying over the provisions & baggage, and in a little upwards of three hours the whole command had crossed, including about 350 animals, thirteen wagons, and their contents (two wagons were sent back to the Fort from this point) & two Howitzers, without the slightest loss or accident having been sustained."—*Journal* of Major Clifton Wharton.

Chapter VIII

12. William Paul Crillon Barton (1786–1856), botanist, teacher, and naval surgeon published various catalogues and compilations in botany and a popular, illustrated work on *Flora of North America*.

13. Governor Isaac I. Stevens exploring the region (Griggs County, North Dakota) for a railroad route in 1853 wrote: "About five miles from camp we ascended to the top of a high hill, and for a great distance ahead every square mile seemed to have a herd of buffalo upon it. Their number

was variously estimated by members of the party—some as high as half a million. I do not think it is any exaggeration to set it down at 200,000." —*Explorations and Surveys to Ascertain the Most Practicable and Economical Route for a Railroad from the Mississippi River to the Pacific Ocean* (Washington, 1860), XII, Book I. Printed in *House Executive Documents*, 1st sess., 36th Cong., Document 56. The quotation is at p. 59.

14. Josiah Gregg (1806–1850) made numerous trips to Santa Fé after 1831 over a period of nine years. His famous work, *Commerce of the Prairies*, which he wrote in the winter of 1843–1844 and which was retouched by John Bigelow was published in the summer of 1844. The work went through about nine editions, including three in German.—John Thomas Lee, "The Authorship of Gregg's *Commerce of the Prairies*," *Mississippi Valley Historical Review* (March, 1930), XVI, 451–466.

CHAPTER IX

15. This was in the vicinity of the modern city of Columbus in Nebraska. Two Pawnees entered the camp this day, one of whom declared that he "*was determined to come forward and speak to us although he might be shot down in the attempt.*"—Major Wharton's *Journal*, August 28.

CHAPTER X

16. See copy of a journal of Captain Nathan Boone of a march over the southwestern prairies from May 14 to July 31, 1843. Lieutenant Carleton's quotation is largely from the entry of Captain Boone for July 2. Josiah Gregg, in the preparation of his *Commerce of the Prairies*, the classic account of the Santa Fé trade, had access to Captain Boone's journal. Quotations describing the "Rock Salt" may be found in Volume II, 187–189 of Gregg's work (1845). The journal is reprinted in Louis Pelzer, *Marches of the Dragoons in the Mississippi Valley* (Iowa City, Iowa, 1917), 181–237 and also in *Chronicles of Oklahoma* (March, 1929), VII, 60–105.

CHAPTER XII

17. Charles Augustus Murray, *Travels in North America During the Years 1834, 1835 & 1836* (London, 1839), 2 vols. Extended accounts of his visits among the Pawnees in the summer of 1834 appear in Chapters XIV–XXII of volume I.

CHAPTER XIII

18. The Reverend John Dunbar was a Presbyterian missionary among these Pawnees from 1834 to 1847. The four bands, Republican Pawnees, Grand Pawnees, Pawnee Loups, and the Tapages numbered between 8,000 and 10,000 in 1834. Major Wharton estimated their numbers at 7,000. Buffalo flesh and corn or "mother" were the principal foods but beans, pumpkins, watermelons, and roots were cultivated. Basketry, pottery, and weaving and hunting were the occupations.—Major Clifton Wharton's

Journal and John Dunbar, "The Presbyterian Mission Among the Pawnee Indians in Nebraska, 1834–1836," *Collections of the Kansas Historical Society 1909–1910*, XI, 323–332.

19. At this council and at the former, Lieutenant's Carleton and Thomas C. Hammond acted as secretaries.

CHAPTER XV

20. This day's movement of twenty-seven miles was in the present county of Platte in Nebraska.

21. Major Wharton wrote: "It derives its name, it is said, from the swarms of butterflies which have been found on its banks. We have remarked them in considerable numbers here, & the fine crop of wild flowers in bloom even at this season evidently is what attracts them."

22. Claude Gellée (1600–1682), commonly called Claude de Lorrain, was born in the ancient province of Lorraine. He produced numerous etchings and about four hundred pictures.

23. The Missouri Fur Company under Joshua Pilcher occupied the site of Bellevue in about 1823. It was purchased by Lucian Fontenelle who turned it over to the American Fur Company when he became its agent. Peter A. Sarpy was in charge of the post for many years but the Indian agency there was designated, "Council Bluffs at Bellevue." A post office was established in 1849 and five years later the village was incorporated. Bellevue became the county seat of Sarpy County, Nebraska in 1875.

24. This was the "Yellowstone Expedition" of 1819, a grandiose project to reach the mouth of the Yellowstone River. Colonel Henry Atkinson, the commander, wished to use keel boats but was overruled by the authorities at Washington. This, added to the difficulties of navigation of the Missouri, and the lack of securities for the contractors caused the failure of the enterprise. The troops passed the winter of 1819–1820 at Council Bluffs (some miles above the present Council Bluffs) in the county of Washington in Nebraska. The name shifted from Council Bluffs to Camp Missouri and finally to Fort Calhoun.

CHAPTER XVI

25. Major Wharton described the Oto as a "thieving, impudent, silly, reckless, people." They were miserably destitute and indifferently armed with bows, arrows, and spears. The numbers of the Otoes and "Missourias," he estimated at 1,000, of whom less than one-third were capable of bearing arms.

26. "The Indians present within, & near the Square formed by the log houses of Mr. Sarpy, a licensed trader, were numerous, Pawnees, Otoes, Pottawatomies and Poncas forming different groups."—Major Wharton's *Journal*.

CHAPTER XVII

27. By the treaty signed with the Sacs and Foxes October 21, 1837 and ratified February 21, 1838, about 1,250,000 acres were ceded to the United States.

28. Fort Croghan, first called "Camp Fenwick," and located on the left bank of the Missouri River near the side of modern Council Bluffs, was established by Captain J. H. K. Burgwin who had come up the Missouri River in a steamboat with sixty or seventy dragoons. The troops were to prevent hostilities between the Pottawatomi and the Sioux and to aid in enforcing law and regulations against the liquor traffic. A map in volume III, p. 471 of *Explorations and Surveys for a Railroad Route to the Pacific Ocean* places "Old Fort Croghan" above the present Council Bluffs and a little below the mouth of the Boyer River. The post was abandoned in September, 1843.

29. The route on September 13 to 17 was through the counties of Atchison and Holt in northeastern Missouri.

CHAPTER XVIII

30. The crossing of the Missouri River was at Jeffrey's or Iowa Point located a few miles below the mouth of Wolf Creek in Doniphan County, Kansas.

31. William Hamilton was a laborer, and S. M. Irvin a missionary at the sub-agency. The next year the Reverend Irvin rendered a discouraging report: "With the single exception of drinking whiskey (which arises more from pecuniary want than moral restraint) they have grown extravagant in all sorts of mischief—stealing, killing cattle, and the like, have, within the last few months, grown more common." The Ioway village near the sub-agency, Major Wharton estimated, contained about four hundred and the Sac village on Wolf River about five hundred.—Report of S. M. Irvin, September 30, 1845, in *Senate Executive Documents*, 1st sess., 29th Cong., I, Document 1, pp. 605, 607.

32. "Reached *Independence creek*, after a march of seven miles—tarried here an hour, and then, leaving the wagons to follow under a Guard, the Squadrons at a *walk out* started for Fort Leavenworth, distant about fifteen miles, which we reached at 4 P.M."—Entry for Saturday, September 21, in Major Wharton's *Journal*.

NOTES AND COMMENTS ON THE LOGBOOK OF 1845

CHAPTER I

33. The Regiment of Dragoons was authorized by the law of March 2, 1833. This became the "First Regiment of United States Dragoons" upon the organization of an additional regiment by the act of May 23, 1836, which then became the "Second Regiment of Dragoons." The designation

of the "First Regiment of Dragoons" was changed to "First Cavalry" on August 3, 1861.

34. "Our people," noted James K. Paulding, "have more of the locomotive principle than any other, not excepting the Israelites and the Arabs . . . . But the people of the 'Great West' beat all the rest together. I hardly met a man, or indeed woman, who had not travelled from Dan to Beersheba, and back again, and 'settled' as they were pleased to term it, in half a dozen places, some hundreds, perhaps thousands of miles distance from each other."

35. See footnote 3 of Chapter I of the first *Logbook.*

36. Thomas Fitzpatrick (1799–1854) trapper, Indian agent, and guide, ranks with Kit Carson and James Bridger among the famous "mountain men." As a guide he was praised by De Smet, Frémont, Kearny, and Abert. —See his biography, LeRoy R. Hafen, *Broken Hand, the Life-Story of Thomas Fitzpatrick.*

CHAPTER II

37. See the account of the journey along this stream in the *Logbook* for August 13, 1844.

CHAPTER III

38. Weston, one of various steamboat landings on the Missouri River, became absorbed by the modern Kansas City. Large numbers of forty-niners arrived there, outfitted there, and departed from it to California.

39. "The horses had a gallant bearing;—fifty blacks led; fifty grays followed; then fifty bays; next fifty chestnuts—and fifty more blacks closed the procession: the arms glittered; the horses' shoes shone twinkling under moving feet." Philip St. G. Cooke, *Scenes and Adventures in the Army* or *Romance of Military Life* (Philadelphia, 1857), 291. Captain Cooke was a participant during the entire expedition. The last one hundred and fifty pages record interesting incidents and details. The scenic descriptions are animated and vivid, but sometimes stilted in style.

40. See entry for August 15 in Chapter III of the first *Logbook.*

CHAPTER VI

41. Francis Parkman, the historian, passed over this route just a year later. On a grassy hill a piece of plank standing upright attracted his notice and there he read a brief story of sorrow on the prairies: Mary Ellis. Died May 7, 1845. Aged two months.

CHAPTER VII

42. Captain Cooke wrote that the buffalo grass "looks like curled gray horsehair" and that "its sod is a near approach to wooden pavements."

CHAPTER VIII

43. On this day Captain Cooke recorded: "Two empty wagons were sent back to Missouri, with a small escort, with broken-down horses: 'all flesh is grass,' and the grass is very poor."

CHAPTER IX

44. Near Ash Hollow or Ash Creek was a fine spring and grass and wood were abundant. The spot (in present Garden County, Nebraska) was well known. Captain Bonneville had passed it in 1832 and seven years later A. Wislizemus, a German physician, had observed it. Fitzpatrick, the dragoon guide, recalled that he had visited the region with Lieutenant Frémont in 1842. In the hegira of 1845 thousands of emigrants hailed this little oasis with delight.

45. Captain Cooke noted that one Frenchman, a Gascon, "joyously spends his ten dollars a month in alcohol, tobacco, coffee, and sugar, and in gaudy presents to some half-breed belle; paying the most incredible prices for these extravagant luxuries."

CHAPTER X

46. A notable guide for the Oregon Trail is *A Topographical Map of the Road from Missouri to Oregon Commencing at the Mouth of the Kansas in the Missouri River, Ending at the Mouth of the Wallah Wallah in the Columbia*, in seven sections. This map was compiled in 1846 by Charles Preuss from the journals and field notes of Frémont and presents a detailed view of the Trail. Its meteorological observations, locations of Indians, and the remarks upon the animal life and vegetation along the route make this map of the highest use and value in studying the Trail.—*House Reports*, 2nd sess., 30th Cong., Document 546.

47. "We are now in advance of the whole emigration; two of their men are with us this evening; they speak of the great discouragement of the women, who even wish to return; and many men have been at times of the same disposition; they have lost many cattle in the first quarter of their journey. They scarcely know where they are going; and these men eagerly question our guide—who has been in Oregon—on the simplest and best known points."—Comment of Captain Cooke for June 12.

48. This stream had piled up large quantities of cedar driftwood on its banks. The perspiring and panting mounts greedily drank its cool water and then browsed or rested in the shade of the clumps of trees.

CHAPTER XI

49. Fort Laramie in Goshen County in Wyoming should not be confused with modern Laramie in Albany County, Wyoming. Fort Laramie had previously borne the names of Fort William and Fort John. An extended account of Fort Laramie is LeRoy R. Hafen and Francis Marion Young,

Fort Laramie and the Pageant of the West, 1834–1890 (Glendale, California, 1938).

50. "The Fort," wrote Captain Cooke, "swarmed with women and children, whose language—like their complections—is various and mixed, —Indian, French, English, and Spanish; they live nearly exclusively on dried buffalo meat, for which the hunters go at least fifty miles." The struggle between half civilization and barbarism was at close quarters—"civilization furnishing house and clothing; barbarism, children and fleas."

CHAPTER XII

51. Francis Parkman, the historian, visited the fort the next summer (1846) and described it in his *The Oregon Trail: Sketches of Prairie and Rocky-Mountain Life.*

52. On June 17 the command marched thirty-six miles over a sterile and desolate country to arrive at Horseshoe Creek (in the northern part of Platte County of Wyoming).

53. On this day the dragoons covered fifteen miles and on the next day arrived at the crossing-place of the Platte River. Few buffalo were seen but on one staring skull the dry air had preserved the hide as well as the ears an inch in thickness.

54. Captain Cooke estimated that Independence Rock was about 120 feet high and 1,000 feet long.

55. The "Camp in Oregon," on June 30, 1845, Captain Cooke estimated as 281 miles from Fort Laramie and 850 miles from Fort Leavenworth.

56. The South Pass was simply a high ridge between the ends of the Sweetwater and the Wind River Mountains and was located in the southern part of what is now Frémont County, Wyoming. The ascent to it is so gradual that it is not easy to determine just when the summit is reached. It had nothing of the gorgelike character of such passes as St. Bernard or Simplon in Europe or the Allegheny passes in America.

57. On July 4 Colonel Kearny, at the request of a group of emigrants, fired the mountain howitzer to celebrate the day. Then the travels led over rocks and sands that glared in the July heat. "So much for the Fourth of July,—and a dry one!" concluded Captain Cooke.

58. On July 5 the command rode twenty-eight miles over soil ground fine by the emigrant trains. They passed Devil's Gate, Independence Rock, and Hot Spring Gap.

59. Lieutenant Carleton's narrative of the march ends at this point. The command skirted the Chugwater River, crossed the south fork of the Platte and travelled 400 miles to Bent's Fort in Colorado. The 600 miles to Fort Leavenworth were covered along the Arkansas River for 200 miles and then along the Santa Fé Trail to Fort Leavenworth or "home." The whole distance travelled in 99 days was 2,200 miles.—*Abstract of Journals* of Lieutenants William B. Franklin and H. S. Turner in *Senate Executive Documents,*

1st sess., 29th Cong., I, Document 1, pp. 214–217. Captain Cooke sketches the return march from Fort Laramie in his *Scenes and Adventures in the Army*, 292–432.

CHAPTER XIII

60. Various estimates of the numbers of emigrants to Oregon exist. Among the best are those of F. G. Young in *The Quarterly of the Oregon Historical Society* (December, 1900), I, 370; in 1842 the estimates are 105 to 137; in the next year, 875 to 1,000; in 1844 the figure is 700; and the following year, 3,000.

61. Senator Mahlon Dickerson on February 26, 1825, opposed the occupation of the Oregon country: "But is this territory of Oregon ever to become a state a member of this Union? Never." A congressman going to Washington and returning would travel 9,300 miles at an expense of $3720; this would require 465 days and "if he should lie by for Sundays" the travel time would be 531 days; to travel at the rate of 30 miles daily would make a schedule of 306 days. With no Sunday travel the journey would take 350 days which would allow the member a fortnight "to rest himself at Washington," before he should commence his journey home. A young, able-bodied Senator might make such a journey, "but he could do nothing else." *Register of Debates in Congress*, 2nd sess., 18th Cong., 689–694.

62. Daniel Webster said of the Oregon region in 1843: "What do we want of that vast and worthless area—that region of savages and wild beasts, of deserts, shifting sands and whirling winds, of dust, of cactus, and prairie-dogs? To what use could we ever hope to put those great deserts and those endless mountain ranges? . . . What could we ever do with the western coast of 3,000 miles, rock-ribbed, cheerless, and uninviting?"—*Guidebook of the United States* by Willis T. Lee *et al.* in Bulletin 612 U.S. Geological Survey, Part B; Overland Route, 7.

63. Senator William L. Dayton of New Jersey in February, 1844, referred to the Oregon country as "one of the most arid, dreary, and miserable wastes of desolation that God ever made." He quoted with approval: "Now, that such a wretched territory should excite the hopes and the cupidity of citizens of the United States, inducing them to leave comfortable homes for its heaps of sand, is indeed passing strange. Russia has her Siberia, and England has her Botany Bay; and if the United States should ever need a country to which to banish its rogues and scoundrels, the utility of such a region as Oregon will be demonstrated."—Reprinted from the *Louisville Journal* in the *National Intelligencer* and quoted in *Appendix to the Congressional Globe*, 1st sess., 28th Cong., 275.

CHAPTER XIV

64. "Dakota" is the largest division of the Siouan family commonly known as "Sioux." Sioux are generally considered as of the highest type—mentally, physically, and perhaps morally—of the western tribes.—F. W. Hodge, *Handbook of American Indians* (Washington, 1907), Part I, 376–381.

APPENDIX

Principal Writings of Members of the First Regiment of United States Dragoons from 1833 to 1847

James Allen, "Report of an expedition into the Indian country made by Company 'I' 1st regiment of dragoons" and "Journal of March into the Indian country in the northern part of Iowa Territory in 1844, by Company 'I' 1st regiment of dragoons from August 11–October 3, 1844." These documents are in *House Executive Documents*, 1st sess., 29th Cong., VI, Document 168, pp. 2–18, and are edited with notes and introduction by J. Van der Zee in *The Iowa Journal of History and Politics* (January, 1913), XI, 68–108.

Nathan Boone, "Journal of an Expedition over the Western Prairies." This is printed in Louis Pelzer, *Marches of the Dragoons in the Mississippi Valley* (Iowa City, Iowa, 1917), 181–237 and is reprinted by W. Julian Fessler with a map in *Chronicles of Oklahoma* (March, 1929), VII, 60–105.

J. Henry Carleton, *Logbook* of 1844 and *Logbook* of 1845 are printed for The Caxton Club of Chicago in this volume.

Philip St. G. Cooke, *Scenes and Adventures in the Army* or *Romance of Military Life* (Philadelphia, 1857). This describes both expeditions of Carleton's *Logbooks*.

Henry Dodge, "A Frontier Officer's Military Order Book." The original in Dodge's handwriting is in the Department of History and Archives at Des Moines, Iowa. A copy is in the library of the Historical Society of Iowa. This document covers his correspondence and orders from April, 1833 to March, 1836. An article by Louis Pelzer describing this document is in the *Mississippi Valley Historical Review* (September, 1919), VI, 260–267.

Hugh Evans, "The Journal of Hugh Evans, Covering the First and Second Campaigns of the United States Dragoon Regiment in 1834 and 1835," edited by Fred S. Perrine and Grant Foreman in *Chronicles of Oklahoma*

(September, 1927), III, 175–215. The journal describes the campaign in Oklahoma from early April to September 8, 1835.

HUGH EVANS, "Journal of Henry Dodge's Expedition to the Rocky Mountains in 1835," edited by Fred S. Perrine in the *Mississippi Valley Historical Review* (September, 1927), XIV, 192–214.

LEMUEL FORD, "Captain Ford's Journal of an Expedition to the Rocky Mountains," edited with introduction and notes by Louis Pelzer in the *Mississippi Valley Historical Review* (March, 1926), XII, 550–579. This account describes the march of 1600 miles through the states of Nebraska, Colorado, and Kansas by dragoon companies from May 29 to September 16, 1835.

JAMES HILDRETH [?], *Dragoon Campaigns to the Rocky Mountains Being a History of the Enlistment, Organization and First Campaigns of the Regiment of United States Dragoons* (New York, 1836). Joseph B. Thoburn in *Chronicles of Oklahoma* (March, 1930), VIII, 35–41, presents evidence that William L. G. Miller, another dragoon, is the author of this book generally ascribed to Hildreth.

A. R. JOHNSON, "Report of the March of the Army of the West from Santa Fé to San Diego," January 25 to December 4, 1846. Printed in *House Executive Documents*, 1st sess., 30th Cong., IV, Document 41, pp. 562–614.

STEPHEN W. KEARNY, Official Letters on the Army of the West (San Diego, California, December 12, 13, 1846, and January 12, 13, 1847) in *Senate Executive Documents*, 1st sess., 30th Cong., I, Document 1, pp. 513–520. Printed also in *Niles' Weekly Register*, LXXII, 170, 171.

STEPHEN W. KEARNY, "Report on the Expedition to the Pawnee Pict Village" (1834), in *Senate Executive Documents*, 1st sess., 29th Cong., I, Document 1, pp. 210–213.

G. P. KINGSBURY, "Report on the Expedition of Dragoons, under Colonel Henry Dodge, to the Rocky Mountains in 1835," in *American State Papers, Military Affairs*, VI, 130–146. This material contains a map of the route, a letter from Colonel Dodge to the Adjutant General, and a letter by General Edmund P. Gaines of the Western Department of the army to the Adjutant General.

"A Journal of Marches by the First United States Dragoons" in *The Iowa Journal of History and Politics* (July, 1909), VII, 331–378. The first journal from May 11 to June 2, 1834 describes the travel from Jefferson Barracks to Fort Gibson. The second from June 15–August 15, 1834, sketches the route from Fort Gibson to the Pawnee Pict and Comanche villages. Considerable portions of this journal are literally transcribed into James Hildreth, *Dragoon Campaigns*. The third narrative from September 3 to 25, 1834, traces a march from Fort Gibson to Fort Des Moines in southeastern Iowa. The fourth account is the record of a march from June 7 to August 19, 1835, from Fort Des Moines to Wabashaw's village in

Minnesota. The author of the journals edited by Louis Pelzer is not known. Two of the accounts are signed by "L-".

ALBERT MILLER LEA, *Notes on Wisconsin Territory with a Map* (Philadelphia, 1836). This volume is largely a geographical description based on data acquired in the author's journey with the dragoons in 1835. A reprint with a map and an introduction was issued by the *State Historical Society of Iowa* (Iowa City, 1935) with the title, *The Book that Gave Iowa its Name.*

PERCIVAL G. LOWE, *Five Years a Dragoon ('49 to '54)* (Kansas City, 1906).

JAMES C. PARROTT, "Reminiscences of Gen. James C. Parrott," edited by Mary B. Whitcomb, *Annals of Iowa* (Third Series, January, 1898), III, 364–383.

EDWIN V. SUMNER, "Report of a march into Iowa Territory," in *Senate Documents*, 1st sess., 29th Cong., I, Document 1, pp. 217–220. This material with introduction and notes by J. Van der Zee is also printed in *The Iowa Journal of History and Politics* (April, 1913), XI, 258–267. Another reprinting is in the *South Dakota Historical Collections* (1918), IX, 369–375. The expedition from Fort Atkinson in the Territory of Iowa to Traverse des Sioux in the Territory of Minnesota was made from June 3, to August 11, 1845.

THOMAS SWORDS, Report to the Quartermaster October 8, 1847 describing march of the Army of the West to California. Printed in *House Executive Documents*, 2nd sess., 30th Cong., I, Document 1, pp. 226–235.

H. S. TURNER and W. B. FRANKLIN. This is a brief extract of the journals of these two officers. *Senate Executive Documents*, 1st sess., 29th Cong., I, Document 1, pp. 214–217.

CLIFTON WHARTON, "Journal of a March of a Detachment of the 1st Rgt. of Dragoons" in *Collections of the Kansas State Historical Society 1923–1925*, XVI, 232–305. This is the expedition in which Lieutenant Carleton participated and describes in his first *Logbook.*

T. B. WHEELOCK, "Journal of the Campaign of the Regiment of Dragoons in the Summer of 1834" in *American State Papers, Military Affairs*, V, 373–382. The route was from Fort Gibson to the Pawnee Pict village from June 21 to August 24, 1834. It is also printed in *House Executive Documents*, 2nd sess., 23rd Cong., I, Document 2, pp. 70–91, and in *Annals of Iowa* (Third Series, January, 1930), XVII, 173–197.